LOVE
Personified

KIND ENDURES BELIEVES BEARS PATIENT HOPES

Is loving tacos the same
as loving my enemies and loving God?

Exploring Biblical Models of REAL Love

TIM WHITEHEAD

LOVE PERSONIFIED
Copyright ©2024 Tim Whitehead

978-1-998815-27-2 Soft Cover
978-1-998815-28-9 E-book

Printed in Canada and the USA

Published by:
Castle Quay Books
Little Britain, Ontario, Canada
Jupiter, Florida, USA
Tel: (416) 573-3249
E-mail: info@castlequaybooks.com | www.castlequaybooks.com

Edited by Marina Hofman Willard PhD
Cover design and book interior by Burst Impressions

All rights reserved. This book or parts thereof may not be reproduced in any form without prior written permission of the publishers
.
Scripture taken from the New King James Version. Copyright © 1982 by Thomas Nelson, Inc. Used by permission. All rights reserved. • Scripture quotations marked (NIV) are taken from the Holy Bible, New International Version®, NIV® Copyright ©1973, 1978, 1984, 2011 by Biblica, Inc.® Used by permission. All rights reserved worldwide. • Scripture quotations marked (NLT) are taken from the Holy Bible, New Living Translation, copyright © 1996, 2004, 2015 by Tyndale House Foundation. Used by permission of Tyndale House Publishers, Inc., Carol Stream, Illinois 60188. All rights reserved.

Library and Archives Canada Cataloguing in Publication
Title: Love personified : "is loving tacos the same as loving my enemies and loving God? Exploring
   biblical models of real love" / by Tim Whitehead.
Names: Whitehead, Tim (Timothy G.), author.
Identifiers: Canadiana (print) 20240455924 | Canadiana (ebook) 20240457544 | ISBN 9781998815272
   (softcover) | ISBN 9781998815289 (EPUB)
Subjects: LCSH: Love—Biblical teaching. | LCSH: Love—Religious aspects—Christianity.
Classification: LCC BS680.L64 W55 2024 | DDC 241/.4—dc23

Contents

Introduction: Another Book on Love?	5
Chapter 1: Joseph Suffers Long	9
Chapter 2: Ruth Is Kind	21
Chapter 3: Jonathan Does Not Envy	33
Chapter 4: Moses Does Not Parade Himself	47
Chapter 5: John the Baptist Is Not Puffed Up	67
Chapter 6: Esther Does Not Behave Rudely	83
Chapter 7: David Does Not Seek His Own	99
Chapter 8: Stephen Is Not Provoked	113
Chapter 9: Jacob *Keeps* a Record of Wrongs	123
Chapter 10: Paul Does Not Rejoice in Iniquity, but Rejoices in the Truth	141
Chapter 11: Daniel, Hananiah, Mishael, and Azariah Bear All Things	159
Chapter 12: Barnabas Believes All Things	173
Chapter 13: Abraham Hopes All Things	187
Chapter 14: Jeremiah Endures All Things	207
Chapter 15: Jesus Never Fails	231
Conclusion	241

Introduction
Another Book on Love?

You may ask, "Do we really need another book about love?" I think so. "But didn't C. S. Lewis already write the definitive book about love? And didn't Gary Chapman already sell millions of copies on how to express love for one another through love languages?" Sure, there are good books on the topic of love, but I think there are two reasons why we can use another one.

First, when Jesus was asked, "Which is the greatest commandment?" He did not respond with any of the Big Ten, or any of the 613 other Levitical laws; and He certainly didn't respond with any of the other thousands of laws the Pharisees had added to protect the Mosaic Law.

Instead, He famously responded,

> "The first of all the commandments is: 'Hear, O Israel, the LORD our God, the LORD is one. And you shall love the LORD your God with all your heart, with all your soul, with all your mind, and with all your strength.' This is the first commandment. And the second, like it, is this: 'You shall love your neighbor as yourself.' There is no other commandment greater than these." (Mark 12:29–31)

So, if Jesus thinks that love is the most important thing in all the world, then for every book we have on leadership, or holiness, or preaching, we ought to have a hundred on love.

Not only does Jesus command us to love God and our neighbour, but we're also to love our enemies (Matthew 5:43–44).

There's more. Love is what should identify us as Christians. It's not how we dress, or what we do on Sundays, or even how we speak. As Jesus ended his earthly ministry, He took His disciples aside and explained to them that it is their love for each other that will identify them as His disciples. He says, "A new commandment I give to you, that you love one another; as I have loved you, that you also love one another. By this all will know that you are My disciples, if you have love for one another" (John 13:34–35).

I know that's technically two reasons, but they're more like 1(a) and (b) as to why we need another book about love: Jesus commands us to love, and love should be what identifies us.

And there is a second reason why we need another book about love.

When you read the word *love*, you may not be thinking about what I am writing about. The media uses the word *love* to describe attraction. Or more specifically lust. Characters on TV programs and movies "make" love, which really means sex. This is not what I'm writing about. This is *eros*. C. S. Lewis covers this in his book *The Four Loves.*

Or perhaps you are a grandparent, and when you read *love*, you think of your grandkids. This is affection. Or for our Greek scholars, *storge*—again, covered by Lewis.

Or my teenagers "love" tacos. I'm not sure where this type of "love" falls, and Lewis didn't cover it either.

I'm sure you have anticipated that what I am writing about is the famous *agape* love. Although Lewis so thoroughly explained what it is, I don't think we have grasped how to express it. Love is a complex, abstract idea. It is not an emotion; it is not infatuation or attraction. It is a purposeful, intentional state of mind that is both tangible and measurable. What does it look like in daily life? How do we translate it into action? It's like trying to understand a mathematical formula. You can see it on paper, but what does it mean?

Nothing Beats Seeing It Put into Practice

I find the best way to learn is through story. Actually, experience is the very best teacher, but a close second is reading the story of someone else's experiences, as it's safer.

Let me share a story to explain. When I was a teenager, I took physics in high school. I was taught the laws of motion, acceleration, and velocity. I was taught formulas and concepts. I even passed the final exam. But I really didn't fully grasp those concepts until one fateful December evening.

I grew up in a small church in Hamilton, Ontario, Canada, and as a teen was part of a small youth group led by my parents. To celebrate Christmas, and to give the youth a chance to get better acquainted with the seniors in our church, we held a "progressive dinner". We started at one home for buns and juice, drove to another for salad, then on to another for the main course. It was on the way from dinner to dessert that I truly learned about both velocity and friction.

When you get a group of teenagers together, the collective IQ drops. Cram them in a van, and it goes even lower. Put those cars in a caravan, and all hope is lost. It started with "Chinese fire drills" at stop signs and progressed to running between vehicles before the traffic lights turned green. My father, who was in the lead vehicle, was sort of playing along but was making very short stops to discourage us from running between vehicles. I took up the challenge. As we approached a stop sign, I opened the sliding door of my friend's van and prepared to jump out and run up to my parents' vehicle before they could drive away.

I mentioned I had learned about velocity and friction in physics class, but that day I truly understood what those formulas meant. I learned as I jumped out of the van that I was travelling at the same speed as it was; and although we were decelerating, going 30 km/h is still pretty fast. Usain Bolt's top speed was clocked at 44.72 km/h, and he had a chance to build up to it. My first step was about 30 km/h, and I never got my other foot down. That's when I learned, profoundly, that I was travelling at the same velocity as the vehicle I was in. I felt like Wile E. Coyote, spinning my legs madly in the air after running off a cliff. Then I hit the ground and learned what that friction formula meant. I skidded along the asphalt, tearing my pants and shirt, scraping my hands and arms.

Did you wince? Could you feel the impact as you read my story? Although experience is the best teacher, just take my word for it: do not try this at home. Just as you can learn basic scientific principles easier through my story than physically experiencing them yourself, we can all learn through the stories of people in the Bible just what it means to love in action, practically and purposefully.

LOVE PERSONIFIED

So, What Does the Bible Say Love Is?

To understand love, let's break it down into the component parts that the apostle Paul used in 1 Corinthians 13.

> Love suffers long and is kind; love does not envy; love does not parade itself, is not puffed up; does not behave rudely, does not seek its own, is not provoked, thinks no evil; does not rejoice in iniquity, but rejoices in the truth; bears all things, believes all things, hopes all things, endures all things. Love never fails. (1 Corinthians 13:4–8)

This list in 1 Corinthians 13 is a list of characteristics, not emotions. Let's take each of these parts and examine the story of someone who personified that characteristic. Let us discover what this love is, bit by bit, and how we can express it. Again, this love we are trying to reclaim is not emotion, infatuation, or attraction.

We are going to examine the successes and failures of real people. We're going to let their experiences teach us, so we don't have to go through the pain of learning the hard way ourselves. We want to turn the abstract idea of agape love into something tangible, achievable, and repeatable. If we truly are to be Jesus's disciples, love should be our defining characteristic. So, let's learn together what Jesus meant when He told us to "Love the Lord your God" and "love your neighbor as yourself".

Chapter 1
Joseph Suffers Long

The first characteristic of the *agape* love that Christ commands us to have and that should identify His followers is most commonly translated "patience". Just like the word *love*, the word *patience* doesn't mean what it used to mean. Patience nowadays is waiting for last night's pizza to heat up in the microwave or for the traffic light to turn green. The better rendering of the Greek word Paul uses is "long-suffering". It's not just waiting for something passively for thirty seconds. It is enduring harm, pain, or sorrow for months or years.

Abused

The best example of this "long-suffering" in the Bible is Joseph. You can read his whole story in Genesis chapters 37 and 39 to 45. Here are some of the most important passages that highlight his love that is long-suffering.

> Joseph, being seventeen years old, was feeding the flock with his brothers. And the lad was with the sons of Bilhah and the sons of Zilpah, his father's wives; and Joseph brought a bad report of them to his father.
> Now Israel loved Joseph more than all his children, because he was the son of his old age. Also, he made him a tunic of many colors. But when his brothers saw that their father loved him more than all his brothers, they hated him and could not speak peaceably to him. (Genesis 37:2–4)

One does not need to be a psychologist to see that this family has issues. In summary, Joseph is the son of the wife that Jacob actually wanted. That wife has since died, so we can forgive Jacob some extra affection towards her sons. There is a special bond here that, through no fault of Joseph's own, causes hatred from his brothers. Although jealousy can never be justified, we can certainly understand why Joseph's brothers hate him. On top of his special status as favoured son, he also appears to be a person of character, and their wrong is exposed by his goodness. We cannot skip by the phrase at the end that they "could not speak peaceably to him", or as the NIV puts it, "could not speak a kind word to him".

I have five children, and nothing breaks my heart more than when they are fighting. It grieves me when one of them speaks condescendingly to another, makes a snide comment, or belittles them for something they said or did, talks in mocking or sarcastic tones, uses passive aggressiveness, or sometimes outright calls them names in order to verbally beat them down. My wife and I try to intervene right away when this starts. With even just a couple of comments, we can see how harsh words can break a spirit, lowering self-esteem and undermining confidence.

The Son Is Cursed by His Father's Favour

I cannot imagine what Joseph has gone through with the constant badgering, name-calling, mocking, and verbal abuse he endures from his brothers. I cannot fathom the effect it has had on his confidence and esteem. But somehow, he endures it. He "suffers long". What about his brothers? I also cannot imagine this level of hatred: to never give a simple "good morning" or "pass the bread", but to always speak with venom, bitterness, and anger.

We next read about Joseph's two dreams (vs 5–11), which compound the problem. God reveals to him that his brothers (sheaves of wheat) and whole family (sun, moon, and stars) will bow down to him. When Joseph shares his dreams with his brothers, they "hate him even more" and become even more jealous. We are now reaching uncharted levels of hatred and jealousy. It's almost not surprising what happens next.

Joseph is looking for his brothers to make sure they are okay. It's good to see that their father loves them too and is concerned about their well-being. As Joseph approaches their camp in the land of Dothan, they see him way in the distance, and these words actually leave the lips of one of them:

> "Look, this dreamer is coming! Come therefore, let us now kill him and cast him into some pit; and we shall say, 'Some wild beast has devoured him.' We shall see what will become of his dreams!" (Genesis 37:19–20)

In all the nasty things I've heard my kids say to or about each other, I've never overheard two of them scheming to kill one of the others. We need to acknowledge the level of hatred and abuse Joseph is enduring. Fortunately, the oldest, Reuben, puts in a kind word and saves Joseph from murder. He *only* has to suffer being stripped and thrown in a pit. But this kindness is short-lived. We don't know where Reuben goes, but when his back is turned, the rest of the family decides to sell Joseph into slavery and just fake his death. You can just feel the love in Judah's words:

> "What profit is there if we kill our brother and conceal his blood? Come and let us sell him to the Ishmaelites, and let not our hand be upon him, for he is our brother and our flesh." (Genesis 37:26–27)

The brothers return home with the infamous technicolour dream coat dipped in goat's blood to complete the deception. When their father falls into a deep grief for "many days", the brothers try to comfort him but refuse to admit their guilt. Even when their father thinks his grief will kill him, their cold, hate-filled, jealous hearts will not allow them to confess. Their hatred for Joseph outweighs their love for their father. Can you imagine letting their father suffer like this instead of letting him know that Joseph is in fact alive?

Can you love someone who abuses you? Can you love God even though He let it happen?

We'll skip chapter 38, Judah and Tamar's story, which indicates that many years pass while Joseph is in his captivity.

Falsely Accused

We catch up with Joseph in Egypt, where he has been sold as a slave to Potiphar, Captain of the Guard. Immediately, we are told that God is with Joseph and that he has been successful and promoted to overseer of Potiphar's house. If we are honest at this point, I'm sure for many of us there would be some moping or outright depression. We might cry out to God, saying, "Why me?" We might try to escape, or at least serve so poorly that we sabotage the work of our master. We see nothing of that with Joseph. In fact, he serves so well that God blesses the Egyptian "for Joseph's sake".

What is Joseph's reward for serving so well and honouring God's will for his life, even in slavery? A false accusation. Potiphar's wife tries to seduce Joseph; when she fails, she falsely accuses him, and he lands in jail.

Can you love someone who lies about you? Can you love God if He lets you go to jail for it?

Now, definitely, it's time for some pouting. Finally, Joseph shakes his fist at God and complains. Wait, that's not what the Bible says. Actually, once again it seems Joseph submits to God's plan, goes to jail, and serves so well there that we read:

> The keeper of the prison committed to Joseph's hand all the prisoners who were in the prison; whatever they did there, it was his doing. The keeper of the prison did not look into anything that was under Joseph's authority, because the Lord was with him; and whatever he did, the Lord made it prosper. (Genesis 39:22–23)

We turn the page to Genesis 40, where we are introduced to Pharaoh's butler and baker, who have also been thrown in jail. Joseph interprets their dreams, the butler is restored to his position, and we see what may be the first crack in Joseph's resolve:

> "Remember me when it is well with you, and please show kindness to me; make mention of me to Pharaoh, and get me out of this house. For indeed I was stolen away from the land of the Hebrews; and also I have done nothing here that they should put me into the dungeon." (Genesis 40:14–15)

Joseph knows that he has been treated wrongly. He knows that he has been abused and unjustly accused. He is not some sort of superhero immune to hurt, who has no feelings. But how much more can he endure?

Neglected

And so, the question is, how do we respond? We're called to love. We are called to love God. We're called to love our enemies. We're called to love each other. We're called to love our neighbour. We're supposed to be long-suffering. The first characteristic of love is that it suffers long. Joseph is suffering long.

Chapter 41: back to our Sunday school story. Pharaoh has his dream: the good sheaves of wheat and the bad ones that swallow them. Then the good, fat cows and the skinny cows.

Finally, the butler slaps his forehead and says, "Oh! I remember the guy that interpreted my dream in jail!" They bring Joseph out of jail, and he interprets the dreams, foretelling seven years of bumper crops, followed by seven years of famine so terrible that the good years will not be remembered. What is important to note here is Joseph's comment, "It is not in me; God will give Pharaoh an answer of peace" (Genesis 41:16). This is love for God: not taking credit when it isn't ours to take but living in humble obedience. John 14:15 says, "If you love Me, keep My commandments." This means not having any god (including ourselves) above God. Joseph lives in obedience even though he has been abused, falsely accused, and neglected. Do you think you would still be able to love God through all of this?

As a contrast, I'm reminded of Numbers 20:12, where God punishes Moses and Aaron because they "did not believe Me, to hallow Me in the eyes of the children of Israel." Loving God means giving Him the honour and respect He deserves and not taking any for ourselves. Joseph loves God.

Joseph volunteers a solution for the upcoming trials that God is warning Pharaoh about. Pharaoh says, "Wow, I will never find anyone wiser than you. You're going to be put in charge of all of Egypt. No one will lift a finger unless you've given them permission." He gives him a role, gives him his signet ring …

And Joseph lives happily ever after. Well, until his brothers show up. Now, here's the test of love. Here are ten people that are the cause of Joseph's suffering. They abused him mercilessly growing up. They sold him as a slave and faked his death. It's because of them that he was in Potiphar's house in the first place, where he got falsely accused, where he got thrown in jail, and sat and rotted for thirteen years.

How Do We Respond to the Chance for Revenge?

Genesis says that Joseph was thirty years old when he became ruler in Egypt. He had endured thirteen years of suffering as a slave. Long suffering! Now his brothers are in front of him, and he's the governor of Egypt; he holds their lives in his hand—literally! He can either give them food or not; he can cause them to starve to death; he can take any revenge he wants; or, being a godly man, he can enact justice and punish them for their crimes and put them in jail. I think that's reasonable.

But what does love do? What does Joseph do? Look at Genesis 42:9. The brothers have arrived, not recognizing Joseph. They are begging for bread.

LOVE PERSONIFIED

Joseph remembers the dreams he had about them bowing before him in worship and says to them, "You are spies. You have come to see the nakedness of the land!" On the spot, he devises a test. He wants to examine their hearts, and he knows just what buttons to press.

> "No, my Lord," they said, "but your servants have come to buy food. We are all one man's sons; we are honest men; your servants are not spies."
>
> But he said to them, "No, but you have come to see the nakedness of the land." [Joseph wants to see if they will crack.]
>
> And they said, "Your servants are twelve brothers, the sons of one man in the land of Canaan; and in fact, the youngest is with our father today, and one is no more." [Nope, they are still holding on to their lie.]
>
> But Joseph said to them, "It is as I spoke to you, saying, 'You are spies!' In this manner you shall be tested: By the life of Pharaoh, you shall not leave this place unless your youngest brother comes here. Send one of you, and let him bring your brother; and you shall be kept in prison, that your words may be tested to see whether there is any truth in you; or else, by the life of Pharaoh, surely you are spies!" (Genesis 42:10–16)

So, Joseph puts them all in prison together. Three days later, he says, "I tell you what: only one of you has to stay. The rest of you can take food home for your family."

In verse 21, they say to one another, "We are truly guilty concerning our brother, for we saw the anguish of his soul when he pleaded with us, and we would not hear; therefore this distress has come upon us."

Now they are starting to crack. They are looking deep into their hearts where their secret sins lie. The wound is being reopened. But will they allow it to be cleaned and dressed?

Reuben answers,

> "Did I not speak to you, saying, 'Do not sin against the boy'; and you would not listen? Therefore, behold, his blood is now required of us." But they did not know that Joseph

> understood them, for he spoke to them through an interpreter. And he turned himself away from them and wept. Then he returned to them again and talked with them. And he took Simeon from them and bound them before their eyes. (Genesis 42:22–24)

Joseph isn't out for revenge; he's not exactly even concerned with justice. He's concerned about their souls. These are troubled people. It's not too hard or too much of a step to suggest that these guys have some issues. Consider that their father didn't want to marry any of their mothers and only really loved Joseph's mother; they were second-class sons, so he treated Joseph better than the rest of them—and then when his wife Rachel died, he more or less neglected his family for a while. So, you know the old saying, "Hurt people hurt people"? They're troubled souls, and they took it all out on Joseph.

Joseph's Little Test

Joseph, somehow, because of God's anointing, His Holy Spirit on him, has God's love in him. And he looks at these other ten men and says, "I love you enough that I want what's best for you. I want healing for you. I want you to see your sin; I want you to repent of your sin. I want you to be reconciled to God, reconciled to me, reconciled to our father. I want you to have the peace that you don't have."

Instead of revenge or justice, Joseph wants what's good and best for them. So, he has this test and he says, "I'll tell you what: one of you has to stay, the rest of you can go."

What do they say? "Oh, yes, you keep Simeon; we'll go." They start to feel a little bit guilty; perhaps they're being punished for their sins. But they're happy that Simeon will stay behind, and they all take off with the food. So, the wound stays opened, but not cleaned or dressed or allowed to heal. The brothers aren't ready for that yet. Healing often hurts.

They go home and have food for the family, but it runs out. Their father Jacob says, "Go back." They debate with him: "We can't go back unless we take Benjamin."

"You're not taking Benjamin! You've already taken Joseph from me. You can't take him."

LOVE PERSONIFIED

"Dad, we're starving. If we don't take Benjamin, the governor won't even see us." After some time and significant belt-tightening, Jacob relents and says, "Okay, take Benjamin." That's the quick summary of the next chapter.

Moving on to Genesis 44: the brothers return to Egypt and Joseph. He receives the brothers, lets Simeon out of jail, and there they are—a family reunion. The eleven brothers, ten abusers and the one brother of his mother, the full brother; Joseph has a feast for them before sending them back with their food. But he can't help himself. He starts to reveal that he knows something. He organizes the table so the brothers sit in birth order. He gives Benjamin an extra portion. He's opening the wound again, getting the brothers talking and thinking.

Any Sunday school kid worth their Bible memory ribbon knows the next step of the little test Joseph has: he puts the silver cup in Benjamin's feed sack. A couple of hours after he lets them go, Joseph sends his servants to bring them back, saying, "Don't you know I'm a man of power? I can see these things and that you've stolen this from me." He declares that the one caught with the silver cup—Benjamin—will stay in Egypt as his slave.

Now, here's the response he's been waiting for, starting in Genesis 44:18: Judah comes near to him and says,

> "Oh my lord, please let your servant speak a word in my lord's hearing, and do not let your anger burn against your servant, for you are even like Pharaoh. My lord asked his servants, saying, 'Have you a father or a brother?' And we said to my lord, 'We have a father, an old man, and a child of his old age, who is young; his brother is dead, and he alone is left of his mother's children, and his father loves him.'
>
> "Then you said to your servants, 'Bring him down to me, that I may set my eyes on him.' And we said to my lord, 'The lad cannot leave his father, for if he should leave his father, his father would die.' But you said to your servants, 'Unless your youngest brother comes down with you, you shall see my face no more.'
>
> "So it was, when we went up to your servant my father, that we told him the words of my lord. And our father said, 'Go back and buy us a little food.'
>
> "But we said, 'We cannot go down unless our brother is with us.'

> "Then your servant my father said to us, 'You know that my wife bore me two sons; and the one went out from me, and I said, "Surely he is torn to pieces and I have not seen him since." But if you take this one also from me, and calamity befalls him, you shall bring down my gray hair with sorrow to the grave.'
>
> "Now therefore, when I come to your servant my father, and the lad is not with us, since his life is bound up in the lad's life, it will happen when he sees that the lad is not with us, that he will die. So your servants will bring down the gray hair of your servant our father with sorrow to the grave. For your servant became surety for the lad to my father, saying, 'If I do not bring him back to you, then I shall bear the blame before my father forever.' Now therefore, please let your servant remain instead of the lad as a slave to my lord, and let the lad go up with his brothers." (Genesis 44:18–33)

It appears that even until now they are okay with their father Jacob suffering the loss of Joseph. When they sat together and saw Joseph afar off and decided to kill him, they thought, "Who cares about Dad? We're going to kill our brother. We're going to dip his coat in blood!" They didn't care about anyone other than themselves. They had no thought or concern about the pain and hurt they were about to cause. They were blinded by their own hurts.

When they go to Egypt for food the first time, they are okay to leave Simeon in jail. Once again, they don't care about the pain and suffering of others. They get their food; they are good.

Are the Brothers Finally Getting It?

On the second trip, we have the second part of the test. We're finally getting to something here, where Judah says, "I can't cause any more suffering. Not on my father, not on Benjamin, not on anybody else. *I'll* take it."

And the rest of the story goes that Joseph reveals himself to them, saying,

> "I am Joseph your brother, whom you sold into Egypt. But now, do not therefore be grieved or angry with yourselves because you sold me here; for God sent me before you to preserve life." (Genesis 45:4–5)

That's a whole other story; there's a whole other lesson we can learn from this story. But it's Joseph's love that allows him to address the behaviour of his abusers in such a way that he brings them finally to healing, into maturity, into reconciliation.

I am not condoning staying in abusive relationships. I am not condoning suffering for no reason. What I am encouraging and suggesting is that Christian love commands us to a higher level of relationship with others—even with our enemies. Jesus commands us to love our enemies.

This is the love we will be discovering throughout our study: the love that says, "Even though you have hurt me, I still want what's best for you." Again, boundaries and self-care are essential, but they don't exclude love for the other.

If someone is in an abusive situation, generally they want revenge. They want something bad to happen to that person. They want them jailed. They want them beaten. But love calls us to want them to get help. Joseph was in a unique situation where he had the power to bring about the change. Most often, we will need to commit our enemies or our abusers to someone who can help them—a counsellor, a therapist. But the desire for the healing of the other is what we are called to. That's a love that suffers long.

A First-Nations Example of Forgiveness

I work for a Christian radio ministry, distributing solar-powered radios and audio Bibles and building radio stations so pastors and missionaries around the world can expand their reach and multiply their impact. One area we work in is Canada's First Nations territories, partnering with the Native Evangelical Fellowship of Canada. One of the main radio presenters and teachers for the NEFC is Gary Quequish. It's heartbreaking to hear Gary talk about his experience in a residential school, suffering separation from his family, having his identity and culture stripped from him, and being abused by older students.

But what is incredible is to hear Gary say that the leaders of those schools "grossly misrepresented Jesus" and to hear him talk about forgiving his abusers and the hope for them to be restored to right relationship with God. The suffering Gary endured pushed him to get a counselling degree and drives him to travel from coast to coast to meet with victims, listen to their stories of heartache and abuse, and then share that through Jesus Christ they can have healing and can forgive their abusers.

CHAPTER 1: JOSEPH SUFFERS LONG

This isn't "Jesus loves me, this I know" nursery school stuff. This level of love, a love that suffers long, is high-level discipleship. This is 1 Corinthians 3:2 meat-versus-milk teaching. And this is what we're all to aspire to—that we respond to people who have abused us, falsely accused us, or neglected us—with what? With true love.

Love is complicated. It is hard work, so we're going to take this in small bites. We're going to look at the next characteristic of love: love is kind. We're going to look at somebody else's story, put ourselves in their shoes, into their situation, and say, "How do I respond?" and "This is how I should respond!"

I said that the second-best way to learn something is through story. The best way is experience. So, before we try to bite off the next characteristic of love, I've got some homework for you.

Sometime this week, maybe even today, you may feel abused. It may be a hurtful comment from someone at work or, even worse, in your family. Maybe you'll get blamed for something that you didn't do, or a nasty rumour will be started by someone who has their own issues. Or maybe you'll be left out, not invited to a party, passed over for a promotion, forgotten on your birthday.

Someone will hurt you. How will you respond? Will you want revenge? Maybe you're more spiritual and you'll want God to get them back; after all. "'Vengeance is Mine,' says the Lord."

Instead, stop and pray. First pray for that person, for whatever hurt they have that has festered and gone untreated, that God will perform a miracle in their life. Then pray for yourself, that God will fill you with His Holy Spirit, that you will not desire revenge or even justice, and that God will give you the wisdom to know how to show love—to suffer the abuse, the accusations, and the neglect and still love.

Jot down the situation below, keep track of your growth as a disciple. Learn how to respond in love; start a habit; learn to pause and pray, asking for God's help, instead of responding with a knee-jerk reaction.

Chapter 2
Ruth Is Kind

I hope that I established why we need to learn about love in the previous chapter, as Jesus teaches in Matthew 22. When asked what the greatest commandment is, Jesus says, "'You shall love the Lord your God with all your heart, with all your soul, and with all your mind.' And the second is like it: 'You shall love your neighbor as yourself.'" In John 13, He says to His disciples, "By this, all will know that you are My disciples, if you love one another."

So, the greatest command Jesus gives us is to love, and our very identity as individual Christians, as a church, as a group of Christians, should be love. Someone comes to your church; it shouldn't be about the type of music you sing or how good the preacher is or the colour of carpets you have, or whether you have pews or chairs. It should be that you are people of love. Love should be the defining characteristic of your local church.

But, as I said, we have this misguided interpretation of what love is. When grandparents think of love, they think of their grandchildren. When kids think of what they love, they think of tacos. If you listen to any type of pop music or watch any type of sitcoms, when anybody uses the term "make love", they're not talking about love; they're talking about sex. And so, as believers, we have this constant bombardment of all these different things of what love *isn't*. It's time for us as Christians to reclaim the idea of what God means when He says to us, "Love your neighbor as yourself."

The passage in 1 Corinthians 13 says, "Love is patient, love is kind. Love does not envy, love does not boast." I've been in church my whole life, and the only time I hear this passage preached is at a wedding. Even with the best of intentions, we were relegating love to weddings, to marriage.

But in Matthew 5:43, Jesus says, "You should love your enemies." Actually, maybe that's why we read this at weddings because of the whole mother-in-law dynamic. (Insert your own favourite mother-in-law joke here; I won't.

LOVE PERSONIFIED

I've got a great mother-in-law—and just in case she's reading: I love you, Rosie!)

We missed what love is about. It's not romantic, dove-eyed wedding talk. It is difficult, high-level discipleship. The first characteristic of love—long-suffering—meant Joseph, our example, endures abuse, neglect, and wrongful accusations; but in the end, he loves his brothers enough to want them restored. He wants them to understand God's forgiveness and wants what is best for them, even after thirteen years of suffering.

Love Is Kind

The next phrase is "love is kind." Our example is Ruth. But kindness, what does that mean? This word *kind* is about action. It's doing something, not just using kind words. You can recite all the love poems you want; you can sing the songs. My dad always said, "You do what you believe. The rest is just talk." Love should be something that we do. If we truly love somebody, we should actually actively *do* something about it. It's not just nice words, just like in James 2, where he talks about our faith without works; I would say, "Love without works is dead."

The Story of Ruth

So, we are going to look at the life of Ruth and her story. Now remember, this is supposed to be an interactive process. You want to imagine yourself in the story, put yourself into the circumstances, into Ruth's sandals. Her story was written between two and three thousand years ago, so perhaps we will have some context issues to work through, but I hope you'll be able to say, "Yeah, I've been in a situation like that." Let's read Ruth chapter 1:

> It came to pass, in the days when the judges ruled, that there was a famine in the land.
> And a certain man of Bethlehem, Judah, went to dwell in the country of Moab, he and his wife and his two sons. The name of the man was Elimelech, the name of his wife was Naomi, and the names of his two sons were Mahlon and Chilion—Ephrathites of Bethlehem, Judah. And they went to the country of Moab and remained there.
> Then Elimelech, Naomi's husband, died; and she was left, and her two sons. Now they took wives of the women of Moab: the name of the one was Orpah, and the name of the

other Ruth. And they dwelt there about ten years. Then both Mahlon and Chilion also died; so the woman survived her two sons and her husband.

Then she then rose with her daughters-in-law that she might return from the country of Moab, for she had heard in the country of Moab that the LORD had visited his people by giving them bread. Therefore she went out from the place where she was, and her two daughters-in-law with her, and they went on the way to return to the land of Judah.

And Naomi said to her two daughters-in-law, "Go, return each to her mother's house. The LORD deal kindly with you, as you have dealt with the dead and with me. The LORD grant that you may find rest, each in the house of her husband."

So she kissed them, and they lifted up their voices and wept. And they said to her, "Surely we will return with you to your people."

But Naomi said, "Turn back, my daughters; why will you go with me? Are there still sons in my womb, that they may be your husbands? Turn back, my daughters, go—for I am too old to have a husband. If I should say I have hope, if I should have a husband tonight and should also bear sons, would you wait for them till they were grown? Would you restrain yourselves from having husbands? No, my daughters; for it grieves me very much for your sakes that the hand of the LORD has gone out against me!"

Then they lifted up their voices and wept again; and Orpah kissed her mother-in-law, but Ruth clung to her.

And she said, "Look, your sister-in-law has gone back to her people and to her gods; return after your sister-in-law."

But Ruth said:

> "Entreat me not to leave you,
> Or to turn back from following after you;
> For wherever you go, I will go;
> And wherever you lodge, I will lodge;
> Your people shall be my people,
> And your God, my God.
> Where you die, I will die,
> And there will I be buried.
> The LORD do so to me, and more also,
> If anything but death parts you and me." (Ruth 1:16–17)

LOVE PERSONIFIED

An Active Kind of Love

Those last verses are another passage you only ever hear at weddings; again, like 1 Corinthians 13, it includes way more than love in a marriage. Christian love, the love God commanded, the love that we're supposed to have for each other, for our neighbour, and for our enemy is to be kind. It is supposed to be active; we are supposed to do things for other people.

I want to just pause here because we need to get some context: what happened in the text is a huge, huge deal. You may not know this about the Moabites, but they are distant relatives of the Israelites—the descendants of Lot. When the Israelites were travelling from Egypt into Israel, the Moabites hired Balaam to curse them. So, God actually reversed the curse, saying that no Moabite should ever be in the sanctuary, up to the tenth generation. So, they're excluded from the sanctuary; they're not enemies, but they are not welcome in the community of believers. And Ruth is a Moabitess.

This was also a big deal because, in Leviticus 27, you have all of the land-inheritance laws. This was a paternalistic society; women could not own land. That's why it was so important that they would have a son; without a husband, their land went to the next male relative.

Naomi is going back to Israel destitute, with no hope, nothing. Ruth is going with her, with nothing promised. She is leaving her home, her comfort and security, to be kind to Naomi. Now, there's a really weird part here for us, in verse 12, where Naomi says, "If I should say I have hope, if I should have a husband tonight and should also bear sons, would you wait for them till they were grown?" What a weird thing to say! But again, you have to go back to Deuteronomy 25. This was another Levitical law. Because women couldn't own land, God put a provision in the Law that if a man died sonless, his brother or closest relative would marry the widow so that she could have a son who would be an heir of the deceased, and then she would have land, food, and security.

So that is what Naomi is referring to here: "Even if I had a son today, are you going to wait twenty years?" How old would Ruth and Naomi be to wait for this? So, there is really no hope for them. If anything, Naomi is using hyperbole to point out to Ruth the hopeless situation that Ruth is joining her in.

CHAPTER 2: RUTH IS KIND

A True Love Passage

And what a beautiful passage follows! Read it again. Ruth says,

> "Entreat me not to leave you,
> Or to turn back from following after you;
> For wherever you go, I will go;
> And wherever you lodge, I will lodge;
> Your people shall be my people,
> And your God, my God.
> Where you die, I will die,
> And there will I be buried.
> The Lord do so to me, and more also,
> If anything but death parts you and me." (Ruth 1:16–17)

We do have it partially correct: this is a love passage. She is giving up everything to be with Naomi. So, they return to the country of Israel, to the Bethlehem area. Chapter 2 reads as follows:

> There was a relative of Naomi's husband, a man of great wealth, of the family of Elimelech. His name was Boaz. So Ruth the Moabitess said to Naomi, "Please let me go to the field, and glean heads of grain after him in whose sight I may find favor."
>
> And she said to her, "Go, my daughter."
>
> Then she left, and went and gleaned in the field after the reapers. And she happened to come to the part of the field belonging to Boaz, who was of the family of Elimelech.
>
> Now behold, Boaz came from Bethlehem, and said to the reapers, "The Lord be with you!"
>
> And they answered him, "The Lord bless you!"
>
> [As an aside, I think we should all greet each other like that, sort of how the Anglicans do at church! Sorry, I'm getting off track.]
>
> Then Boaz said to his servant who was in charge of the reapers, "Whose young woman is this?"
>
> So the servant who was in charge of the reapers answered and said, "It is the young Moabite woman who came back with Naomi from the country of Moab. And she said, 'Please let me glean and gather after the reapers among the sheaves.'

> So she came and has continued from morning until now, though she rested a little in the house."
>
> Then Boaz said to Ruth, "You will listen, my daughter, will you not? Do not go to glean in another field, nor go from here, but stay close by my young women. Let your eyes be on the field which they reap, and go after them. Have I not commanded the young men not to touch you? And when you are thirsty, go to the vessels and drink from what the young men have drawn." (Ruth 2:1–9)

And she bows down, and she thanks him.

Acre after Acre of Love

Have you ever gleaned? And I don't mean volunteering with the Gleaners, which is a wonderful organization (look them up online), but do you understand what gleaning is? Gleaning is walking behind the harvesters, bent over all day, picking up whatever scrap you can find to make a meal out of—all day bent over. This is *literally* backbreaking labor. You've heard that as a kind of colloquialism, but this is where it comes from, bent over, trying to glean.

To put gleaning in a little bit more context: Leviticus 19 is where God gives the gleaning rules; he says to the Israelites,

> "When you reap the harvest of your land, you shall not wholly reap the corners of your field, nor shall you gather the gleanings of your harvest. And you shall not glean your vineyard, nor shall you gather every grape of your vineyard; you shall leave them for the poor and the stranger: I am the Lord your God." (Leviticus 19:9–10)

So this was a common practice. Ruth, in her kindness, goes and performs backbreaking labor, acre after acre, trying to find enough to create a loaf of bread for her and her mother-in-law. Kindness—love is kind.

I want to bring us back to the beginning of the book of Ruth: "In the days when the judges ruled." Ever read the book of Judges? It is not a children's book. So, when we get to chapter 2, I want to emphasize that when Boaz says, "Stay close by my young women … Have I not commanded the young men not to touch you?" Some translations use "harm", others "strike", and one even uses the strongest possible English translation, "that they will not molest you."

CHAPTER 2: RUTH IS KIND

Ruth was a Moabite; she had no rights in Israel. She had no land, no security, no one to look after her. And if you think of the book of Judges, without me having to get explicit, you understand the risk that she was taking by going into a stranger's field and gleaning by herself to provide food for her mother-in-law.

So, she's left home and family and security. She spends all day in the hot sun, performing backbreaking work, trying to scratch up enough food for her mother-in-law and herself. She puts herself at physical risk to do this—love is kind. To acknowledge her kindness to Naomi, Boaz allows Ruth to eat with his servants. She has her lunch but saves most of it and brings it back to Naomi.

Naomi is amazed at how much food she has, because Boaz tells the young men to let some drop so she won't have to work so hard and can more easily get enough. She gleans until evening and brings home the food, and explains to Naomi at the end of chapter 2 whose field she was in. Naomi says in verse 22, "It is good, my daughter, that you go out with his young women, and that people do not meet you in any other field."

Have you ever let the Word of God act as a mirror on your life? Really let the Holy Spirit show you in the light of God's perfect way of doing things? I was preparing to preach this chapter of *Love Personified* as a sermon at a church to fill in while the pastor was on vacation. The day before, my youngest son and I were working hard in our yard, digging up some grass and dirt, filling in some low spots, trimming branches, and pulling up weeds. We worked hard, filling a trailer with brush to take to the dump.

When we were driving back, trailer empty, work done, I said to my son, "I'm exhausted and *starving!*" I had some blisters forming, and my back ached. When we got home, it was about 12:30; we had been working for at most four hours. I went to the fridge and grabbed a hot dog bun and scarfed it down plain while I looked for some other leftovers to heat up and eat. I actually said, "Hey, Tobias, you're on your own; grab what you want." That's right! After only four hours of work, I was so selfish and self absorbed, I didn't even feed my son. Then after eating, I took a nap. Contrast that to Ruth, who worked from sunrise to sundown, twelve hours, saved part of her lunch to give to Naomi, and presented her with the fruit of her labour.

As I further let the Holy Spirit expose issues in my life, I reflected on this act of presenting the grain to Naomi. There's that chauvinistic voice in the back of my head: "I'm the breadwinner in my family, so I get final say in how we spend our money." Wow, when I write that down, it really does sound misogynistic and chauvinistic. Ruth is literally the breadwinner in her little family, but out of kindness and respect, she presents the grain to Naomi. She could certainly have used this as leverage: "I worked for this, so we're going to do things my way!" But no, she submits herself to Naomi's plan—and Naomi has a plan!

Naomi's Plan

Just one more time let's remember this warning for Ruth's safety; we can't emphasize this enough. "So she stayed close by the young women of Boaz, to glean until the end of barley harvest and wheat harvest; and she dwelt with her mother-in-law" (Ruth 2:23). Naomi then says to her in chapter 3, "My daughter, shall I not seek security for you?" Remember, even after all of Boaz's kindness, they may have food, but they are still squatters on somebody else's land. Once Naomi is gone, Ruth, the foreigner, will not be welcome in the community of Israel.

> "My daughter, shall I not seek security for you, that it may be well with you? Now Boaz, whose young women you were with, is he not our relative? In fact, he is winnowing barley tonight at the threshing floor. Therefore wash yourself and anoint yourself, put on your best garment and go down to the threshing floor; but do not make yourself known to the man until he has finished eating and drinking. Then it shall be, when he lies down, that you shall notice the place where he lies; and you shall go in, uncover his feet, and lie down; and he will tell you what you should do."
> And [Ruth] said to her, "All that you say to me I will do." (Ruth 3:1–5)

Now, I spent some time trying to research this advice from Naomi. This is the only time in the Bible that this idea of uncovering someone's feet or lying at their feet is mentioned, and commentators have different ideas of what it means. Basically, Ruth is throwing herself at Boaz. She's saying, "I am here, I will be your wife."

Boaz wakes up, startled, and he says (starting at verse 10),

> "Blessed are you of the LORD, my daughter! For you have shown more kindness at the end than at the beginning, in

> that you did not go after young men, whether poor or rich. And now, my daughter, do not fear. I will do for you all that you request, for all the people of my town know that you are a virtuous woman. Now it is true that I am a close relative; however, there is a relative closer than I. Stay this night, and in the morning it shall be that if he will perform the duty of a close relative for you—good; let him do it. But if he does not want to perform the duty for you, then I will perform the duty for you, as the LORD lives! Lie down until morning." (Ruth 3:10–13)

So, back to Leviticus and the whole rule about land inheritance. If someone dies, the land goes to a brother, or if he doesn't have a brother, it goes to a cousin, and so on to a near kinsman, or some versions will say a "kinsman redeemer". And they have the right to own that land. And no matter who took the land when Elimelech left, Boaz, or this other man who's unnamed, has the right to go and "buy" it. Not really buy it; they can claim it. So, this is how Ruth is going to gain security for herself and Naomi.

Now, we've already read how Boaz refers to her as daughter. We're not told exactly how old Boaz is, but we get the idea that there is a substantial age difference. Again, we're trying to recapture what Christian love is. There is no mention of attraction here for Ruth to Boaz—no infatuation for Ruth to Boaz. It is possible that he is already married with a family of his own. This is out of duty. This is out of kindness for her mother-in-law. And that's why Boaz says, "You have shown more kindness [presenting yourself to me] at the end than at the beginning [even greater than you going out, doing backbreaking work, gathering grain and gleaning in the fields]."

Boaz to the Rescue

Moving on to chapter 4,

> Boaz went up to the gate and sat down there; and behold, the close relative of whom Boaz had spoken came by. So Boaz said, "Come aside, friend, sit down here." So he came aside and sat down. And he took ten men of the elders of the city, and said, "Sit down here." So they sat down. Then he said to the close relative, "Naomi, who has come back from the country of Moab, sold the piece of land which belonged to our brother Elimelech. And I thought to inform you, saying,

> 'Buy it back in the presence of the inhabitants and the elders of my people. If you will redeem it, redeem it; but if you will not redeem it, then tell me, that I may know; for there is no one but you to redeem it, and I am next after you.'"
>
> And he said, "I will redeem it." (Ruth 4:1–4)

Our unnamed friend is probably thinking "Great, free land. I get land, wonderful. More food for my family, more security for my family."

Then Boaz adds,

> "On the day you buy the field from the hand of Naomi, you must also buy it from Ruth the Moabitess, the wife of the dead, to perpetuate the name of the dead through his inheritance." (Ruth 4:5)

So again, this idea that a brother, a cousin, an uncle, or whatever male relative was to marry the woman so that she would have a son in the name of her dead husband and have security, have land. And the near kinsman says, "I cannot redeem it for myself, lest I ruin my own inheritance. You redeem my right of redemption for yourself, for I cannot redeem it" (Ruth 4:6).

Now, this is basically an excuse. He doesn't lose his inheritance by taking another one. Whatever his excuse is, he does not want to marry Ruth, the Moabitess. He doesn't want this hassle. He realizes this isn't a quick land grab increasing his possessions. Ruth's first son will inherit the land to carry on Elimelech's line. This man is *not* kind.

> This was the custom in former times in Israel concerning redeeming and exchanging, to confirm anything: one man took off his sandal and gave it to the other, and this was a confirmation in Israel. (Ruth 4:7)

Wouldn't you love to buy a house for a sandal? No further commentary on current house prices.

And so that day, Boaz then claims the land, takes Ruth as his wife; and, as we know, they have a child named Obed, who has a child named Jesse, who has a child named David.

CHAPTER 2: RUTH IS KIND

Kindness Is Rewarded

Very much like the previous chapter, what seemed like a terrible, horrible situation, God uses for good. God redeems it. Here again is a lesson for another book. What we want to focus on, though, is kindness—showing love to each other, to our neighbour, to our enemy, with kindness—active, self-sacrificing kindness. Just to reiterate, one more time: Ruth in chapter 1 leaves her home, her family, her comfort, her security, out of kindness, out of love for Naomi, to take care of her.

Have you ever been in a situation where you could easily stay home and just not get involved? And it's perfectly all right? Naomi says, "Just go home. It's hopeless! Orpah went home. Go home, Ruth." Have you ever been in that situation where you could choose comfort versus love, security versus love?

In chapter 2, Ruth goes on and she gleans in the field hour after hour. The Bible says that she did it through the entire barley and wheat harvest, day after day, week after week, bent over, scratching out whatever she could get to make a loaf of bread at home. Have you ever been in a situation where you're asked to give a little bit of blood, sweat, and tears for somebody else? And you had the option to just get enough for yourself and not worry about others, or you could just mail it in?

Have you ever put yourself, the way Ruth did, at physical risk by going out there by herself as a Moabitess in this time and age in Israel, the time of the judges, where the Bible says that people did whatever they thought was good in their own eyes, and it was terrible? She puts herself in harm's way to show love to someone else. Have you ever been put in a situation where you've got to risk your own safety and health to show love for someone else?

Finally, she chooses to marry Boaz, an older man, out of duty to provide security for her and her mother-in-law. In chapter 1, Naomi is saying, "Go back to Moab, find a young man, fall in love, get married, have kids, and live happily ever after." Out of duty, Ruth chooses the opposite, sacrificing pleasure, comfort, and happiness—out of duty, out of kindness, out of love.

Have you ever been faced with doing something out of duty for someone else? See, this doesn't sound romantic! I hope you're getting the point here. This love that God calls us to has nothing to do with romance, affection, emotion, or feelings. Jesus Christ came to the cross and said, "Not My will, Father, but Thine be done." Out of duty, out of love, He gave His life for us.

One more quick story from our family. We attend a church downtown in our city, right beside a Salvation Army drop-in centre. When pandemic lockdowns restricted the number of men allowed in the shelter, we started seeing a dozen guys sleeping on the front steps of our church. What is a church to do? Kick them off? Call the cops? The leadership decided we needed to show kindness. So, we started feeding them and gathering donations of clothes. We even started a Thursday service called "Church at the Table" where they are provided a hot meal. To do all this, they hired my wife Melody to organize the outreach.

Once again, God's Word is a mirror and exposes my sin. Melody is constantly giving, going, and answering calls late into the evening. The outreach has grown to meeting the needs of refugee families. The other day, she loaned our Crockpot to a family. I was really upset, that was mine. I had no plans to use it, but for whatever reason, I resented her lending it out, and I wanted it back. It eventually came back, full of some incredible food as a thank you. Maybe you're like me (say "yes" so I don't feel like such a monster)—you are self-absorbed and focused on your own needs and wants. Love is putting others first in a tangible, self-sacrificing way. That is kindness.

My wife gets it, even when she is taken advantage of, even when those she is helping disappoint her and fall back into old habits of drug addiction or crime. She keeps showing kindness to those guys on our church steps. It doesn't matter if we are ever paid back. We are to show love. "For God so loved the world," but not everyone accepts God's gift of love. Not everyone will accept your kindness. It doesn't matter; be kind anyway.

Sacrifice Ends in Blessing

I have some homework for you. I guarantee that before one week is out, you will be faced with a choice. To either stay home and not get involved, to take care of your own needs and comfort or sacrifice some time, perhaps some resources, and definitely some emotions to show kindness to someone in need. Love is a choice. Choose kindness. I won't promise that everything will work out great for you, but I know that when we do things God's way, there are always blessings that follow.

Chapter 3

Jonathan Does Not Envy

We've been learning about love. This is not church nursery–level stuff. I hope you've seen from the examples of Joseph and Ruth that this is difficult, high-level discipleship, suffering, kindness, and self-sacrifice.

And it doesn't get any easier when we talk about envy. In Acts chapter 7, when Stephen is being tried in front of the Sanhedrin for his testimony about Jesus Christ, he gives an account of the history of Israel. He talks about the story of Joseph and his brothers, and he says, "The patriarchs, becoming envious, sold Joseph into Egypt" (Acts 7:9). This is the same word Paul uses in 1 Corinthians 13. Envy is the outward expression of our most base human characteristics of selfishness, greed, lust, and pride.

Let's read 1 Corinthians 13:4–8 again:

> Love suffers long and is kind; love does not envy; love does not parade itself, is not puffed up; does not behave rudely, does not seek its own, is not provoked, thinks no evil; does not rejoice in iniquity, but rejoices in the truth; bears all things, believes all things, hopes all things, endures all things. Love never fails.

When I read that list, it goes right over my head. I can't absorb all of those things. That's why we're taking the time to look, one at a time, at people who each personify one of those characteristics, to help us understand and apply it.

So, we have this concept of love not envying. And we have the negative example of Joseph's brothers, whom we studied at length, who really did envy. And you saw all the damage that envy caused; they hated their brother, treated him abusively, planned his murder, and sold him into slavery. Envy does terrible things; jealousy does terrible things.

LOVE PERSONIFIED

I wanted to find someone who could serve as an example for us, someone who could look across at somebody else and not envy. Not like Joseph's brothers, who said, "Look at everything he has: he got the coat. Dad loves him best. I want that kind of relationship. I hate that guy." So, take your Bible and turn to 1 Samuel 13. I want to look at someone who had every right to say, "That should have been me; I deserve that. It's been taken from me," but didn't, and instead acted in love.

Birthright

This is the story of the crown prince of Israel, Jonathan. Just to get us up to speed, we have come out of the era of the judges, where we were studying Ruth. This is a terrible time, so the people want a king who they think will bring law, order, justice, and deliverance to the people. They go to Samuel, the prophet, and say, "Give us a king." So, he anoints Saul. Saul has a couple of sons, one of them being Jonathan.

Let's pick up the story in 1 Samuel 13:1:

> Saul reigned one year, and when he had reigned two years over Israel, Saul chose for himself three thousand men of Israel. Two thousand were with Saul in Michmash in the mountains of Bethel, and a thousand were with Jonathan in Gibeah of Benjamin. The rest of the people he sent away, every man to his tent.
> And Jonathan attacked the garrison of the Philistines that was in Geba, and the Philistines heard of it. Then Saul blew the trumpet throughout all the land, saying, "Let the Hebrews hear!" Now all Israel heard it said that Saul had attacked a garrison of the Philistines, and that Israel had also become an abomination to the Philistines. And the people were called together to Saul at Gilgal.
> Then the Philistines gathered together to fight with Israel, thirty thousand chariots and six thousand horsemen, and people as the sand which is on the seashore in multitude. And they came up and encamped in Michmash, to the east of Beth Aven.
> When the men of Israel saw that they were in danger (for the people were distressed), then the people hid in caves, in thickets, in rocks, in holes, and in pits. (1 Samuel 13:1–6)

So, what happens here? Jonathan starts the battle to deliver Israel, and his father gets involved. And then the people get a look at the enemy and get scared, and they take off.

Right by Deed

Let's jump ahead to Chapter 14 to pick up Jonathan's story. We'll be doing this a lot because even though Jonathan is the crown prince, he is only a supporting character in this drama.

> Now it happened one day that Jonathan the son of Saul said to the young man who bore his armor, "Come, let us go over to the Philistines' garrison that is on the other side." But he did not tell his father. And Saul was sitting in the outskirts of Gibeah under a pomegranate tree which is in Migron. The people who were with him were about six hundred men. Ahijah the son of Ahitub, Ichabod's brother, the son of Phinehas, the son of Eli, the Lord's priest in Shiloh, was wearing an ephod. But the people did not know that Jonathan had gone.
>
> Between the passes, by which Jonathan sought to go over to the Philistines' garrison, there was a sharp rock on one side and a sharp rock on the other side. And the name of one was Bozez, and the name of the other Seneh. The front of one faced northward opposite Michmash, and the other southward opposite Gibeah.
>
> Then Jonathan said to the young man who bore his armor, "Come, let us go over to the garrison of these uncircumcised; it may be that the Lord will work for us. For nothing restrains the Lord from saving by many or by few."
>
> So his armorbearer said to him, "Do all that is in your heart. Go then; here I am with you, according to your heart."
>
> Then Jonathan said, "Very well, let us cross over to these men, and we will show ourselves to them. If they say thus to us, 'Wait until we come to you,' then we will stand still in our place and not go up to them. But if they say thus, 'Come up to us,' then we will go up. For the Lord has delivered them into our hand, and this will be a sign to us."
>
> So both of them showed themselves to the garrison of the Philistines. And the Philistines said, "Look, the Hebrews are coming out of the holes where they have hidden." Then the

> men of the garrison called to Jonathan and his armorbearer, and said, "Come up to us, and we will show you something."
>
> Jonathan said to his armorbearer, "Come up after me, for the LORD has delivered them into the hand of Israel." And Jonathan climbed up on his hands and knees with his armorbearer after him; and they fell before Jonathan. And as he came after him, his armorbearer killed them. That first slaughter which Jonathan and his armorbearer made was about twenty men within about half an acre of land.
>
> And there was trembling in the camp, in the field, and among all the people. The garrison and the raiders also trembled; and the earth quaked, so that it was a very great trembling. (1 Samuel 14:1–15)

Then it goes on to recount how the Philistines flee from Jonathan and his armour-bearer. The whole army of Israel is gathered. They go pursuing them across the countryside; the fight is so fast and furious that Saul says, "No one stops for food. We're going to pursue them until we've slaughtered them."

Right by Popular Demand

And so, as they're chasing the Philistines (if you know the story), Jonathan is going past a tree, and he sees a honeycomb. He sticks it on his spear and takes some of the honey to strengthen his body, because he didn't know that Saul had pronounced a curse on anyone that stopped to eat during this battle because he wanted so badly to kill the Philistines all in one fell swoop.

Now the rest of chapter 14 recounts the battle, and then we come to verse 37. They've been pursuing the Philistines all day. It gets to be nighttime, and they take a break, finally stopping to eat, but because they are so hungry, they are eating their meat raw. Saul, knowing God's laws about eating meat with the blood still in it, commands them to stop and properly cook it. After this short break Saul wants to rejoin the battle.

> Saul asked counsel of God, "Shall I go down after the Philistines? Will You deliver them into the hand of Israel?" But He did not answer him that day. And Saul said, "Come over here, all you chiefs of the people, and know and see what this sin was today. For as the LORD lives, who saves Israel, though it be in Jonathan my son, he shall surely die." But not a man among all the people answered him. Then he said to all

CHAPTER 3: JONATHAN DOES NOT ENVY

Israel, "You be on one side, and my son Jonathan and I will be on the other side."

And the people said to Saul, "Do what seems good to you."

Therefore Saul said to the LORD God of Israel, "Give a perfect lot." So Saul and Jonathan were taken, but the people escaped. And Saul said, "Cast lots between my son Jonathan and me." So Jonathan was taken. Then Saul said to Jonathan, "Tell me what you have done."

And Jonathan told him, and said, "I only tasted a little honey with the end of the rod that was in my hand. So now I must die!"

Saul answered, "God do so and more also; for you shall surely die, Jonathan."

But the people said to Saul, "Shall Jonathan die, who has accomplished this great deliverance in Israel? Certainly not! As the LORD lives, not one hair of his head shall fall to the ground, for he has worked with God this day." So the people rescued Jonathan, and he did not die. (1 Samuel 14:37–45)

They call off the battle and go back home, even though they still have the problem with the Philistines. I highlight this story because I want to demonstrate Jonathan's character. First of all, by birthright he is the future king of Israel, the crown prince. Number two: his character, faith, and trust in God are evident as he turns to his armorbearer and says, "God can deliver with many or with few." You see his faith when he goes out and starts to deliver Israel from the hand of the Philistines. What courage! He is an incredible man.

Then in verse 44, when Saul says that Jonathan has disobeyed the command and it is his fault they didn't completely wipe the Philistines out, he declares that Jonathan must die. But the people gather and respond, "No, we choose Jonathan!" By the voice of the people, they want Jonathan. By birthright, character, faith, and his relationship with God, Jonathan deserves to be king; he has earned that right, and the people choose him. Now we're getting to see who Jonathan is.

But Jonathan is not even the main character in this story; he's a supporting actor for someone else. "And he's the crown prince? This story doesn't make sense!" Just to establish some context we have to mention the main character, David. To be brief, we first meet David when, out of nowhere, he is anointed by Samuel to be king. His career in the palace starts out with him just singing

LOVE PERSONIFIED

to Saul whenever the king is in a bad mood, and in chapter 17, he defeats Goliath. It seems that only after that does he first meet our guy, Jonathan.

Their Souls Are Knit Together

This is where we pick up the story, in chapter 18.

> Now when he [David] had finished speaking to Saul, the soul of Jonathan was knit to the soul of David, and Jonathan loved him as his own soul. Saul took him that day, and would not let him go home to his father's house anymore. Then Jonathan and David made a covenant, because he loved him as his own soul. And Jonathan took off the robe that was on him and gave it to David, with his armor, even to his sword and his bow and his belt.
> So David went out wherever Saul sent him, and behaved wisely. And Saul set him over the men of war, and he was accepted in the sight of all the people and also in the sight of Saul's servants. Now it had happened as they were coming home, when David was returning from the slaughter of the Philistine [Goliath], that the women had come out of all the cities of Israel, singing and dancing, to meet King Saul, with tambourines, with joy, and with musical instruments. So the women sang as they danced, and said:
> "Saul has slain his thousands,
> And David his ten thousands."
> Then Saul was very angry, and the saying displeased him; and he said, "They have ascribed to David ten thousands, and to me they have ascribed only thousands. Now what more can he have but the kingdom?" So Saul eyed David from that day forward. (1 Samuel 18:1–9)

The Contrast of Father and Son

When it says, "Saul eyed David," it means he eyed him with suspicion or jealousy, envy. Jonathan could have been in that parade as well. You remember who started the deliverance? Jonathan. Do you remember who won those battles? It was Jonathan. Jonathan heard the songs as well about Saul and David. And guess what? He didn't even get a verse. He didn't get "hundreds" or even "dozens"; he didn't get anything! Yet we don't hear about Jonathan

CHAPTER 3: JONATHAN DOES NOT ENVY

envying David. We certainly hear about Saul. We have this incredible contrast now between Saul and Jonathan and their view of David. One loves David, the other is threatened by him, despises him.

Then Saul tries to pin David to the wall with a spear—twice. That doesn't work, so he thinks that to get rid of David, he'll send him out to fight the Philistines with bad odds, which doesn't work. Again, the story is all about David; Jonathan is just a supporting actor.

In chapter 19, David has just come back from another successful vanquishing of the Philistine armies, and everyone loves him.

> Now Saul spoke to Jonathan his son and to all his servants, that they should kill David; but Jonathan, Saul's son, delighted greatly in David. So Jonathan told David, saying, "My father Saul seeks to kill you. Therefore please be on your guard until morning, and stay in a secret place and hide. And I will go out and stand beside my father in the field where you are, and I will speak with my father about you. Then what I observe, I will tell you."
>
> Thus Jonathan spoke well of David to Saul his father, and said to him, "Let not the king sin against his servant, against David, because he has not sinned against you, and because his works have been very good toward you. For he took his life in his hands and killed the Philistine, and the LORD brought about a great deliverance for all Israel. You saw it and rejoiced. Why then will you sin against innocent blood, to kill David without a cause?"
>
> So Saul heeded the voice of Jonathan, and Saul swore, "As the LORD lives, he shall not be killed." Then Jonathan called David, and Jonathan told him all these things. So Jonathan brought David to Saul, and he was in his presence as in times past. (1 Samuel 19:1–7)

And they lived happily ever after.

No! Next verses:

> And there was war again; and David went out and fought with the Philistines, and struck them with a mighty blow, and they fled from him.

> Now the distressing spirit from the LORD came upon Saul as he sat in his house with his spear in his hand. And David was playing music with his hand. Then Saul sought to pin David to the wall with the spear, but he slipped away from Saul's presence; and he drove the spear into the wall. So David fled and escaped that night. (1 Samuel 19:8–10)

Broken Promises

So much for his promise, "As the LORD lives, he shall not be killed." We go three verses down, and he tries it again! Saul then sends messengers to try to kill David in his bed, and he tries to kill him at Samuel's house. The envy, the hatred, the fear of David taking over his kingdom is all-consuming for Saul, but not Jonathan. Why not? Jonathan is the rightful heir to the throne; he has earned it by his character, and the people love him.

Skipping ahead to 1 Samuel 20:27, the New Moon feast is approaching, and David should be there at the king's table.

> It happened the next day, the second day of the month, that David's place was empty. And Saul said to Jonathan his son, "Why has the son of Jesse not come to eat, either yesterday or today?"
> So Jonathan answered Saul, "David earnestly asked permission of me to go to Bethlehem. And he said, 'Please let me go, for our family has a sacrifice in the city, and my brother has commanded me to be there. And now, if I have found favor in your eyes, please let me get away and see my brothers.' Therefore he has not come to the king's table."
> Then Saul's anger was aroused against Jonathan, and he said to him, "You son of a perverse, rebellious woman! Do I not know that you have chosen the son of Jesse to your own shame and to the shame of your mother's nakedness? For as long as the son of Jesse lives on the earth, you shall not be established, nor your kingdom. Now therefore, send and bring him to me, for he shall surely die."
> And Jonathan answered Saul his father, and said to him, "Why should he be killed? What has he done?" Then Saul cast a spear at him to kill him, by which Jonathan knew that it was determined by his father to kill David.

CHAPTER 3: JONATHAN DOES NOT ENVY

> So Jonathan arose from the table in fierce anger, and ate no food the second day of the month, for he was grieved for David, because his father had treated him shamefully. (1 Samuel 20:27–34)

The Crown Prince and the Anointed One

Now we have the famous Sunday school story of the boy with the bow and arrow. Jonathan goes out to the field and says, "My father is going to kill you; you have to run." And they embrace and weep, and David leaves. If there is any doubt that Jonathan didn't understand what was happening, it has certainly been cleared up here. If he didn't know that David had been anointed by Samuel to be the next king of Israel, Saul certainly made sure he knew now.

So here again, we need to put ourselves in the story. How would you feel if it was not only your birthright but you'd earned it and the people endorsed you to be king, and some usurper came by to take your place?

Now, I know you are most likely not the crown prince or princess and in line to inherit the throne of some kingdom. But here's the situation: Maybe you're at work. You have worked hard and with loyalty. You've been there for years. You deserve the promotion. You've done everything right. You put in the extra hours, and your performance shows it; your coworkers say, "Yes, Tim's the guy.," Then you get passed over; and you look at the other person who got the job. What is your feeling towards them?

You may not believe it to look at me, but I was a basketball star. Two-time city all-star for my junior varsity team. In my first year playing senior ball, my coach gathered the team at the end of the season to let us vote on who would represent us at the all-star game. One of my teammates asked, "Who would you choose?" He responded, "Tim."

Right away there was pushback: "No, one of the seniors should go; Tim has more years left." Then there was debate over my worthiness. I was sitting in the room listening to all this. So, we had the vote after all, and another guy was picked: Jeremy, a senior. I could live with that, but it was still hard to swallow. But for reasons I never found out he ended up not playing, and another guy was chosen as the all-star for our team. Why was I left out?

Looking back, that all-star nod to Kevin was pivotal. The next year, we were co-captains, and he came out of nowhere to be the best player on our team. The all-star nod was a huge boost to his confidence. I'm still a little burned by it, such a trivial thing that I still remember vividly. But our team was better for it. I know what it's like to feel slighted and to envy.

Envy Is an Enemy to Love

That's the crux: that's the advanced discipleship that we're talking about here when we're talking about love. When God commands us to love our neighbour, to love each other, and to love our enemy, it's these situations that He's talking about. We must consider what to do with that person, how to treat them, and what our speech towards them should be. We see this in Saul's attempt to kill David, and the envy, jealousy, and hatred that boils up within him. The Greek word for jealousy is the same word used for a boiling pot, indicating an uncontrollable, spilling-over emotion. We see this same emotion in Joseph's brothers, who are willing to kill him.

Envy is an enemy to love. So, how do we respond? Jonathan is willing to give up his rightful place as king—and not only give it up, but help David get away, help him escape Saul, and help him become the king.

Again, 1 Samuel isn't about Jonathan; we must skip ahead to the last chapter of the book before we see Jonathan again. The rest is all about David, some shepherd boy who shouldn't be king. In 1 Samuel 31, the Philistines haven't been dealt with yet, and here they are again.

> The Philistines fought against Israel; and the men of Israel fled from before the Philistines, and fell slain on Mount Gilboa. Then the Philistines followed hard after Saul and his sons. And the Philistines killed Jonathan, Abinadab, and Malchishua, Saul's sons. (1 Samuel 31:1–2)

And that's the end of the story of Jonathan. He dies in battle beside his father, loyal to the end, despite Saul's threatening to kill him, name-calling, and insisting that he will never have the kingdom.

He fights to the end beside his father.

The Song of the Bow

One last little bit about Jonathan; it's in 2 Samuel chapter 1. And just because he is such an incredible person, with such an incredible character, I think he

CHAPTER 3: JONATHAN DOES NOT ENVY

deserves that we read the song written for him; it begins in 2 Samuel 1:19. We need to give Jonathan his due; he doesn't get a lot of ink. We've been skipping over, what, fifteen, twenty chapters and he's barely mentioned. But let's read his song here. This is David's song for Saul and Jonathan:

> "The beauty of Israel is slain on your high places!
> How the mighty have fallen!
> Tell it not in Gath,
> Proclaim it not in the streets of Ashkelon—
> Lest the daughters of the Philistines rejoice,
> Lest the daughters of the uncircumcised triumph.
>
> "O mountains of Gilboa,
> Let there be no dew nor rain upon you,
> Nor fields of offerings.
> For the shield of the mighty is cast away there!
> The shield of Saul, not anointed with oil.
> From the blood of the slain,
> From the fat of the mighty,
> The bow of Jonathan did not turn back,
> And the sword of Saul did not return empty.
>
> "Saul and Jonathan were beloved and pleasant in their lives,
> And in their death they were not divided;
> They were swifter than eagles,
> They were stronger than lions.
>
> O daughters of Israel, weep over Saul,
> Who clothed you in scarlet, with luxury;
> Who put ornaments of gold on your apparel.
>
> "How the mighty have fallen in the midst of the battle!
> Jonathan was slain in your high places.
> I am distressed for you, my brother Jonathan;
> You have been very pleasant to me;
> Your love to me was wonderful,
> Surpassing the love of women.
>
> "How the mighty have fallen,
> And the weapons of war perished!" (2 Samuel 1:19–27)

Choosing to Love

I've been saying all along that we've got to recapture what God means when He says love. At first, we read this song through our cultural lens and think, "Well, that's kind of weird!" because it doesn't fit what we mean when we say the word *love*. But this love, this bond of love—unemotional devotion—it's not fleeting. It's not an infatuation. Jonathan chose to love David. It says Jonathan knit his heart with David. Jonathan cared about David so much that Jonathan would rather let David be king than fight against him. Phenomenal love. Phenomenal grace. Not envy.

So how did Jonathan do it? How was Jonathan able to stand by and watch David take the throne right from under him? How was Jonathan able to help David? Jonathan could have just stepped back and said, "Okay, my dad's going to get him, and then I'll be king, and everything's going to be okay!" But instead, Jonathan *helped* David get the throne.

Turn to Philippians 4:11–13:

> Not that I speak in regard to need, for I have learned in whatever state I am, to be content. I know how to be abased, and I know how to abound. Everywhere and in all things I have learned both to be full and to be hungry, both to abound and to suffer need. I can do all things through Christ who strengthens me.

First Timothy 6:6 says: "Godliness with contentment is great gain."

Hebrews 13:5 says: "Let your conduct be without covetousness; be content with such things as you have. For He Himself has said, 'I will never leave you nor forsake you.'"

Contentment

Contentment. "Now, wait a minute, Tim! That doesn't fit with the whole relationship between Jonathan and David." But we're not just discussing the love between Jonathan and David. Jonathan loved David and did not envy him; but contentment is a demonstration of our love for God. The first and greatest commandment is to love the Lord your God with all your heart, soul, mind, and strength.

CHAPTER 3: JONATHAN DOES NOT ENVY

Here's the key to not envying: to love God so much that you trust His plan for your life. That way, you can celebrate His plan in somebody else's life. Until you can accept what God has called you to be and to do, and find contentment with that, you will never be able to love others or live without envy and jealousy of what God's plan is for others.

Jonathan dies in battle. In our storybook, happily-ever-after culture, someone who is so noble, who trusts God so much, and who is such a great friend should have a happy ending. We hear it in his speeches to his armorbearer. He says, "If God wills it, we can do it." Jonathan says to Saul when he's defending David, "It was God who brought this deliverance." His trust, his faith in God is so profound that he is content with God's plan for his life, even though it means not getting what he deserves and becoming king. That is high-level discipleship; that is deep love for God.

I have five kids, as I mentioned, and with each of them, when they were younger, we would read through *The Chronicles of Narnia.* My favourite book was *The Horse and His Boy.* Quick synopsis with only mild spoilers: a little boy named Shasta is rescued from the land of Calormen, along with a little girl named Aravis. They get to the country bordering Narnia, Archenland. If you haven't read the books, please read the books! Come on, it's *The Chronicles of Narnia!*

What Is It to You?

Shasta is left alone with Aslan the lion—God—and Shasta turns to Aslan and asks about Aravis. And Aslan says to Shasta, "I am telling you your story, not hers. I tell no one any story but his own." And it reminded me of the passage in John 21:21.

We have this beautiful scene of Jesus on the beach with His disciples after the Resurrection, and he says to Peter, "Peter, do you love Me?"

"Of course, Jesus. You know." They go back and forth, and then Peter looks over and sees John, and he says, "What about him?"

Jesus replies, "What is it to you? You follow Me."

That is the message that we learn from Jonathan's life: if we are to truly love as God has commanded us to love, if we're to love each other as we're commanded, all people will know we are His disciples. That should be the defining characteristic of our lives, of our churches: love. We should love our neighbour. We should love our enemies.

Love Means Trust

If love is to be the defining characteristic of us as Christians, we need to love God enough to trust that His story for us, His plan for us, is enough and to be content and to even celebrate what He does in the lives of others.

An overly simplified example (this one burns me): I don't know if it can be classified as a pet peeve, but when it's the Sunday church service on Mother's Day, the pastor doesn't come up and say, "Happy Mother's Day" anymore. They've changed it to: "Happy Mother's Day to all the women here, whether they're mothers or not." This is a symptom of our culture, where it's all about *me.* And we're not willing to say (or trust others to say), "God has a plan for me that right now does not include children, and I'm willing to celebrate others who are mothers." They've got to mention everybody because we can't leave anybody out. We don't want to hurt anybody's feelings. We couldn't hurt their feelings if they were content with what God gave them and they could celebrate what God has done for somebody else.

That's just a practical example, since none of us are crown princes of Israel and might not be able to relate to Jonathan's story.

Contentment. Celebrate with others; love God enough to trust Him with the plan for your life.

We Are Supporting Actors

The homework on this chapter is simple. The next time you see someone else succeed, even if it is at your expense, celebrate it. Authentically. First, stop and say a silent prayer telling God that you love Him and that you trust His plan for your life. Then go up to that person and let them gush with all the enthusiasm that good news brings. Pray a blessing on them. Then write about it down below. It will do good for your heart as well.

Chapter 4

Moses Does Not Parade Himself

Growing up, I used to sing a song in church based on Hebrews 13:15, "We bring the sacrifice of praise into the house of the Lord." It was a catchy tune. Although I never really understood what it meant, I knew what a sacrifice was. You can go through Leviticus 23 and Deuteronomy 18 and find all sorts of rules there for the ancient Israelites on how they are to worship God by sacrificing things.

In Leviticus, it talks about sacrificing the first fruits of your crops, and all throughout Exodus, Leviticus, and Deuteronomy, there are numerous commands: sacrifices for sin, atonement of sin, peace offerings—all these offerings where you bring an animal, kill it, and offer it as a sacrificial substitute. The punishment for sin is death; something must die, and God allowed the ancient Israelites to bring an animal as a substitute in their place.

There's a great passage in the life of David, in 1 Samuel, where God initiates a plague due to David's sin. In response, David goes out to make an offering to stop the plague. He goes to the threshing floor of Araunah the Jebusite, and when the man offers the oxen and wood for free, David refuses, stating, "I will not sacrifice something that doesn't cost me; otherwise, it's no sacrifice."

Sacrifice Costs

Sacrifice: the idea of giving something up. In this context, with David, giving up something of our livelihood to God. We are saying, "God, I trust You that You will be my provider. I'm not relying on my own assets, my own things, or my own ability; but in faith, I'm going to trust You to provide." And that's what part of sacrifice is.

Even now, in the New Testament era, I believe in sacrifice being an important part of worship. I know we are free from the Law, but I believe in tithing. As children, we were always taught to tithe, and our church continues to teach it.

I think tithing predates the Levitical and Deuteronomic laws, tracing back to Abraham when he gave a tenth of a battle's plunder to Melchizedek, the priest of the Lord.

There's a covenant relationship with God through tithing that is more than keeping the Law. There's something about giving God a sacrifice from our first fruits; it's a way of acknowledging Him as our provider and relying on Him. Wait, how did I get here? I just looked up from my keyboard and realized that I have gone down a very long bunny trail. Back to the point.

What's this idea of a sacrifice of praise? That's the part I never got. What do I give up by singing? My time? A little energy? No, I believe the idea revolves around what praise includes.

But How Is Worship Sacrifice?

When we exalt God, or even just praise someone else, we are essentially positioning them in relation to us. We're saying, "You're better than me; you're worthier than me"; I take a subservient spot when I praise. With God, when we sing a song like "Holy, Holy, Holy," we admit that God is separate and superior to us. Similarly, when we sing, "Not I, but Christ through me," we acknowledge that our good deeds are due to Christ working within us. Or my wife's favourite chorus, "Lord, I need you": again, we're positioning God in a place of provision and authority, and we're making ourselves subservient.

And I believe that's a sacrifice, especially in our current culture where everything is "me, me, me". We live in an era of influencers and followers, and everyone is exalting themselves, parading themselves. This is where we find ourselves in our study of 1 Corinthians 13—Love does not parade itself.

A Parade Doesn't Always Involve Clowns

Now, the Oxford dictionary provides several good definitions for *parade*. A parade can involve clowns and marching bands going down your street, but that's the noun. The verb form means to make a formal procession, and it can have a negative connotation—to be ostentatious or attention-seeking, putting yourself in front of others in order to get people to look at you.

To summarize, a parade in its most positive meaning is to celebrate the accomplishments of someone. I'm a big sports fan, and although I have never attended a championship parade for my favourite teams, I have watched with envy

CHAPTER 4: MOSES DOES NOT PARADE HIMSELF

the TV footage of thousands of people lining the streets to cheer on their sports heroes.

But I think, in the context of what Paul is speaking about here, we may need to lean more towards the negative connotation of the word: someone acting in a prideful, arrogant manner. In the Authorized Version, the old King James Bible, it says, "Love vaunteth not itself." Think of someone who accomplishes something and just can't wait to tell you what a great job they've done. The modern term for this behaviour is *virtue signaling*. "Look at me: I'm important, and I've done something special." Love does not act this way: it is quiet and humble. It does its good deeds in secret (Matthew 6:1–4). Love gives up its opportunity to parade itself, even when it has done something commendable.

The reason I wanted to address this "sacrifice of praise" is that I believe it to be one of the tangible ways to express our love for God. In Matthew 25, Jesus explains that service to others is service to God, and I would add that love for others is love for God. But often we don't link the two. It's far easier for me to express love for others. We're all innately programmed with the notion of affection or attraction. I embrace my children to show my love. But remember, that's not the paradigm of love we're discussing here. However, these images and emotional actions are ever-present in our minds, so it raises the question: how do we show love for God, when we can't perform these tactile acts like giving Him a present or hugging Him? There's always an intermediary when we do things for God. This is why the idea of "sacrifice of praise" is so important.

We express our love for God by repetitively affirming that God is superior to us. "You're holy. You're wonderful. I need You. Without You, I can't do anything. Everything I have is from You." This shows God love because it puts Him in His proper place as *Lord* while recognizing that we are not. This is how we love Him with all our heart, soul, mind, and strength. It is a purposeful action to put Him on a pedestal, to give Him attention, and not to take the attention for ourselves.

The Most Humble Man

Who models this type of behaviour of not parading themselves so that we can follow their example? Well, turn to the book of Exodus in your Bible. We're going to study the life of the most humble man who ever lived, Moses.

> A man of the house of Levi went and took as wife a daughter of Levi. So the woman conceived and bore a son. And

> when she saw that he was a beautiful child, she hid him three months. But when she could no longer hide him, she took an ark of bulrushes for him, daubed it with asphalt and pitch, put the child in it, and laid it in the reeds by the river's bank. And his sister stood afar off, to know what would be done to him.
>
> Then the daughter of Pharaoh came down to bathe at the river. And her maidens walked along the riverside; and when she saw the ark among the reeds, she sent her maid to get it. And when she opened it, she saw the child, and behold, the baby wept. So she had compassion on him, and said, "This is one of the Hebrews' children."
>
> Then his sister said to Pharaoh's daughter, "Shall I go and call a nurse for you from the Hebrew women, that she may nurse the child for you?"
>
> And Pharaoh's daughter said to her, "Go." So the maiden went and called the child's mother. Then Pharaoh's daughter said to her, "Take this child away and nurse him for me, and I will give you your wages." So the woman took the child and nursed him. And the child grew, and she brought him to Pharaoh's daughter, and he became her son. So she called his name Moses, saying, "Because I drew him out of the water." (Exodus 2:1–10)

The Bible skips over Moses's formative years. Still, if you've ever seen the Charlton Heston classic *The Ten Commandments* or the more recent animated *Prince of Egypt*, you probably have a fair idea of the privileged life Moses has led. He's had the finest education, food, companionship, and even chariot races, complete with well-arranged background music for whatever he was doing at the moment—if we're to believe the cartoon. Regardless of the movies' accuracy, Moses has led the life of a prince, a ruler, and a leader.

Ruler to Judge

So, it's not surprising when we reach verse 11 of chapter 2 that Moses takes matters into his own hands and acts as judge, jury, and executioner in the case of *Egyptian slave-driver versus Hebrew slave*. Unsurprisingly, his unmediated, irrational immediate reaction leads to exile in the Midian wilderness. But note this: when interacting with the slave and the slave master, there is no record of Moses asserting his authority or even identifying himself. He simply acts. He doesn't announce, "I am the prince. Stop what you're doing." He just acts.

CHAPTER 4: MOSES DOES NOT PARADE HIMSELF

Now, let's accompany Moses into the desert.

> When Pharaoh heard of this matter, he sought to kill Moses. But Moses fled from the face of Pharaoh and dwelt in the land of Midian; and he sat down by a well.
>
> Now the priest of Midian had seven daughters. And they came and drew water, and they filled the troughs to water their father's flock. Then the shepherds came and drove them away; but Moses stood up and helped them, and watered their flock.
>
> When they came to Reuel their father, he said, "How is it that you have come so soon today?"
>
> And they said, "An Egyptian delivered us from the hand of the shepherds, and he also drew enough water for us and watered the flock."
>
> So he said to his daughters, "And where is he? Why is it that you have left the man? Call him, that he may eat bread."
>
> Then Moses was content to live with the man, and he gave Zipporah his daughter to Moses. (Exodus 2:15–21)

Once again, we don't find Moses parading himself or even disclosing his rank.

Exile to Shepherd

Perhaps out of fear, considering he is a criminal on the run, he stands up for Reuel's daughters and serves them by drawing water for them. That's certainly not something he would have been used to doing, having grown up in Pharaoh's palace. Notably, he doesn't even boast about performing this good deed.

And after he accomplishes this act of kindness, the daughters leave him sitting at the well and return home. His good deed isn't even acknowledged until their father sends them back to express his appreciation. Then, this once-prince-of-Egypt marries the daughter of this backwoods shepherd and goes to work tending his sheep.

Perhaps we're too familiar with this story. Maybe we've heard too many sermons on how God used these years as a training ground for Moses, preparing him to lead the people of Israel through the wilderness. Yet, if we consider it from a human perspective, not knowing the end of the story, Moses is just days removed from palace life. He is accustomed to breakfast in bed and servants fanning him to keep him cool—all the comforts that ancient Egypt has to offer.

Now picture Moses sitting on a rock with the sun blazing down on his head, watching over a herd of mindless sheep that he's inherited because he chose to marry a shepherd's daughter from the backwoods, a girl he happened to help get some water for one day.

I can imagine him asking himself, "What happened? How did I get here?" Compared to palace life, his current situation is a mess! But still, he humbly serves his father-in-law.

I initially thought it strange that the Bible skipped over the first forty years of his life. But skipping over the next forty years, which were admittedly uneventful, doesn't seem so odd.

Forty years is a long time for nothing to be happening, but then God appears. Let's revisit Moses's character. Remember, we aren't examining Moses as the great leader of Israel but as an example for us: how to show love that neither parades itself nor seeks attention for its good deeds.

When God calls Moses to lead the Israelites out of slavery, how does Moses respond? He doesn't say, "It's about time—why didn't we collaborate when I was trying to help that Hebrew forty years ago?" or "Of course You want me; I was trained in Pharaoh's palace." Instead, his genuine response lies in verse 11 of chapter 3: "Who am I that I should go?" Perhaps this response shows more than just humility—maybe there's a hint of self-consciousness and fear when he says, "But what if they don't believe me?" or "I'm slow of speech and of tongue." Moses does not think very highly of himself; perhaps that's why God chose to use him in the first place.

Shepherd to God's Leader

If you're familiar with the movies, we don't need an in-depth review of the ten plagues or the crossing of the Red Sea, but we should highlight some of the dialogue between Moses, Pharaoh, and others. These exchanges illustrate Moses's view of himself, his perception of God, and his love for God that does not parade itself. All through his dialogue with Pharaoh, Moses is careful to always say, "This is what the Lord, the God of Israel, says." Or "The Lord, the God of the Hebrews, has sent me." "This is what the Lord says." Not Moses, but God.

After Pharaoh designates a day for the plague of frogs to leave Egypt, Moses answers, "It will be as you say, so that you may know that there is no one

CHAPTER 4: MOSES DOES NOT PARADE HIMSELF

like the Lord our God" (Exodus 8:10). The pattern repeats through to chapter 10. Moses never takes credit for any of the miracles, instead repeating God's words faithfully, following His commands unequivocally, and attributing all the merit to God. Love for God does not parade itself.

If you think Moses only acts and speaks this way when dealing publicly with Pharaoh, fast-forward to chapter 13, verse 11:

> "It shall be, when the Lord brings you into the land of the Canaanites, as He swore to you and your fathers, and gives it to you, that you shall set apart to the Lord all that open the womb, that is, every firstborn that comes from an animal which you have; the males shall be the Lord's." (Exodus 13:11–12)

Moses declares to the Israelites that it's the Lord who will lead them to the Promised Land, not him. And how do they express their gratitude to God? Through sacrifice.

> "It shall be, when your son asks you in time to come, saying, 'What is this?' that you shall say to him, 'By strength of hand the Lord brought us out of Egypt, out of the house of bondage. And it came to pass, when Pharaoh was stubborn about letting us go, that the Lord killed all the firstborn in the land of Egypt, both the firstborn of man and the firstborn of beast. Therefore I sacrifice to the Lord all males that open the womb, but all the firstborn of my sons I redeem.' It shall be as a sign on your hand and as frontlets between your eyes, for by strength of hand the Lord brought us out of Egypt." (Exodus 13:14–16)

God gets all the credit. Love says that God gets all the credit. In Exodus 15, we encounter the song of Moses and Miriam, a sacrifice of praise. I recommend reading the whole passage yourself, but here are some highlights: "I will sing to the Lord, for He has triumphed gloriously … The Lord is my strength and song. He has become my salvation. He is my God. I will praise Him. My father's God, I will exalt Him … Your right hand, O Lord, has become glorious in power … The Lord shall reign forever and ever."

Well, Moses and the Israelites leave the Egyptians behind, but now they've got the wilderness ahead and a plethora of new challenges. It doesn't take long before everyone starts complaining to Moses that they wish they had things as good as they were back in Egypt. In chapter 16, the Israelites approach Moses grumbling, asking him, "What are you going to do? We're starving out here."

Your Complaints Are Not Against Us

But Moses, although he's the leader, never takes credit *or blame* for anything. He continually redirected people toward God. Look at chapter 16, from verse 6:

> Moses and Aaron said to all the children of Israel, "At evening you shall know that the Lord has brought you out of the land of Egypt. And in the morning you shall see the glory of the Lord; for He hears your complaints against the Lord. But what are we, that you complain against us?" Also Moses said, "This shall be seen when the Lord gives you meat to eat in the evening, and in the morning bread to the full; for the Lord hears your complaints which you make against Him. And what are we? Your complaints are not against us but against the Lord." (Exodus 16:6–8)

This claim, I believe, isn't an example of false modesty. It's not Moses trying to shrug off responsibility. Instead, he truly sees God as the sole provider. The situation is completely out of his control, completely out of his hands. It is God who is responsible for the success and provision of the Israelites. Love does not parade itself.

If I still haven't made my point clear, let's move ahead to chapter 17. The Israelites are now not only hungry but also thirsty, so they demand water from Moses. "Give us water to drink!" they bark (v. 2 NLT). Moses replies, "Why do you quarrel with me? Why do you put the Lord to the test?" (NIV). Again, he understands that it's not about him and follows God's instructions to strike the rock in front of the people. Water bursts forth!

Immediately after this miraculous event, they're attacked by the Amalekites. This is their first real test. And how do they win the battle? By Moses lifting up his hands in prayer. Whenever his hands lower, the people start to lose. When his hands are held up, they are victorious. He names the place "The Lord, my banner," acknowledging again that it's God, not Moses, who gets the credit. That's the name of the place where God gave them victory over their enemies on their journey to Canaan.

CHAPTER 4: MOSES DOES NOT PARADE HIMSELF

Public Man and Private Man

Until now, we've examined some very public displays of Moses's behaviour regarding self-promotion or credit-taking. However, even outside of the public view, this characteristic is evident in Moses. Advancing to chapter 18, the Israelites are deep into the wilderness, and Moses's father-in-law, Reuel (it might be Jethro in your Bible translation), pays a visit, having heard about their adventures. Moses recounts the story for him. Verse 8 states that Moses tells his father-in-law about everything *the Lord* had done. Even in private, away from the public eye, Moses gives credit to God rather than boasting or promoting himself—he does not parade himself but gives credit to God.

This chapter is best known for Reuel's advice to Moses to delegate his authority—a classic lesson in leadership. You've probably read books about this wonderful advice on decentralizing authority and power. I believe it's not a stretch to interpret Moses's decision to relinquish his sole authority over the people of Israel as an act of love. He's not concerned about being the one out front, receiving all the glory, honour, and responsibility. By taking this advice, Moses exhibits love as he appoints others to positions of influence and prominence. Love, after all, doesn't parade itself; it's content to give credit to others and always acts humbly.

What God Does for Moses

Over the next few chapters, we accompany Moses in his interactions with God on Mount Sinai. In these verses, familiarity with the story can overshadow the significance of what we're reading. Therefore, let me repeat: Moses meets with God, converses with Him, and is permitted to see God's glory—not His face, but His back. God passes by Moses, declaring Himself as

> "The LORD, the LORD God, merciful and gracious, longsuffering, and abounding in goodness and truth, keeping mercy for thousands, forgiving iniquity and transgression and sin, by no means clearing the guilty, visiting the iniquity of the fathers upon the children and the children's children to the third and the fourth generation." (Exodus 34:6–7)

Over the years, I've met some famous, important, and powerful people—mayors, politicians, judges, and influential figures. They do carry themselves a touch differently than the Average Joe. Spending years walking red carpets, having their photographs taken, attending high-profile parties and meetings, signing autographs, being interviewed on TV—I think it does something to their personal self-image, which in turn dictates their conduct.

I'm sure we have all heard stories of celebrities acting with contempt and impatience towards hotel or restaurant staff, appearing condescending. So, let me repeat this once more: *Moses met with God, the LORD, the Creator and Sustainer of the universe, Yahweh!* As the rest of the Israelite nation cowered in fear at the base of Mount Sinai, Moses "drew near the thick darkness where God was," according to Exodus 20:21.

Now, one could develop some sort of superiority complex, being the only one to meet with God; they might think themselves more important and better than others. Moses spends so much time with God that his face begins to glow. What a contrast between Moses's behaviour and that of today's celebrities! There is nothing more important Moses could have ever done than meet with God face-to-face.

It sure sounds like he's the most important person on the planet! You would think he would come down and lord it over other people, like a celebrity might in a similar position. But not Moses. Love does not parade itself. Now, aside from a brief anecdote in chapter 24 about another meeting with God, where Moses is treated preferentially compared to the other leaders of Israel, the next chapters merely detail the laws given by God to His people. These laws are important, and reading them can be enlightening. But our purpose here is to learn how to live a life of love towards God. So, let's jump over to Chapter 32.

What Moses Does for His People

After forty days and nights on the mountain, Moses returns to the camp to find the people worshipping an idol. Following a particularly creative punishment, forcing them to consume the ground-up gold and purging the camp of three thousand rebellious men with the help of fellow Levites ...

> Moses returned to the LORD and said, "Oh, these people have committed a great sin, and have made for themselves a god of gold! Yet now, if You will forgive their sin—but if not, I pray, blot me out of Your book which You have written." (Exodus 32:31–32)

CHAPTER 4: MOSES DOES NOT PARADE HIMSELF

What? Moses—the chosen one, the privileged one, the leader—offers to take the punishment for the rebellion and sin of the people. He demonstrates love that doesn't flaunt itself, that doesn't expect any preferential treatment.

Let's skim quickly over the next few chapters, but pause long enough to acknowledge all the print Bezalel and Aholiab get for the construction of the Tabernacle and everything in it used for worship.

Interesting, isn't it? Now, off the top of your head, try to recall the name of the builders of the first temple. I'll wait! It may require flipping over to 1 Kings. We often find the temple casually referred to as "Solomon's Temple" or "the temple that Solomon built". Are any of the builders or craftspeople who contributed mentioned? Certainly, there's a brief mention of some who brought lumber and lent their hand, but not quite like the tributes to Bezalel and Aholiab throughout this passage in Exodus.

Moses, commonly thought to be the author of the Pentateuch, is quite content to distribute credit where it's due—he never craves the spotlight. Speaking of prominence, have you ever wondered why God chooses Moses's brother Aaron and his descendants to serve as priests? Moses is well-versed in law, even inscribing it himself. He has a special relationship with God; he has sons capable of continuing the priesthood.

Consider a perusal of Leviticus, especially the first ten chapters, which establish the priesthood and outline their duties and privileges. These are the most respected and honoured men in the nation. As you journey through these Scriptures, try to find a moment where Moses grumbles to God about being sidelined or replaced as the leader. I can't find the place where he asks, "What about my sons?" Love does not parade itself.

Because I'm so grateful that you've picked up my book, I've read through the rest of Leviticus for you, in order to glean any additional nuggets of wisdom from the life of Moses. While there's a wealth of stuff here about things like sacrifices (have I mentioned about sacrifices?), that's for another book.

God's Spirit Is Not to Be Kept Selfishly

For our current purpose, we skip ahead to the book of Numbers, where there's a little more action. Let's look at chapter 11. Once again, Moses's authority is being shared among others, as God pours His Spirit upon seventy elders. I fear sounding redundant, but it's not the most human characteristic to give up authority, power, and influence to others voluntarily.

In fact, two of the men who miss the ceremonial anointing of the Spirit, but who stay comfortably in their tents within the camp, start to prophesy like the other elders. Joshua, Moses's assistant, has a much more natural human reaction: jealousy.

> Joshua the son of Nun, Moses' assistant, one of his choice men, answered and said, "Moses my lord, forbid them!"
> Then Moses said to him, "Are you zealous for my sake? Oh, that all the LORD's people were prophets and that the LORD would put His Spirit upon them!" (Numbers 11:28–29)

Once again, I think that there is something divine happening in Moses's heart, a divine love. Chapter 12 provides an even starker contrast between loving humility and selfish pride.

Moses's siblings, Aaron and Miriam, feel like they are not getting their due. Why aren't they being elevated to higher positions, and why aren't they being paraded in front of the nation? I've heard a lot of comments about the irony of verse 3: "Now, the man Moses was very humble, more than all men who were on the face of the earth." If Moses indeed penned Numbers, could this truly denote humility? Consider the context where Moses's authority is continually questioned, yet he makes no effort to defend himself. Perhaps he is indeed the most humble. Just look at what God has to say about his relationship with Moses when he confronts Aaron and Miriam. He declares,

> "Hear now My words:
> If there is a prophet among you,
> I, the LORD, make Myself known to him in a vision;
> I speak to him in a dream.
> Not so with My servant Moses;
> He is faithful in all My house.
> I speak with him face to face,
> Even plainly, and not in dark sayings;
> And he sees the form of the LORD.
> Why then were you not afraid
> To speak against My servant Moses?" (Numbers 12:6–8)

CHAPTER 4: MOSES DOES NOT PARADE HIMSELF

Moses is special—God says so. Yet, Moses's love for God does not allow him to flaunt it, to parade it. When God punishes Miriam for her jealousy and pride, Moses pleads on her behalf. Now, I've got a good sister, and we have a pretty harmonious relationship. But I think I would have indulged in an "I told you so" or "serves you right" if we found ourselves in the same situation.

Once Miriam recovers, the nation of Israel arrives at the doorstep of the Promised Land. Twelve spies are dispatched: ten deliver a bad report, while Joshua and Caleb encourage the people to trust in God. Disheartened, the mob contemplates returning to Egypt and even electing a new leader (Numbers 14:4).

So, does Moses retaliate by raising his rod and calling down divine fire on the rebels? No. Rather, in verse 5, we read, "Moses and Aaron fell on their faces before all the assembly of the congregation of the children of Israel." Alternatively, we could say they lay prostrate, a sign of submission. You can't get any further from parading yourself than prostrating yourself.

God's Offer to Moses

Again, God threatens to exterminate the Israelites as punishment for their lack of faith (if this sounds familiar, I am indeed repeating myself! The Israelites are continually unfaithful!), promising to establish a new, greater nation with Moses as its leader. What does Moses do? Moses pleads on their behalf, appealing to God that His reputation will be tarnished if He destroys the nation of Israel just as they are about to re-enter the land. I can only compare Moses's words and actions to what would come out of my own heart and mind: I get a nation, I become famous, and my enemies are wiped out? Sounds good to me!

But Moses cares more about preserving God's reputation than his own. He shows more concern for the people he is leading—rather, serving—than focusing on himself. Those who incite the rebellion are punished by God; they die from a plague. Other leaders perish in a reckless attack against the Amalekites and Canaanites. All others of the generation who disobey die over the next forty years, which they spend wandering aimlessly in the wilderness.

Love for God says, "I humbly obey and trust that He is truly in control. He has a plan and will do what is best." It doesn't put our plans first, parading them around for self-glorification.

Now, we can bypass the next few chapters about tassels and grain offerings and get back to the action. You're welcome. So, flip ahead in your Bible to Numbers 16:

> Now Korah the son of Izhar, the son of Kohath, the son of Levi, with Dathan and Abiram the sons of Eliab, and On the son of Peleth, sons of Reuben, took men; and they rose up before Moses with some of the children of Israel, two hundred and fifty leaders of the congregation, representatives of the congregation, men of renown. They gathered together against Moses and Aaron, and said to them, "You take too much upon yourselves, for all the congregation is holy, every one of them, and the Lord is among them. Why then do you exalt yourselves above the assembly of the Lord?" So when Moses heard it, he fell on his face. (Numbers 16:1–4)

Korah Reveals His Own Motives

Have you ever heard of projecting—the phenomenon where someone ascribes their feelings, motives, or emotions to someone else? The telltale signs are phrases such as "You must be scared" or "That must really bother you." These types of comments illustrate how a person applies their own feelings to a situation and expects you to react similarly. Korah, looking at Moses, sees all the blessings God has poured out on him. Yet, through his own perspective, he accuses Moses of exalting himself.

Now, let's consider Moses's response. He falls prostrate, submissive in front of them. As if to add insult to injury, while Korah and the Levites complain that Moses has exalted himself too highly, Dathan and Abiram also question not only his leadership but his integrity. They say,

> "Is it a small thing that you have brought us up out of a land flowing with milk and honey, to kill us in the wilderness, that you should keep acting like a prince over us? Moreover you have not brought us into a land flowing with milk and honey, nor given us inheritance of fields and vineyards. Will you put out the eyes of these men? We will not come up!" (Numbers 16:13–14)

Finally, we get a little humanity from Moses in verse 15. Overcome with anger, he seeks divine intervention saying to God, "Do not respect their offering. I

CHAPTER 4: MOSES DOES NOT PARADE HIMSELF

have not taken one donkey from them, nor have I hurt one of them." I sense Moses is almost at the breaking point, a point that I would have reached ten problems or rebellions ago.

Moses, however, does not lord it over them or act princely. He doesn't seek accolades or praise, but instead faithfully obeys and serves God's people. Once again, Moses trusts God to act. The ground opens up, swallowing Korah, Dathan, and Abiram into an abyss, and fire from the Lord consumes the remaining 250 rebellious leaders.

This is too much for the people to bear. The following day, an even larger crowd challenges Moses. Once again, God is on the brink of wiping out the entire nation, and in fact, sends a plague that results in 14,700 deaths. But what is Moses's response? He doesn't gloat or say, "I told you so." Instead, he sends Aaron out with an incense censer to save the nation and halt the spread of the plague.

Why would he endure so many complaints, so much envy, false accusations, and hatred? As I've argued before, the love God calls us to is not based on emotion. If it were, Moses would have retaliated long ago. It's not based on affection either, as there is clearly no warm relationship between him and many of the other Israelites.

Moses has chosen to love. Christian love is a choice, regardless of the situation or our position. Love calls us to humility. There's much more to learn in the subsequent chapters of Numbers, which I encourage you to read at another time. But for our study of love, let's skip ahead to chapter 20. Often, the best way to understand a concept is to define what it isn't.

When Moses Fails

Love does not parade itself. So, what happens when your actions or words expose your natural, fleshly pride? Well, the Israelites find themselves without water yet again—no surprise, given that they are in a desert. Let's resume the narration from verse 7.

> The Lord spoke to Moses, saying, "Take the rod; you and your brother Aaron gather the congregation together. Speak to the rock before their eyes, and it will yield its water; thus you shall bring water for them out of the rock, and

> give drink to the congregation and their animals." So Moses took the rod from before the LORD as He commanded him.
>
> And Moses and Aaron gathered the assembly together before the rock; and he said to them, "Hear now, you rebels! Must we bring water for you out of this rock?" Then Moses lifted his hand and struck the rock twice with his rod; and water came out abundantly, and the congregation and their animals drank.
>
> Then the LORD spoke to Moses and Aaron, "Because you did not believe Me, to hallow Me in the eyes of the children of Israel, therefore you shall not bring this assembly into the land which I have given them." (Numbers 20:7–12)

That fateful "we" in "must *we* bring water for you"! Despite humbly serving God throughout his lifetime without taking credit or parading himself as anything special, Moses claims that he has worked alongside God in providing the water. He presents himself as an equal to God in this action. Now, let's extend some sympathy towards Moses—I know I would have failed far earlier.

The punishment Moses receives for his prideful action is hard to accept—he, like those who lacked faith and were condemned to forty years wandering the wilderness, will never enter the Promised Land after his years of faithful service. As we trusted God's wisdom and sovereignty with His punishment of Korah and the others who rebelled, we have to believe that God is just in His decisions here in His punishment of Moses.

The story does not end there. Once again, the Israelites complain and rebel. This time, God sends venomous snakes. We have a fascinating anecdote that Jesus refers to in John 3:14–16:

> "As Moses lifted up the serpent in the wilderness, even so must the Son of Man be lifted up: that whoever believes in Him should not perish, but have eternal life. For God so loved the world that He gave His only begotten Son, that whoever believes in Him should not perish but have everlasting life."

In summary, Moses has returned to exalting and glorifying God—all eyes are on the Lord, not Moses. God provides the salvation and healing for His people.

CHAPTER 4: MOSES DOES NOT PARADE HIMSELF

Turning Their Eyes to God's Deliverance

God's deliverance is seen as it is paraded through the camp—faith and belief in God's power is what heals them. John uses this as a metaphor or allegory to point towards how Christ takes our punishment and provides healing for our sins on the cross. It's entirely about faith and belief in God and the work of Jesus Christ for us as sinners.

However, it all centers around God's healing power for the Israelites, not Moses. The book of Numbers is rich with fascinating stories, like talking donkeys, water miracles, incredible battles, and lessons about trust, obedience, and holiness—but not as much for our purposes to learn about love. Let's conclude with a brief summary of Moses's final days from the book of Deuteronomy.

By studying the character of Moses and mentally stepping into his shoes, we see the significance of love that threads through the entire book. Why? Because when Jesus was asked what the greatest commandment was, he responded, "Love the Lord your God with all your heart, soul, mind, and strength."

Jesus was quoting Deuteronomy 6:5. Before Moses begins his review of the law, before he dies and the Israelites enter into the Promised Land, he starts with the most important command. In fact, the phrase "Love the LORD" appears 16 times in the book of Deuteronomy. This is Moses's final reciting of the Law, but he repeats over and over, "Love the LORD your God."

The only way we can hope to obey any of God's commandments is by having a heart and mind filled with love for Him. This brings to mind Jesus's words in John 14:15 "If you love Me, you will keep My commandments" (NASB). I'm only human, so my love is weak and often conditional. I think Moses understood this when he wrote in Deuteronomy 8:11–17, "Do not forget what God has done." When we look back at the highs and lows of our lives, we see God's love and care for us.

Loving God back means crediting Him for all that's accomplished in our lives, not claiming the credit for ourselves for the good and acknowledging God's help in the bad. In verse 14, Moses warns the Israelites, "Do not become proud." There is a strong link between love for God and humility. We don't want to make ourselves our own God.

Finishing Well

Let's conclude Moses' story by reminding ourselves of just how incredible he is. Deuteronomy 34:5 states,

> Moses the servant of the Lord died there in the land of Moab, according to the word of the Lord. And He buried him in a valley in the land of Moab, opposite Beth Peor; but no one knows his grave to this day. Moses was one hundred and twenty years old when he died. His eyes were not dim nor his natural vigor diminished. And the children of Israel wept for Moses in the plains of Moab thirty days. So the days of weeping and mourning for Moses ended.
> Now Joshua the son of Nun was full of the spirit of wisdom, for Moses had laid his hands on him; so the children of Israel heeded him, and did as the Lord had commanded Moses.
> But since then there has not arisen in Israel a prophet like Moses, whom the Lord knew face to face, in all the signs and wonders which the Lord sent him to do in the land of Egypt, before Pharaoh, before all his servants, and in all his land, and by all that mighty power and all the great terror which Moses performed in the sight of all Israel. (Deuteronomy 34:5–12)

Moses was one of the greatest men to ever live, with a unique and special relationship with God.

But he never, ever—well, I guess just that once—put himself on par with God. He never paraded himself before others or puffed out his chest, never *vaunteth*-ed himself. Loving God means humbling ourselves, submitting to His revealed will in His Word, obeying His law, and refraining from placing ourselves on a pedestal or flaunting our accomplishments. Bringing a "sacrifice of praise".

Parade or Prostrate?

Think about this as you delve into the next chapter. This week, someone might offer you a compliment, or you might receive a promotion. Perhaps you're already in a leadership role; maybe you're the CEO, the senior pastor, or a parent. A genuine love for God implies prioritizing Him, not misusing your authority or flaunting it, but serving humbly and attending to others. So, this week, when faced with the decision to either parade or prostrate, choose to serve someone humbly and write about it below.

Chapter 5

John the Baptist Is Not Puffed Up

This section of our love poem in 1 Corinthians seems very similar to our last study that "Love does not parade itself." It is "Love is not puffed up." In looking up word definitions and synonyms from older Bible translations these two can't be beat. I still haven't been able to include *vaunteth*, that fancy word we learned last chapter, in everyday speech, but I think I can with a synonym for our current study on the phrase "love is not puffed up." I came across another posh-sounding word: *vainglorious*, meaning meritlessly proud, full of hot air, puffed up, vain, worthless, boastful, and empty. I can picture an overweight aristocrat in some cartoon popping his buttons as he puffs out his chest in pride. But he's empty, shallow, full of hot air.

Love Is Not Puffed Up

In our journey through Scripture, we are trying to find real people who, through their stories, are examples for us so that when we're faced with certain situations, we can emulate their behaviour, responding out of love. Love is multifaceted, and now we come to this next particular expression—"love is not puffed up." Just slightly different then our last subject, Moses, who was not arrogant and did not parade himself. Now we want to look at someone who specifically did not have an inflated opinion of themselves. Who constantly made themselves smaller in the public view. Remember, this love is complex.

This is not an emotional response. It's not infatuation or attraction. This is a purposeful choice to behave in a certain way as God commanded us to love. I wanted to choose someone who obviously was not puffed up, who never got up in front of everybody and said, "Look at me." I first thought Paul as a good example. He had that vision, and he says, "I know a man … caught up to the third heaven … Of such a one I will boast; yet of myself I will not boast" (2 Corinthians 12:2–5). But most scholars think that he was really talking about himself. So, did he never, ever boast about himself? For full effect, I needed to choose someone who was really important. They were told they were really important, they achieved an incredible amount, and people said they were great. But they never got a swelled head.

The Story of John the Baptist Throughout the Four Gospels

Let's look at John the Baptist's story and see how he, who achieved much, both in the eyes of God and people, who had popularity and influence, never promoted himself, never inflated his own worth. Now, this one's a little more difficult than the Old Testament passages, because, of course, there are four accounts. And I'm going to try to put them in a chronological order. We'll be skipping back from Luke to Matthew to Mark to John to try to get this in order. Hang with me!

As you may know, Matthew, Mark, and Luke are the Synoptic Gospels. They tell the same story from three different perspectives. I've tried to choose the most appropriate account of each story to share here, but there are other texts that you can look at and cross-reference to get an even fuller view. Let's start with John's story in Luke chapter 1.

Zacharias and Elizabeth

I'm going to be recounting lots of Scripture because I want to stay true to the story, and I want you to kind of start interpreting it yourself and get that "Aha!" moment of application. We'll let the Holy Spirit work through the Scriptures. So, let's get to this then!—from Luke 1:5:

> There was in the days of Herod, the king of Judea, a certain priest named Zacharias, of the division of Abijah. His wife was of the daughters of Aaron, and her name was Elizabeth. And they were both righteous before God, walking in all the commandments and ordinances of the Lord blameless. But they had no child, because Elizabeth was barren, and they were both well advanced in years.
> So it was, that while he was serving as priest before God in the order of his division, according to the custom of the priesthood, his lot fell to burn incense when he went into the temple of the Lord. And the whole multitude of the people was praying outside at the hour of incense. Then an angel of

CHAPTER 5: JOHN THE BAPTIST IS NOT PUFFED UP

the Lord appeared to him, standing on the right side of the altar of incense. And when Zacharias saw him, he was troubled, and fear fell upon him.

But the angel said to him, "Do not be afraid, Zacharias, for your prayer is heard; and your wife Elizabeth will bear you a son, and you shall call his name John. And you will have joy and gladness, and many will rejoice at his birth. For he will be great in the sight of the Lord, and shall drink neither wine nor strong drink. He will also be filled with the Holy Spirit, even from his mother's womb. And he will turn many of the children of Israel to the Lord their God. He will also go before Him in the spirit and power of Elijah, 'to turn the hearts of the fathers to the children,' and the disobedient to the wisdom of the just, to make ready a people prepared for the Lord."

And Zacharias said to the angel, "How shall I know this? For I am an old man, and my wife is well advanced in years."

And the angel answered and said to him, "I am Gabriel, who stands in the presence of God, and was sent to speak to you and bring you these glad tidings. But behold, you will be mute and not able to speak until the day these things take place, because you did not believe my words which will be fulfilled in their own time."

And the people waited for Zacharias, and marveled that he lingered so long in the temple. But when he came out, he could not speak to them; and they perceived that he had seen a vision in the temple, for he beckoned to them and remained speechless.

So it was, as soon as the days of his service were completed, that he departed to his own house. Now after those days his wife Elizabeth conceived; and she hid herself five months, saying, "Thus the Lord has dealt with me, in the days when He looked on me, to take away my reproach among people." (Luke 1:5–25)

Skipping ahead to verse 41, this is now when Mary visits Elizabeth, the next part of John's story.

It happened, when Elizabeth heard the greeting of Mary, that the babe leaped in her womb; and Elizabeth was filled with the Holy Spirit. Then she spoke out with a loud voice and said, "Blessed are you among women, and blessed is the fruit of your womb!" (Luke 1:41–42)

Skipping ahead now to verse 57:

> Now Elizabeth's full time came for her to be delivered, and she brought forth a son. When her neighbors and relatives heard how the Lord had shown great mercy to her, they rejoiced with her.
> So it was, on the eighth day, that they came to circumcise the child; and they would have called him by the name of his father, Zacharias. His mother answered and said, "No; he shall be called John."
> But they said to her, "There is no one among your relatives who is called by this name." So they made signs to his father—what he would have him called.
> And he asked for a writing tablet, and wrote, saying, "His name is John." So they all marveled. Immediately his mouth was opened and his tongue loosed, and he spoke, praising God. Then fear came on all who dwelt around them; and all these sayings were discussed throughout all the hill country of Judea. (Luke 1:57–65)

Then Zacharias sang a song, and we're just going to read a little bit of that, starting at verse 76. He said:

> "You, child, will be called the prophet of the Highest;
> For you will go before the face of the Lord to prepare His ways,
> To give knowledge of salvation to His people
> By the remission of their sins,
> Through the tender mercy of our God,
> With which the Dayspring from on high has visited us;
> To give light to those who sit in darkness and the shadow of death,
> To guide our feet into the way of peace."
> So the child grew and became strong in spirit, and was in the deserts till the day of his manifestation to Israel. (Luke 1:76–80)

CHAPTER 5: JOHN THE BAPTIST IS NOT PUFFED UP

John, the Extra-Special One

Did you have your birth prophesied? Did your mom get a visit from an angel, letting her know how special you were going to be? Were you born of a miraculous conception with aged parents? Were you conscious of the world around you while in the womb? No? So, maybe you're having trouble relating to this right now. But I think you can see what it was like for John: everyone knew about him; everyone marvelled at him. Everyone said this child would be great.

I marvel that this didn't affect John negatively. Of the people we've studied so far, this is actually the one who hits home most to me. I've never suffered like Joseph. I've never been in a situation like Ruth, with the sacrifice of kindness that she performed. I've definitely never been in a situation like Jonathan, to the extent where he absolutely deserved something but was passed over.

But this one I relate to. I've mentioned before that when I was younger, I was quite an athlete. In fact, I stopped growing in about grade 7, and I'm quite an average height now. But for a grade-7 kid, I was tall and athletic. I was the captain of all the sports teams; we won championships and, as I mentioned before, made high school city all-star teams in basketball. I had a lot of people telling me, "Tim, you're really good, you're going places, you're going to play college ball, you're a star."

Arrogant Youth

And you know what happens when a lot of people start telling you how special and good you are? You believe them. Then you start repeating that to others. You get an inflated ego, you are puffed up. Thinking of yourself as a bigger deal than you really are.

If we look back at the 1 Corinthians 13 passage in the New King James Version: "Love suffers long and is kind; love does not envy. love does not parade itself, is not *puffed up.*" It is important to remember that this love is a mindset, a lifestyle. We need to get away from the cultural view of love as a reaction to another person. Love is a character trait.

I look back at my youth; I look back with regret at the way I treated people and talked to people in my arrogance. My parents built me up and encouraged me, but in my humanity, because I didn't have the character trait of love, I acted boastfully, full of hot air, puffed up, and empty. This is what boasting does, and it shows a real lack of love, a significant self-centeredness. Being arrogant and boastful doesn't allow us to love others.

The Wild Prophet

So, we have John, who is prophesied about by an angel and born to an aged priest—everyone is talking about him. "The child became strong in spirit." We have to go forward in his story by going backwards in the Bible to Matthew chapter 3. Read verses 1–17:

> In those days John the Baptist came preaching in the wilderness of Judea, and saying, "Repent, for the kingdom of heaven is at hand!" For this is he who was spoken of by the prophet Isaiah, saying:
> "The voice of one crying in the wilderness:
> 'Prepare the way of the LORD;
> Make His paths straight.'"
> Now John himself was clothed in camel's hair, with a leather belt around his waist; and his food was locusts and wild honey. Then Jerusalem, all Judea, and all the region around the Jordan went out to him and were baptized by him in the Jordan, confessing their sins.
> But when he saw many of the Pharisees and Sadducees coming to his baptism, he said to them, "Brood of vipers! Who warned you to flee from the wrath to come? Therefore bear fruits worthy of repentance, and do not think to say to yourselves, 'We have Abraham as our father.' For I say to you that God is able to raise up children to Abraham from these stones. And even now the ax is laid to the root of the trees. Therefore every tree which does not bear good fruit is cut down and thrown into the fire. I indeed baptize you with water unto repentance, but He who is coming after me is mightier than I, whose sandals I am not worthy to carry. He will baptize you with the Holy Spirit and fire. His winnowing fan is in His hand, and He will thoroughly clean out His threshing floor, and gather His wheat into the barn; but He will burn up the chaff with unquenchable fire."
> Then Jesus came from Galilee to John at the Jordan to be baptized by him. And John tried to prevent Him, saying, "I need to be baptized by You, and are You coming to me?"

> But Jesus answered and said to him, "Permit it to be so now, for thus it is fitting for us to fulfill all righteousness." Then he allowed Him.
> When He had been baptized, Jesus came up immediately from the water; and behold, the heavens were opened to Him, and He saw the Spirit of God descending like a dove and alighting upon Him. And suddenly a voice came from heaven, saying, "This is My beloved Son, in whom I am well pleased." (Matthew 3:1–17)

John has an immeasurable popularity. Everyone is coming from Jerusalem, Judea, and all the region; everyone is coming to hear John preach. The only way I can explain it is that he is a rock star; people are flocking to hear him.

The Rock Star Knows His Place

And he has authority! No one gets away with talking to the Pharisees and Sadducees like this, and he lambastes them, and they don't argue with him. The authority with which he carries himself with is unparalleled. Jesus comes by, and John says, "I should be baptized by You. You're the greater one. I should be baptized as Your disciple, not the other way around." He says earlier, "I don't have the right to even undo his sandal straps." There are many sermons about Jesus washing the disciples' feet, and a lot of preachers emphasize that the lowliest job of a slave was washing people's feet when they came into a house, and so the lowliest thing to do was to untie someone's sandal in order to wash their feet. John's saying, "I'm not even worthy of that. I am so low compared to Jesus." Here's the most popular guy in the country saying this.

Let's go over to the Gospel of John. We're going to get some overlap here, but I think it is important to get the character of John and understand truly what it means to love and not boast. John chapter 1:

> John bore witness of Him and cried out, saying, "This was He of whom I said, 'He who comes after me is preferred before me, for He was before me.'"
> And of His fullness we have all received, and grace for grace. For the law was given through Moses, but grace and truth came through Jesus Christ. No one has seen God at any time. The only begotten Son, who is in the bosom of the Father, He has declared Him.

Now this is the testimony of John, when the Jews sent priests and Levites from Jerusalem to ask him, "Who are you?"

He confessed, and did not deny, but confessed, "I am not the Christ."

And they asked him, "What then? Are you Elijah?"

He said, "I am not."

"Are you the Prophet?"

And he answered, "No."

Then they said to him, "Who are you, that we may give an answer to those who sent us? What do you say about yourself?"

He said: "I am the voice of one crying in the wilderness: 'Make straight the way of the Lord,' as the prophet Isaiah said."

Now those who were sent were from the Pharisees. And they asked him, saying, "Why then do you baptize if you are not the Christ, nor Elijah, nor the Prophet?"

John answered them, saying, "I baptize with water, but there stands One among you whom you do not know. It is He who, coming after me, is preferred before me, whose sandal strap I am not worthy to loose."

These things were done in Bethabara beyond the Jordan, where John was baptizing.

The next day John saw Jesus coming toward him, and said, "Behold! The Lamb of God who takes away the sin of the world! This is He of whom I said, 'After me comes a Man who is preferred before me, for He was before me.' I did not know Him; but that He should be revealed to Israel, therefore I came baptizing with water."

And John bore witness, saying, "I saw the Spirit descending from heaven like a dove, and He remained upon Him. I did not know Him, but He who sent me to baptize with water said to me, 'Upon whom you see the Spirit descending, and remaining on Him, this is He who baptizes with the Holy Spirit.' And I have seen and testified that this is the Son of God."

Again, the next day, John stood with two of his disciples. And looking at Jesus as He walked, he said, "Behold the Lamb of God!"

The two disciples heard him speak, and they followed Jesus. (John 1:15–37)

CHAPTER 5: JOHN THE BAPTIST IS NOT PUFFED UP

Now, I don't think it's a matter of John not understanding the whole baptism/disciple thing. I think he clearly understands. But this is what would happen in this time: a teacher, a prophet, would gather disciples, baptizing them. The word "baptism" comes from a textile term; it's when you take a white cloth and dip it in a dye, and it becomes a different colour. You're now identified with that teacher. Of course, it means so much more to us now when we look at it through Jesus Christ's death and resurrection, but this is where it originates from.

Incredible Humility

So, John gathers these disciples and baptizes them, and they're now his followers. He's the most popular guy in the country. He has all this influence and power. And as soon as he sees Jesus, he says, "Behold the Lamb of God who takes away the sin of the world," and he's implying to his disciples, "Don't follow me; follow Him." Incredible! And his disciples leave.

For the next part of the story, we need to go back to Luke 3:10–20. John has baptized Jesus, and the people come to John and say, "What shall we do?" He stops his sermon …

> He answered and said to them, "He who has two tunics, let him give to him who has none; and he who has food, let him do likewise."
> Then tax collectors also came to be baptized, and said to him, "Teacher, what shall we do?"
> And he said to them, "Collect no more than what is appointed for you."
> Likewise the soldiers asked him, saying, "And what shall we do?"
> So he said to them, "Do not intimidate anyone or accuse falsely, and be content with your wages."
> Now as the people were in expectation, and all reasoned in their hearts about John, whether he was the Christ or not, John answered, saying to all, "I indeed baptize you with water; but One mightier than I is coming, whose sandal strap I am not worthy to loose. He will baptize you with the Holy Spirit and fire. His winnowing fan is in His hand, and He will thoroughly clean out His threshing floor, and gather the wheat into His barn; but the chaff He will burn with unquenchable fire."

> And with many other exhortations he preached to the people. But Herod the tetrarch, being rebuked by him concerning Herodias, his brother Philip's wife, and for all the evils which Herod had done, also added this, above all, that he shut John up in prison. (Luke 3:11–20)

Shunning the Spotlight

John is so influential, so popular, so well regarded that everyone is convinced that he's the Messiah. It has happened before, and this is the second time; the first time was after the baptism of Jesus, where he has had to convince people, "No, I am not the Messiah sent by God. There's someone else coming that's better than I am." He is constantly taking the spotlight and shining it on Jesus instead of himself, even at the height of his popularity. And then we have this event where he gets thrown in jail by Herod.

For the next part of John's story, we need to go back to Matthew chapter 11. John's ministry has ended, and Jesus's ministry is now in full swing. Jesus is now healing and performing miracles and preaching, while John rots in Herod's jail.

And in Matthew chapter 11, we get back to John, just as with Jonathan in a previous chapter, who wasn't the main character, but David was. Jonathan kind of came in and out of the story; the same thing with John. Of course, the Gospels are all about Jesus, and John comes in and out, so I am trying to bring out his story in some sort of cohesive manner. Matthew 11:1–15:

> Now it came to pass, when Jesus finished commanding His twelve disciples, that He departed from there to teach and to preach in their cities.
> And when John had heard in prison about the works of Christ, he sent two of his disciples and said to Him, "Are You the Coming One, or do we look for another?"
> Jesus answered and said to them, "Go and tell John the things which you hear and see: the blind see and the lame walk; the lepers are cleansed and the deaf hear; the dead are raised up and the poor have the gospel preached to them. And blessed is he who is not offended because of Me."
> As they departed, Jesus began to say to the multitudes concerning John: "What did you go out into the wilderness to see? A reed shaken by the wind? But what did you go out to

see? A man clothed in soft garments? Indeed, those who wear soft clothing are in kings' houses. But what did you go out to see? A prophet? Yes, I say to you, and more than a prophet. For this is he of whom it is written:

'Behold, I send My messenger before Your face,
Who will prepare Your way before You.'

"Assuredly, I say to you, among those born of women there has not risen one greater than John the Baptist; but he who is least in the kingdom of heaven is greater than he. And from the days of John the Baptist until now the kingdom of heaven suffers violence, and the violent take it by force. For all the prophets and the law prophesied until John. And if you are willing to receive it, he is Elijah who is to come. He who has ears to hear, let him hear!" (Matthew 11:1–15)

The Greatest Prophet

I want to take this in two parts. The first is this question from John the Baptist when he sends his disciples to ask, "Is Jesus really the Messiah?" Some commentaries and thoughts on this suggest that John is disillusioned. He has been serving God, reached the height of popularity, and had all these crowds come to hear him preach. Now he's in jail, and he's now wondering, "Was it all worth it?"

I don't think this is the case. Yes, it's probably how I would feel. But John's absolute confidence that, when he saw Jesus, he said, "Behold, the Lamb of God! I was told by God that whoever I saw the Spirit descending on like a dove was the Messiah." With all that absolute confidence, I think John asking his disciples to go and ask Jesus if he's the Messiah is more in sync with what we read first in John 1:37, where he said, "Behold, the Lamb of God," and John's disciples followed Jesus. I think what's happened here is that John is sitting in jail, and his disciples are hanging around, moping, because they haven't got the point. John has been telling them, "I'm not the Messiah; you're not supposed to follow me. I'm just making the way straight for the Messiah." So, he says, "Go and ask Jesus if he's the Messiah; go and see." And Jesus performs miracles in front of them and preaches. And I believe they realize, "Ah! He's the Messiah; we're supposed to follow Him." That's what I'd like to interpret here, as opposed to John moping and wasting away in prison.

LOVE PERSONIFIED

If you want to check out another version of the story, Luke 7:18–35 has the same account. You can see the dialog between Jesus and these disciples and John and his disciples.

The next part of John's story: he's still in jail. We need to go to Mark now, chapter 6.

Oh, before we go there, lets mention this comment from Jesus: "Among those born of women there has not risen one greater than John the Baptist; but he who is least in the kingdom of heaven is greater than he." Jesus, God in the flesh, regards John the Baptist as the greatest prophet of all prophets; he is their pinnacle, their completion, when John is making the way for Jesus. If you were wondering about that rock star status, that movie star draw, John is the best, most popular, most influential prophet ever. The part about "but he who is least in the kingdom …"—I'm hypersensitive about taking things out of context, so I prefer to quote the whole verse, but that part is for another book by another author. Let's keep our focus on love.

Herod's Rash Promise

All right, now to Mark 6:14–29:

> King Herod heard of Him [Jesus], for His name had become well known. And he said, "John the Baptist is risen from the dead, and therefore these powers are at work in him."
> Others said, "It is Elijah."
> And others said, "It is the Prophet, or like one of the prophets."
> But when Herod heard, he said, "This is John, whom I beheaded; he has been raised from the dead!" For Herod himself had sent and laid hold of John, and bound him in prison for the sake of Herodias, his brother Philip's wife; for he had married her. Because John had said to Herod, "It is not lawful for you to have your brother's wife."
> Therefore Herodias held it against him and wanted to kill him, but she could not; for Herod feared John, knowing that he was a just and holy man, and he protected him. And when he heard him, he did many things, and heard him gladly.
> Then an opportune day came when Herod on his birthday gave a feast for his nobles, the high officers, and the chief men of Galilee. And when Herodias' daughter herself came

in and danced, and pleased Herod and those who sat with him, the king said to the girl, "Ask me whatever you want, and I will give it to you." He also swore to her, "Whatever you ask me, I will give you, up to half my kingdom."

So she went out and said to her mother, "What shall I ask?"

And she said, "The head of John the Baptist!"

Immediately she came in with haste to the king and asked, saying, "I want you to give me at once the head of John the Baptist on a platter."

And the king was exceedingly sorry; yet, because of the oaths and because of those who sat with him, he did not want to refuse her. Immediately the king sent an executioner and commanded his head to be brought. And he went and beheaded him in prison, brought his head on a platter, and gave it to the girl; and the girl gave it to her mother. When his disciples heard of it, they came and took away his corpse and laid it in a tomb. (Mark 6:14–29)

And that's the end of the story of John the Baptist. What I'm trying to pull out of this and emphasize is how powerful, how popular, how influential John is, to the point that Herod is convinced that Jesus is a resurrected John the Baptist. In Matthew 16:13–14, Jesus asks the disciples, "Who are the people saying that I am?" Their response: "John the Baptist." John the Baptist is an incredible preacher with incredible influence. People think Jesus is John the Baptist.

Whose Authority?

One last passage, Mark 11:27–33:

> They came again to Jerusalem. And as He [Jesus] was walking in the temple, the chief priests, the scribes, and the elders came to Him. And they said to Him, "By what authority are You doing these things? And who gave You this authority to do these things?"
>
> But Jesus answered and said to them, "I also will ask you one question; then answer Me, and I will tell you by what authority I do these things: the baptism of John—was it from heaven or from men? Answer Me."
>
> And they reasoned among themselves, saying, "If we say, 'From heaven,' He will say, 'Why then did you not

> believe him?' But if we say, 'From men'"—they feared the people, for all counted John to have been a prophet indeed. So they answered and said to Jesus, "We do not know."
> And Jesus answered and said to them, "Neither will I tell you by what authority I do these things." (Mark 11:27–33)

And that's the last comment about John the Baptist in the Bible.

Love does not boast; it does not parade itself; it is not puffed up. Love does not behave—what were those fancy words again? Love *vaunteth* not itself, it is not *vainglorious*. It is love that restrained John from boasting.

I mentioned the trouble I had as a kid. Well, guess what: I didn't grow out of it. So, I worked for ten years at Crossroads, at 100 Huntley Street. I oversaw the Circle Square Ranch ministry and travelled around Africa with legendary missionary Cal Bombay. I did all these important, wonderful things.

And then God called me to the ministry of Galcom. I truly believe this was a call from God. I'm not a technician; I'm an accountant. When I was at Crossroads, I spent a lot of time fundraising and working in administration. When I went to Galcom and met with the board, they hired me to come in and take this little ministry of eight people and grow it to its potential.

And you know, I heard, "Tim, you're the man. You can do this!" And what happens when people start saying good things about you? Your head inflates! And I was certain that I was going to take Galcom, and we'd become this big ministry, like the Billy Graham Association or something like that, a huge ministry. And we'd all be famous around the world, with our radios, and I'd be famous and all that. I don't know—I've got this problem with pride, I really do.

The Wake-Up Call at Galcom

But this was 2008. Remember what happened in 2009? They've made movies about it—the subprime mortgage housing crisis happened, and the economy tanked. Well, all the giving at Galcom tanked, and I remember sitting in my office saying, "I can't do anything. I am completely helpless to fix this problem." Our giving was down 70 percent from what it had been before the crash.

And God graciously spoke to me and said, "Tim, it was never about you. It was never up to you. I'm in charge here. Your job is to have personal integrity and to be a good steward."

CHAPTER 5: JOHN THE BAPTIST IS NOT PUFFED UP

And I sat and I thought, *You know what? Yeah, that's all.*

So, here's the story again: it's not about us. And when we think it's all about us, we can get in the habit of bragging, boasting, being puffed up. "It's about me. I'm the important one here."

John Knew It Wasn't about Him

But if you look at John the Baptist, amazingly, because of his love for God, never once do you hear him say, "Come to me, listen to me." It was always, "Follow Him. I'm not worthy. Follow Him. That's the Lamb of God."

And that's the example for us in our love. For anyone here who ever gets the chance to be up in front of others, with fancy spotlights on them—for anyone who has their name on the bottom of a book—the difficulty, the danger, is if we don't love God enough, we might take His glory for ourselves. Hebrews 13:15 says, "By Him let us continually offer the sacrifice of praise to God, that is, the fruit of our lips, giving thanks to His name." We learned about this as we studied the life of Moses, this term, the "sacrifice of praise". When you're praising somebody else, what are you doing? You're abasing yourself; you're lowering yourself. So, when we sing to God and proclaim His name, we are lowering ourselves to where we should be.

And this is why I think the secret for us is to keep ourselves in the right perspective; and if we praise God, worship God for who He is, it's all about *His* glory. We understand who He is and who we are, and then we're able to love as we are commanded to love. And that is the lesson of John the Baptist.

As I said, this is not easy stuff. This one hits home for me. I have a problem with pride, and I have to show love for God and continue to remind myself who I am in relation with God so that I will humble myself and bring that sacrifice of praise.

For you, maybe it is one of the other people that we've studied so far. Maybe you've had a life of suffering and you want revenge. Or you're in a situation like Ruth, but you don't want to help anybody; you're happy to be comfortable. "Don't ask me to help." Maybe we haven't studied one yet who has really hit you. But we will; we're going to keep working through this list in 1 Corinthians 13, and you're not perfect either. I'm sure you have some room to improve in the area of loving God and others.

LOVE PERSONIFIED

Before I give you your homework, pray this prayer:

> Father, we want to thank You again for the example of real humans who succeeded and failed, who had good things and bad things happen to them. Help us to put ourselves in their shoes in some way and ask, "How would I respond? What would I do? Can I love You with all my heart, soul, mind, and strength, and love my neighbour as myself, as You have commanded me?" Lord, help me to fulfill the great commandment this week. Help me to be humble, to give a sacrifice of praise to You, and not to boast, be puffed up, or think of myself too highly. Lord, help us to love in Jesus's name. Amen.

This week something great is going to happen to you. You will be acknowledged for your hard work, and the chance will come to stand in front of everyone, in the spotlight. When it happens, however big or small the crowd is, take that spotlight and point it at Jesus.

Chapter 6
Esther Does Not Behave Rudely

As we try to understand Jesus's command to love God with all our heart, soul, mind, and strength, and to love our neighbours as ourselves, as we try to recapture the true definition of love that Jesus is talking about, let's study 1 Corinthians 13 in Paul's personal "Amplified Version". In Paul's list of love's varying characteristics, some aspects are easier to understand than others, like love is kind. That chapter just about wrote itself! In nearly every English translation of the Bible, the words "kind" and "kindness" appear multiple times throughout the New Testament, making it straightforward to interpret. However, other characteristics and phrases aren't as clear, which brings us to this chapter's phrase: "Love does not behave rudely."

So, Just What Is "Rude"?

Many different English translations render this Greek word differently, making it difficult to grasp its true meaning. Turning to the Greek text to understand what Paul is conveying isn't much help, since this word is found only twice in the entire Bible: our passage in 1 Corinthians 13, and in 1 Corinthians 7:36, which says:

> If any man thinks he is behaving improperly toward his virgin, if she is past the flower of youth, and thus it must be, let him do what he wishes. He does not sin; let them marry.

The word translated as "rudely" in First Corinthians 13 is translated as "improperly" in this passage.

The noun version of the word appears only twice: in Romans 1:27 and in Revelation 16:15. Let's read them together:

> Likewise also the men, leaving the natural use of the woman, burned in their lust for one another, men with men committing

what is shameful, and receiving in themselves the penalty of their error which was due. (Romans 1:27)

"Behold, I am coming as a thief. Blessed is he who watches, and keeps his garments, lest he walk naked and they see his shame." (Revelation 16:15)

The Greek word used in these verses is translated as "shameful" and "shame". It will help us to look at the context of these verses to determine the semantic field of meaning. What is the meaning of this word in its context?

In each instance where this word is used, it pertains to topics such as sex, marriage, and celibacy. In 1 Corinthians 7, Paul discusses marriage, sexual relationships, serving God, and whether it's better to be single or married. In Romans 1:27, it's pretty clear what God is talking about—this shameful sexual act outside of His design for creation. In Revelation 16:15, the discussion is about modesty. Although the book of Revelation often speaks allegorically, the idea of nakedness is associated with shame and being exposed.

Earlier, in 1 Corinthians, Paul references the members of our body in relation to parts of the church, emphasizing that the more modest parts deserve more honour. This implies modesty and propriety concerning the parts of our body used for sexual encounters. Therefore, it's a responsible hermeneutic to interpret "love does not behave rudely" as referring to sexual purity, modesty, and virtue. So, where do we find someone who is an example to us for our behaviour?

Now, remember, the whole point of this book is to recapture the definition of love. Too many times in our society, we use the term "make love" when we're not talking about love at all—we're talking about sex. TV and movies constantly bombard us with the idea that sex equals love or that making love is simply a sexual act. Our culture is consumed with sexual identity.

Everything seems to be about sex. The most popular TV show of the 1990s was *Seinfeld*. The self-professed show about nothing? Well, not quite—it was about sex. A quick Google search reveals that Jerry, the main character, had seventy-three different girlfriends with entire episodes about him trying to have sex with them.

The other leading character, Elaine, had fifty different boyfriends throughout the series, and there were entire episodes about birth control. This show's

CHAPTER 6: ESTHER DOES NOT BEHAVE RUDELY

driving force was sex. This seemed to be the main point of the characters' lives: to have as much sex as possible.

Acclimatizing Ourselves to Impropriety

Growing up, I had an uncle with an old Beta VCR, and there were two cassettes I remember him having; one was the thirtieth anniversary of Disneyland. I encourage you to go to YouTube and search for David Hasselhoff's epic "Do You Love Me?" performance with Minnie Mouse. The other tape was *Thunderball*, the classic James Bond movie. Whenever we visited their house, I'd watch it, becoming a huge James Bond fan.

I still love action movies—the more karate chopping, bombs exploding, and car chasing, the better. But, as you know with any James Bond movie, there's all sorts of sexual innuendo and gratuitous sex scenes. While there's never nudity, it's all there on the surface. As a child, I don't think I caught it, so I started collecting James Bond movies.

I would go to the video store whenever I had enough money, and I would buy a VHS tape of a James Bond movie; we didn't have a Beta VCR. I had the entire collection by the time I got married. I loved watching them, but I compromised my faith and life in Christ by thinking it didn't affect me.

It's okay, I thought. I would dismiss the names of the female characters or ignore the little comments and innuendo. Fast-forward several years; I'm now married, and my son is around seven or eight. We were at my in-laws' house during the holidays, just wasting time in the middle of the day.

A James Bond movie comes on one of the movie channels, and we start to watch. Great scenes, James Bond with all his gadgets, saving the world. It goes to a commercial, and when we come back, there's the usual viewer discretion advisory. "This movie contains violence and sexuality" was the phrase.

What Does Sexuality Mean?

There wasn't any swearing or nudity in James Bond movies; so, aren't they good? Then my son asked, "Dad, what does 'sexuality' mean?"

Well, seeing as he was around eight years old and I wasn't prepared for this conversation yet, I said, "I'll tell you when you're older." But then I remembered an upcoming scene in the movie where James Bond was going to seduce the evil villainess, and they were going to start making out, and all sorts of things were going to be implied! I decided that we had better change the channel and find a good cartoon instead.

Sexuality, impropriety, and pornography are pervasive in our society. There are movies and TV shows all about teenagers wanting to lose their virginity. This concept is pervasive in our culture. Too much of our identity comes from our sexuality, which is not what God intended. When we're talking about love, we need to recapture the idea of loving others outside of any type of physical attraction or sexual gratification.

So, do we have as an example in the Bible who stands for modesty, virtue, and propriety in the midst of a society that is filled with debauchery and an overly sexualized atmosphere?

Let's turn to the book of Esther. It begins with a 180-day party held by King Ahasuerus—which is quickly followed by another seven-day after-party, where, in verse seven, we read that they were served drinks in golden vessels, each cup different from the other, and royal wine in abundance. Just in case you were wondering about the type of party this was, I like how the author subtly and gracefully describes it; he keeps it classy! He is understated in his description of the situation.

> On the seventh day, when the heart of the king was merry with wine, he commanded Mehuman, Biztha, Harbona, Bigtha, Abagtha, Zethar, and Carcas, seven eunuchs who served in the presence of King Ahasuerus, to bring Queen Vashti before the king, wearing her royal crown, in order to show her beauty to the people and the officials, for she was beautiful to behold. (Esther 1:10–11)

Merry with wine? Read that as drunk out of his mind! If 180 days of drunken revelry doesn't make it clear what kind of society we are reading about, how does King Ahasuerus decide to raise the bar? With a public display of Queen Vashti's beauty. Now, I'm always careful not to read too much into things, specifically in Scripture; we have to be careful not to project things in our culture or understanding onto events from the past. But, considering what happens in chapter 2, I think we can conservatively extrapolate that this culture and this drunken party isn't a wholesome presentation of the queen and her beauty, which is why she refuses to come out (see v. 12).

CHAPTER 6: ESTHER DOES NOT BEHAVE RUDELY

She is perhaps about to objectified, and while it might not be a commonly held idea, it may be that she is asked to wear *only* her royal crown. If you're familiar with the story, her refusal infuriated the king. In a knee-jerk reaction, he and his advisers decide that Vashti should be dethroned, fearing that if word got out of the queen disobeying the king, there would be anarchy across the kingdom with women not honouring their husbands as they should.

The Plan to Cheer Up the King

Early in chapter 2, the king begins to regret his decision and feels a little lonely, so his advisers devise a new plan:

> "Let beautiful young virgins be sought for the king; and let the king appoint officers in all the provinces of his kingdom, that they may gather all the beautiful young virgins to Shushan the citadel, into the women's quarters, under the custody of Hegai the king's eunuch, custodian of the women. And let beauty preparations be given them. Then let the young woman who pleases the king be queen instead of Vashti."
> This thing pleased the king, and he did so. (Esther 2:2–4)

Once again, the author delicately leaves the interpretation of "pleasing the king" to the reader's imagination. But the bottom line is that we find ourselves in a culture centered around the king's sexual gratification and his desire for scores of beautiful women at his exclusive disposal. He would choose the best to be queen, while the rest would become his concubines.

It is in this context that we are finally introduced to our hero, Esther, a young Jewish orphan raised by her cousin Mordecai in a foreign land, where they were taken captive.

Esther's Beauty

Her beauty condemns her to be part of this royal charade. Something about her demeanor endears her to the chief eunuch in charge of the women—perhaps grace, propriety, or modesty. I can only imagine that some of the ambitious young ladies saw this only as an opportunity to become queen, even at the cost of their dignity or self-worth.

Again, I must be careful not to view this through the lens of our culture, where young women expose themselves on social media for followers, fame, and popularity. But I think our society is more like this Babylonian Persia than we might like to admit. Now, we must consider the terms of the competition.

> Each young woman's turn came to go in to King Ahasuerus after she had completed twelve months' preparation, according to the regulations for the women, for thus were the days of their preparation apportioned: six months with oil of myrrh, and six months with perfumes and preparations for beautifying women. Thus prepared, each young woman went to the king, and she was given whatever she desired to take with her from the women's quarters to the king's palace. In the evening she went, and in the morning she returned to the second house of the women, to the custody of Shaashgaz, the king's eunuch who kept the concubines. She would not go in to the king again unless the king delighted in her and called for her by name. (Esther 2:12–14)

Again, thank you to the author of Esther for handling the situation so delicately, but I think we all know what is going on here.

> When the turn came for Esther the daughter of Abihail the uncle of Mordecai, who had taken her as his daughter, to go in to the king, she requested nothing but what Hegai the king's eunuch, the custodian of the women, advised. And Esther obtained favor in the sight of all who saw her. So Esther was taken to King Ahasuerus, into his royal palace, in the tenth month, which is the month of Tebeth, in the seventh year of his reign. The king loved [air quotes here!] Esther more than all the other women, and she obtained grace and favor in his sight more than all the virgins; so he set the royal crown upon her head and made her queen instead of Vashti. Then the king made a great feast, the Feast of Esther, for all his officials and servants; and he proclaimed a holiday in the provinces and gave gifts according to the generosity of a king. (Esther 2:15–18)

You may be questioning how much Esther's modesty, virtue, and decorum play into this story, but we need to take the context of her situation into account. The contrast of how Esther conducts herself in a degraded, perverted society is quite telling.

CHAPTER 6: ESTHER DOES NOT BEHAVE RUDELY

This brings us back to our topic of love. Esther is not acting out of ambition or as part of the sexually driven, debased, depraved culture around her. She gets no pleasure from this; she is a victim, trying to survive and live as best she can.

We have skipped over passages where Mordecai constantly commands her not to reveal her nationality. Jews lived differently than the countries around them, even in the midst of a captive society where they had been transplanted. Chronologically, the book of Daniel is just before Esther, even though it doesn't appear that way in most of our Bibles. We read the story of Daniel, Hananiah, Mishael, and Azariah and their quest to remain true to their beliefs and convictions about food and worship in the midst of a pagan land.

Obedience Amidst Depravation

Esther is in the same situation, trying to live a life of obedience to God in the midst of a pleasure-seeking, sexually driven, depraved culture. Out of respect for your time and to save a few trees, I've been skipping over a lot and will continue to skip a lot of content in the Bible as we pull out the information on our topic of love, exploring how we truly understand the command to love and how we live it out. However, I try not to do so at the expense of context.

We need to look a little at the next part of Esther's story to understand her actions better. Here is a quick summary: Mordecai, Esther's guardian and de facto father, paces outside the palace during this whole process because of his concern and love for Esther. While there, he overhears a couple of the king's eunuchs plotting to kill the king. He quickly tells Esther, who informs the king. The plot is discovered, the king is saved, the two eunuchs are executed, and it's recorded that Mordecai is the one who discovered the plot. Keep that in mind (if you haven't heard this story already through Sunday school or VeggieTales).

The Villain of the Piece

Now we're introduced to the villain of our story, Haman. We don't know why, but the king promotes him. He must have been one of his trusted advisors, maybe manipulative, as evidenced by his actions later on in the story—spoiler alert! Mordecai, who's still at the gate worried about Esther, never bows when Haman goes by. This infuriates Haman, and he decides to kill Mordecai—but not just Mordecai.

LOVE PERSONIFIED

Knowing that Mordecai is a Jew, Haman wants to kill everyone related to him, including the entire Jewish population. The Jews are different; they stand out. I'm sure their obedience to God's laws silently yet unavoidably exposes the evil of the society around them. Also, I would hazard a guess that Haman projects Mordecai's unyielding spirit onto all the Jewish population. Yes, that includes Esther, which is why Mordecai warned her, "Don't let anybody know you're a Jew."

Haman goes to the king and convinces him that the Jewish people are dangerous. The king agrees and gives Haman the king's signet ring to make a law. Haman creates the law, stating that on the thirteenth day of the twelfth month, all of the people of Babylon can annihilate, kill, and loot anyone who is Jewish. The law is proclaimed around the city and the empire. When Mordecai hears about it, in true Jewish fashion he tears his clothes, puts on sackcloth pours ashes on his head as a symbol of mourning, and starts to pray, asking God for relief.

Esther's maids see Mordecai, who is still outside the palace no matter what is going on, and inform her of his attire. She sends them to find out the story and get him some proper clothes. Then, we arrive at the most famous verse in Esther:

> Mordecai told them to answer Esther: "Do not think in your heart that you will escape in the king's palace any more than all the other Jews. For if you remain completely silent at this time, relief and deliverance will arise for the Jews from another place, but you and your father's house will perish. Yet who knows whether you have come to the kingdom for such a time as this?" (Esther 4:13–14)

Such a Time as This

Well, I think that Esther does accept that she has been put in the palace for such a time as this. There was a purpose for her being there, enduring the abuse she suffered at the hands of the king and being removed from her family and everything she knew, being put in this place. And she sends a message back with her eunuch to Mordecai, revealing a problem. In verse 11, she says,

> "All the king's servants and the people of the king's provinces know that any man or woman who goes into the inner court to the king, who has not been called, he has but one

> law: put all to death, except the one to whom the king holds out the golden scepter, that he may live. Yet I myself have not been called to go in to the king these thirty days." (Esther 4:11)

Why would the queen not be in the presence of the king for thirty days? I thought he "loved" her! Again, I try not to read too much into things, but this is clearly a commentary on the culture and the king who sets it. He does not love her but uses her for his sexual gratification. With a few dozen concubines, he has plenty of options to satisfy his own pleasure.

Esther needs to advocate for her people, so she asks for three days fasting. She asks Mordecai and all the Jews to fast, while she and her maids do the same, seeking God's help in deliverance. I love this next line. Esther bravely says, "My maids and I will fast likewise. And so I will go to the king, which is against the law; and if I perish, I perish!" (Esther 4:16).

This may seem off-topic, but in the greater study of love, John 15:13 does have some merit: "Greater love has no one than this, than to lay down one's life for his friends." Esther is ready to lay down her life and is motivated by love for others. This love is evident in her statement and her day-to-day conduct. Let's jump ahead to chapter five.

> It happened on the third day that Esther put on her royal robes and stood in the inner court of the king's palace, across from the king's house, while the king sat on his royal throne in the royal house, facing the entrance of the house. So it was, when the king saw Queen Esther standing in the court, that she found favor in his sight, and the king held out to Esther the golden scepter that was in his hand. Then Esther went near and touched the top of the scepter.
> And the king said to her, "What do you wish, Queen Esther? What is your request? It shall be given to you—up to half the kingdom!"
> So Esther answered, "If it pleases the king, let the king and Haman come today to the banquet that I have prepared for him."
> Then the king said, "Bring Haman quickly, that he may do as Esther has said." So the king and Haman went to the banquet that Esther had prepared.

> At the banquet of wine the king said to Esther, "What is your petition? It shall be granted you. What is your request, up to half the kingdom? It shall be done!"
>
> Then Esther answered and said, "My petition and request is this: If I have found favor in the sight of the king, and if it pleases the king to grant my petition and fulfill my request, then let the king and Haman come to the banquet which I will prepare for them, and tomorrow I will do as the king has said." (Esther 5:1–8)

I like to think that even though she hasn't been in the presence of the king for thirty days, Esther's reputation, grace, and class allowed her to approach the king at a moment's notice, uninvited, and request his presence at a banquet the same day. The king likely has plans and schedules for weeks ahead, perhaps another 180 days of drunken revelry, for example. But he drops everything to attend Esther's banquet. It seems that she remains separate from the culture of concubines and sexual gratification. She seems separate from everything else—apart from this pleasure-seeking, debauched culture. The word *holy* in the Bible means separate or "set apart". The king offers her a gift, but I don't know if he's trying to appease her or win her over, or if he's feeling guilty. There's an interesting dynamic going on here.

Irony Personified

We press on to verse 9. Now, if this book were called *Irony Personified*, this would be the only chapter. This is an incredible bit of literature we read here. We briefly touch on the backstory to understand the cultural context and Esther's situation.

Haman, the only guest invited to a banquet with the king and queen, heads home bragging to his family. But instead of feeling a sense of accomplishment, that "he's made it," he's unsatisfied because Mordecai the Jew still won't bow to him. Honestly, he's just received an incredible honour, but it is still not enough to overcome his resentment that Mordecai doesn't honour him as he wants. For people who need to be important, there's never enough fame or honour to truly satisfy them. His wife and friends advise him to build huge gallows to hang Mordecai on, the notion of which delights Haman. Consumed with revenge, he's determined to punish Mordecai for not honouring him.

In chapter 6, we're told that, that night, the king can't sleep, so he calls in the royal scribes to read from the chronicles of his reign. Maybe this is how he

CHAPTER 6: ESTHER DOES NOT BEHAVE RUDELY

usually falls asleep—I know reading textbooks or leadership books helps me doze off. (Maybe this book is helping you fall asleep!) While reading, they come to the account of Mordecai saving the king's life. The king wonders, "Did we ever acknowledge or reward Mordecai for his loyalty?" Well, no, they haven't. By now it must be dawn; they've been reading a long time, and the king still can't sleep. Perhaps the stories are too action-packed. His life was almost taken in this account, so this isn't going help him fall asleep!

Haman has already arrived, the first guy at work—a loyal worker or a brown noser. The king invites him into the court and asks, "What would you do for someone who's been loyal to the king and has done something special?"

Haman, of course, thinks, *The king must be talking about me! I'm his number one guy, I've got his signet ring, I'm even able to make laws in his name, and I'm getting exclusive invites to dinner with him and the queen.* He devises a grandiose parade. Didn't we talk about love not parading itself in a previous chapter? He imagines wearing the royal robes, riding the king's horse, and having someone walk ahead announcing who he is.

However, the king commands him to do this for Mordecai instead—and you can't write a better description of irony! Haman must fetch Mordecai, put him on the horse, dress him in the robes, and walk in front of him, shouting, "This is what is done for the man the king delights to honour."

Furious, embarrassed, and enraged, Haman finally gets home but has to quickly attend the banquet. Then we pick up Esther's story again.

> Queen Esther answered and said, "If I have found favor in your sight, O king, and if it pleases the king, let my life be given me at my petition, and my people at my request. For we have been sold, my people and I, to be destroyed, to be killed, and to be annihilated. Had we been sold as male and female slaves, I would have held my tongue, although the enemy could never compensate for the king's loss."
> So King Ahasuerus answered and said to Queen Esther, "Who is he, and where is he, who would dare presume in his heart to do such a thing?"
> And Esther said, "The adversary and enemy is this wicked Haman!" (Esther 7:3–6)

Even Haman's Begging Backfires

Suddenly, Haman realizes that Esther is a Jew, like Mordecai, and his plan has backfired. The king, enraged and furious, charges out into the garden to decide what to do. Haman falls at Esther's feet, begging for his life. When the king returns, it *looks* like Haman is on top of her. In verse 8, the king asks, "Will he also assault the queen while I am in the house?"

We can see that this culture is so filled with sexual objectification of women that this is where the king's mind quickly goes. He calls for his servants, who blindfold Haman—not a good omen. Harbonah, one of the eunuchs, says to the king, "Look! The gallows, fifty cubits high, which Haman made for Mordecai, who spoke good on the king's behalf, is standing at the house of Haman." The king orders Haman to be hanged on it, and we have the completion of the irony when he dies on his own gallows—gallows he had prepared for Mordecai.

The story concludes with Mordecai being promoted to Haman's position, obtaining the king's signet ring to make a law. He sets up the law for the Jews to defend themselves in the twelfth month, just a few months until this will take place. The Jews conquer their enemies, overcoming those who hated them and sought to destroy and loot them, taking advantage of Haman's hatred for Mordecai for their own gain.

It's a great story, and I encourage you to read through Esther slowly, enjoying the irony, as well as God's hand of provision and protection. But we need to return to the idea of the way Esther carries herself throughout the story—within this culture. Love does not behave rudely. Her love for God commands decorum, class, and dignity.

Esther's Dignity and Grace

Even in the midst of this terrible so-called "beauty pageant", where she is used and abused, and a victim of this culture, she stands out. You can see it between the lines: she carries herself differently than any of the women in the palace or any of the concubines. She also carries herself differently than Haman; she is welcomed in, and the king treats her with such deference in this passage.

Despite being surrounded by debauchery and wine-drinking banquets, she is different—perhaps in the way she talks, the way she acts, or her respect for others. She doesn't put people in uncomfortable positions. I think this is what

Paul is getting at in this little phrase from 1 Corinthians 13: "Love does not behave rudely."

That's the call to us, in a culture that is quick to tell dirty jokes, objectify women, and take pleasure in sexuality and pornography. We're supposed to rise above all that. It's essential to understand that love—*agape* love—has nothing to do with attraction, infatuation, or lust. It's not an erotic love at all. We need to keep that in mind in our day-to-day behaviour, acting with love, respect, dignity, morality, and holiness.

Love Versus Sex

Let's talk a little more about love and sex—or maybe better put, love versus sex. In deference to and in honour of the author of Esther, who handled the subject delicately, I'll try to do the same.

God obviously created sex for procreation—that's the first purpose. But for some reason, God also made it so that it brings pleasure and enjoyment to the people participating in it.

But God sets limits and boundaries on *eros* love, intending it to be exclusive and intimate between one husband and one wife. Throughout Scripture, God uses sex and marriage as metaphors for His relationship with His people, first with the people of Israel. God frequently rebukes them for committing adultery—not just idolatry—as they've chased after other gods, violating their intimate spiritual relationship with Him. They've gone off and, as God often puts it, prostituted themselves with idols. Marriage is supposed to provide the framework for maintaining this intimate sexual relationship, serving as an allegory for our exclusive, spiritual connection with God.

However, we often cast aside this allegory and, like the people of Israel, prostitute ourselves by worshipping other things. We give intimate, exclusive feelings spiritually—which are intended for God—toward other things and pleasures.

We have also done the same with sex, and in doing this, we lose sight of what love for God means: an intimate, exclusive love for Him. Sex is supposed to be special between two people, but sometimes I'm put off by Christian authors going into explicit details, and I question how this honours their spouse. Love should not behave rudely; it should demonstrate propriety, modesty, and care.

If we speak too openly, it can disrespect the honour and modesty of our spouse. Sex is meant to be private and intimate.

Now let's consider what Paul says about love: it should have decorum, be respectful, and handle things that deserve extra honour with care. In 1 Corinthians 11, he discusses the body of Christ and its parts—albeit allegorically—using common sense to suggest that certain areas should be covered and treated with greater honour, respect, modesty, and privacy.

What Love Does

As Christians, we should conduct ourselves in a way that neither brings shame nor is rude. We need to speak with respect and modesty about our bodies, sex, and the opposite gender, without objectifying them.

Throughout the story of Esther, we see women being treated as mere objects for the pleasure of men. However, Esther carries herself with grace and modesty, holding her head high as best she can. That is what love does, and love for God does the same. She conducts herself respectfully and with decorum, never becoming unseemly or crass.

We need to recapture this attitude, as it demonstrates love for our marriage partner, the opposite gender, and people in general. In the New Testament, there is a verse that says, "Do not let any unwholesome talk come out of your mouths" (Ephesians 4:29 NIV). As a child, I thought this only applied to swearing, but I believe it also relates to dirty jokes and offhand comments. Getting back to those James Bond movies and the names given to many of the female characters—they're rude! There's no other way to put it. The innuendos and comments—we don't need to talk that way, to be that way. Love for others has a gentleness and a modesty.

So, our homework this week: when you're in a locker room, or around the lunch table when the dirty jokes are going around, or when you're speaking to or about your spouse, or watching television and movies, strive to show love and respect in all that you do by not being or engaging in things that are rude. It may mean removing yourself from temptation, leaving certain friend groups, cancelling the cable package.

For me, watching action movies led to a compromise in my Christian faith. We're called to holiness and purity, yet I allowed myself to be drawn in by the action, overlooking the swearing, the bit of nudity, and sexual innuendo. No!

We're called to better. Love for God and love for others calls us to modesty, decorum, class, and holiness. This week, choose not to watch those shows, participate in those conversations, or engage in disrespectful behaviour. Speak and act with decorum, dignity, class, and modesty.

Oh, and what about my James Bond collection? Sometimes God intervenes when we won't act ourselves. We suffered a flood in our neighbourhood not too long after that conversation with my son. A whole bunch of stuff in our basement was ruined, including my VHS collection. I never replaced it.

Chapter 7

David Does Not Seek His Own

On our journey through 1 Corinthians 13, we have been trying to recapture what it means to love as Christians are commanded to love. In John 13, Jesus says, "All will know that you are My disciples, if you have love for one another." In Mark 12, when Jesus is tested by a lawyer, asking what's the most important commandment, He says, "Love the Lord your God with all your heart, with all your soul, with all your mind, and with all your strength … and love your neighbor as yourself." In Matthew 6, He says, "Love your enemies." We're trying to understand what this means. It's not emotion, it's not infatuation; it is an act of the will.

A Bit of Review

To review, we looked at Scripture for examples of the characteristics that Paul uses to describe love:

> First: Joseph suffered at the hands of his brothers, Potiphar and the jailor. But he loved. Love suffers long.
> Second: Ruth gave up security, gave up the comfort of her own home, and went to be with Naomi and helped with backbreaking work in the fields. Love is kind.
> Third: Jonathan, the crown prince of Israel, did not envy God's plan for David; he was content and did not envy what David was given and served him right to the end. Love does not envy.
> Next: Moses, Prince of Egypt, hand-picked by God, continually served his people humbly. Similarly, with John the Baptist, who Jesus himself said was the greatest man ever born of woman, and people thought Jesus was John the Baptist himself—because who else could do such great things? It must have been John the Baptist, raised from the dead. That's how great John the Baptist was! But all he ever said was "He

> must increase, I must decrease. Go follow Him." Love does not parade itself, is not puffed up.
>
> Lastly: Esther practised modesty, in the midst of a depraved, sex-driven culture. Love does not behave rudely.

And now we've come to "Love does not seek its own."

It is a bit difficult to find someone who regularly puts others first, always thinks of the impact their actions will have on others, and considers others' feelings, the baggage they carry, and the cultural norms they are coming from.

I've been married more than twenty-five years, but as a rule I don't give any marriage advice. The only thing I ever say is "When I got married, I learned just how selfish I was. When you're single, you just do what you want; you wake up when you want, eat what you want. But when you're married, suddenly, you have to take the other person into consideration all the time. What do they want to watch on TV, how warm do they want the house temperature." That is for a successful marriage, at least. I guess you can do what you want, but there are consequences when you act selfishly.

So, looking at Scripture, perhaps the best we can do is find someone who thinks of others first *most* of the time. This one's a bit of a trick.

We won't find a perfect example in Scripture apart from Jesus, but there is someone who, nine times out of ten, never is selfish and always thinks of others; and the times that they actually act selfishly, it is a disaster. Introducing King David. So, grab a Bible and turn to 1 Samuel chapter 16, and follow along David's story to see what happens when we love or when we act selfishly.

David's Story

In verse 6, Samuel has been sent by God to anoint a new king. He's done with Saul. God sends Samuel to the family of Jesse, and Samuel examines each of Jesse's sons. Samuel thinks each of David's older brothers fit the bill to be the new king, but God says:

> "Do not look at his appearance or at his physical stature, because I have refused him. For the LORD does not see as man sees; for man looks at the outward appearance, but the LORD looks at the heart." (1 Samuel 16:7)

CHAPTER 7: DAVID DOES NOT SEEK HIS OWN

David was out with the sheep, but God tells Samuel to have David called in and reveals to Samuel that David is His choice.

> Then Samuel took the horn of oil and anointed him in the midst of his brothers; and the Spirit of the LORD came upon David from that day forward. So Samuel arose and went to Ramah. (1 Samuel 16:13)

David is now, by God's anointing through his prophet Samuel, king over Israel. Practically speaking, however, we know he is not the king yet; Saul is still the king. But David has been appointed by God to be the king; keep that in mind.

Let's jump ahead in the story to chapter 17: David and Goliath. The scene starts with David bringing food to his brothers at the camp of the army of Israel. Running a simple errand for others in obedience to his father. Not a very kinglike action.

It's All Coming Up Roses for David

Well, we know the Sunday school story: David takes his stone and sling and kills Goliath. We're just establishing the plot here: first, anointed king; now, after killing Goliath, he is going to be a prince; marrying the king's daughter, and his father's house will be exempt from taxes in Israel. He will receive great honour and praise and riches.

The Israelites go on to conquer the Philistines. Let's pick up the story in 1 Samuel 18:5:

> David went out wherever Saul sent him, and behaved wisely. And Saul set him over the men of war, and he was accepted in the sight of all the people and also in the sight of Saul's servants ... [In fact, on the way back from the battle the women line the streets literally singing his praises,]
> "Saul has slain his thousands,
> And David his ten thousands." (1 Samuel 18:5–7).

Let's pause there for a second: God is building up David's right to be king. He is anointed as the king, he is given a princess for his wife, he is honoured among the people, and now he is named head of the army. What kind of effect are all these honours and privileges having on David? My son is

101

in the military. He has learned that when a commanding officer says something, you say, "Yes, sir." You don't question it. The general gets his way; he doesn't serve anybody, he is served. The crown prince gets served; the anointed king gets served. It's all about them. They don't have to think of others. There is no indication that David let these honours go to his head.

But David Has It Too Good

Then things go sideways. Read 1 Samuel 18:8:

> Saul was very angry, and the saying displeased him; and he said, "They have ascribed to David ten thousands, and to me they have ascribed only thousands. Now what more can he have but the kingdom?" So Saul eyed David from that day forward. (1 Samuel 18:8–9)

We can see the popularity of David. Just like John the Baptist, who was an absolute rock star and had everyone fawning over him and wanting to hear him, coming out into the wilderness.

The same with David: "He's so wonderful that he killed ten thousand men." This is where David is: a future king, a general in the army, and all of this fame is his. All of this praise is for him. But in chapter 18, we know the story of how Saul is suspicious of David and tries to kill him a few times, even throwing a spear at him. Eventually, Jonathan tells David that it is hopeless, and he needs to run and hide.

And so, David runs off, and we pick up the story in chapter 22.

> David therefore departed from there and escaped to the cave of Adullam. So when his brothers and all his father's house heard it, they went down there to him. And everyone who was in distress, everyone who was in debt, and everyone who was discontented gathered to him. So he became captain over them. And there were about four hundred men with him.
>
> Then David went from there to Mizpah of Moab; and he said to the king of Moab, "Please let my father and mother come here with you, till I know what God will do for me." So he brought them before the king of Moab, and they dwelt with him all the time that David was in the stronghold. (1 Samuel 22:1–4)

CHAPTER 7: DAVID DOES NOT SEEK HIS OWN

This can be easily skipped over, but I just want to pause here for a second. Here is David, who has all these rights, and people should be serving him; but the king wants to kill him, so he runs for his life. He is in hiding and just trying to save his own neck, when he suddenly becomes responsible for all the outcasts of Israel. He even detours to make sure that his parents and family are taken care of. I think that is actually worth noting, that in the midst of all of his own problems and troubles, David is concerned about somebody else's safety.

David Has His Big Chance

We then skip ahead to 1 Samuel 24:1–11. Here is the big test, and we are probably familiar with these stories; but let's read these in full and drink them in. First Samuel 24:

> Now it happened, when Saul had returned from following the Philistines, that it was told him, saying, "Take note! David is in the Wilderness of En Gedi." Then Saul took three thousand chosen men from all Israel, and went to seek David and his men on the Rocks of the Wild Goats. So he came to the sheepfolds by the road, where there was a cave; and Saul went in to attend to his needs. (David and his men were staying in the recesses of the cave.) Then the men of David said to him, "This is the day of which the LORD said to you, 'Behold, I will deliver your enemy into your hand, that you may do to him as it seems good to you.'" And David arose and secretly cut off a corner of Saul's robe. Now it happened afterward that David's heart troubled him because he had cut Saul's robe. And he said to his men, "The LORD forbid that I should do this thing to my master, the LORD's anointed, to stretch out my hand against him, seeing he is the anointed of the LORD." So David restrained his servants with these words, and did not allow them to rise against Saul. And Saul got up from the cave and went on his way.
>
> David also arose afterward, went out of the cave, and called out to Saul, saying, "My lord the king!" And when Saul looked behind him, David stooped with his face to the earth, and bowed down. And David said to Saul: "Why do you listen to the words of men who say, 'Indeed David seeks your harm'? Look, this day your eyes have seen that the LORD delivered you today into my hand in the cave, and someone urged me to kill you. But my eye spared you, and I said, 'I will not stretch out my hand against my lord, for

> he is the LORD's anointed.' Moreover, my father, see! Yes, see the corner of your robe in my hand! For in that I cut off the corner of your robe, and did not kill you, know and see that there is neither evil nor rebellion in my hand, and I have not sinned against you. Yet you hunt my life to take it." (1 Samuel 24:1–11)

This is a real test. Love does not seek its own. We've already established that David has been anointed to be the king. Yet instead of seeking his own, he considers Saul. He considers the consequences. He considers God's plan. Saul is still anointed as well. It's not his place to take Saul's life; it's in God's control.

Will David Seek His Own This Time?

It happens again in 1 Samuel 26. Maybe David's patience has come to an end, maybe this time he'll watch out for himself.

> David therefore sent out spies, and understood that Saul had indeed come.
> So David arose and came to the place where Saul had encamped. And David saw the place where Saul lay, and Abner the son of Ner, the commander of his army. Now Saul lay within the camp, with the people encamped all around him. Then David answered, and said to Ahimelech the Hittite and to Abishai the son of Zeruiah, brother of Joab, saying, "Who will go down with me to Saul in the camp?"
> And Abishai said, "I will go down with you."
> So David and Abishai came to the people by night; and there Saul lay sleeping within the camp, with his spear stuck in the ground by his head. And Abner and the people lay all around him. Then Abishai said to David, "God has delivered your enemy into your hand this day. Now therefore, please, let me strike him at once with the spear, right to the earth; and I will not have to strike him a second time!"
> But David said to Abishai, "Do not destroy him; for who can stretch out his hand against the LORD's anointed, and be guiltless?" David said furthermore, "As the LORD lives, the LORD shall strike him, or his day shall come to die, or he shall go out to battle and perish. The LORD forbid that I should stretch out my hand against the LORD's anointed. But please, take now the spear and the jug of water that are by his head,

and let us go." So David took the spear and the jug of water by Saul's head, and they got away; and no man saw or knew it or awoke. For they were all asleep, because a deep sleep from the LORD had fallen on them. (1 Samuel 26:4–12)

After they escape, David shouts back at Saul, "Saul, look, I'm not trying to kill you. Stop hunting me. I'm not going to hurt you."

The reason why we're spending so much time talking about love is because we keep on thinking of love as affection at best; or just animal attraction, infatuation—lust, whatever gets in our mind with popular culture. But we're trying to understand that when God commands His disciples, His followers, to love, we need to obey. No matter what, David loved Saul. It seems weird even writing it down, but David did, in the way that God commands. He loved his enemy. He wanted what was best for him, and he was not going to take anything for himself. As anointed king, as general of the army, all these rights, he wasn't going to use them. Love does not seek its own.

You should remember the story from the chapter on Jonathan, where Saul and his sons are fighting the Philistines, and Saul and Jonathan are killed. David is now king, but one part of the story we didn't mention is that after their death one of Saul's sons, Ishbosheth, still holds some power.

David Thinks of Mephibosheth

There's a rarely taught passage of Scripture about these years, when David is king only of Hebron, and there is fighting back and forth with Ishbosheth. We're going to fast-forward just a bit to get to 2 Samuel 4. Ishbosheth, son of Saul, is murdered by a couple of people who think they're doing David a favour. Which is not uncommon; if you've ever read the book of 2 Kings, you'll notice a pattern: whenever a new king comes into power, he kills all of the sons and everybody else affiliated with the former king.

It happens over and over—at least a half a dozen times. This was the common practice in the ancient Near East. New king? Get rid of anyone who might threaten you. So, these people think they're doing David a favour. David, however, punishes them by execution for killing Ishbosheth.

In chapter 9, David unequivocally and absolutely establishes his rule as king of Israel, and the Philistines are now subdued. So what does David do?

> David said, "Is there still anyone who is left of the house of Saul, that I may show him kindness for Jonathan's sake?"
>
> And there was a servant of the house of Saul whose name was Ziba. So when they had called him to David, the king said to him, "Are you Ziba?"
>
> He said, "At your service!"
>
> Then the king said, "Is there not still someone of the house of Saul, to whom I may show the kindness of God?"
>
> And Ziba said to the king, "There is still a son of Jonathan who is lame in his feet."
>
> So the king said to him, "Where is he?"
>
> And Ziba said to the king, "Indeed he is in the house of Machir the son of Ammiel, in Lo Debar."
>
> Then King David sent and brought him out of the house of Machir the son of Ammiel, from Lo Debar.
>
> Now when Mephibosheth the son of Jonathan, the son of Saul, had come to David, he fell on his face and prostrated himself. Then David said, "Mephibosheth?"
>
> And he answered, "Here is your servant!"
>
> So David said to him, "Do not fear, for I will surely show you kindness for Jonathan your father's sake, and will restore to you all the land of Saul your grandfather; and you shall eat bread at my table continually."
>
> Then he bowed himself, and said, "What is your servant, that you should look upon such a dead dog as I?" (2 Samuel 9:1–8)

Mephibosheth understands what is supposed to happen: he is supposed to get killed by David. He's groveling for his life, expecting full well to be executed. But instead David is putting at risk his own rule and authority by giving back to Mephibosheth all that was Saul's. This is ridiculous if you compare it to all of the other kings in the area. But again, it is David's love for Saul, for Jonathan, for his family, and for God that dictates his behaviour. He doesn't seek his own; he isn't concerned about his own health, well-being, and security of the crown. He is concerned about somebody else—in this case, Mephibosheth.

The Pattern Is Broken

We see this wonderful pattern of David always putting other people first, always loving God and doing things His way, never grabbing and striving for

CHAPTER 7: DAVID DOES NOT SEEK HIS OWN

things that by right are his. Although anointed king as a teenager, he never strives, never takes things into his own hands, always waits on and trusts God, and always acts in love—until 2 Samuel 11.

> It happened in the spring of the year, at the time when kings go out to battle, that David sent Joab and his servants with him, and all Israel; and they destroyed the people of Ammon and besieged Rabbah. But David remained at Jerusalem.
> Then it happened one evening that David arose from his bed and walked on the roof of the king's house. And from the roof he saw a woman bathing, and the woman was very beautiful to behold. So David sent and inquired about the woman. And someone said, "Is this not Bathsheba, the daughter of Eliam, the wife of Uriah the Hittite?" Then David sent messengers, and took her; and she came to him, and he lay with her, for she was cleansed from her impurity; and she returned to her house. And the woman conceived; so she sent and told David, and said, "I am with child." (2 Samuel 11:1–5)

David acts absolutely selfishly, with total disregard for Bathsheba, Uriah, the consequences to his rule, the lives of his soldiers, his relationship with God—absolute self-seeking behaviour—and it is a disaster. To cover up his sin, David brings Uriah back and tries to get him to sleep with his wife, but he won't. This isn't just some random guy who is just in and out of the story. There's a list of David's mighty men in both Samuel and Chronicles, and Uriah the Hittite is one of his top thirty fighters; he's not just an extra in this story, he is a trusted friend and loyal soldier. David has him killed to cover up his sin, because Uriah will know that he had not slept with his wife and could expose David. He thinks he has covered it all up. So because of his selfishness he has committed adultery and murder.

In chapter 12, the Lord sends Nathan the prophet to David. He tells the king a story about two men, where one steals the other one's sheep to serve a meal to a guest. Verse 5:

> David's anger was greatly aroused against the man, and he said to Nathan, "As the LORD lives, the man who has done this shall surely die! And he shall restore fourfold for the lamb, because he did this thing and because he had no pity."
> Then Nathan said to David, "You are the man! Thus says the LORD God of Israel: 'I anointed you king over Israel, and

> I delivered you from the hand of Saul. I gave you your master's house and your master's wives into your keeping, and gave you the house of Israel and Judah. And if that had been too little, I also would have given you much more! Why have you despised the commandment of the LORD, to do evil in His sight? You have killed Uriah the Hittite with the sword; you have taken his wife to be your wife, and have killed him with the sword of the people of Ammon. Now therefore, the sword shall never depart from your house, because you have despised Me, and have taken the wife of Uriah the Hittite to be your wife.'" (2 Samuel 12:5–10)

God says, "The child of Bathsheba is going to die and I am going to bring an adversary to harm you, and the sword will never leave your house. This sin you have committed of adultery is now a curse on your house, on your home, on your family." One selfish act undermined all of his previous acts of love for God and others.

The Curse Bears Fruit

The curse happens almost immediately. Let's quickly summarize chapter 13 because it's messy and hard to read; I often tell youth groups I teach that the Bible is not a kid's book. You may know the story: Amnon lusts after his half-sister, Tamar, and rapes her. Absalom, her full brother, kills Amnon, his half-brother. Absalom is exiled. Absalom pleads to come back, but David doesn't deal with the issue. Perhaps because of the guilt of his own adultery and murder, he doesn't want to deal with somebody else's; we don't know what his problem is here, but he doesn't deal justly in the whole situation. And it just keeps on devolving, and getting worse and worse.

Absalom finally convinces David to let him come back, but not into the palace. So, Absalom sets up shop outside the Jerusalem gate. Any time someone's coming by to get justice, Absalom says, "Hey, friend, come here. If only I could help you." He listens to them and they're overwhelmed by his charm and good looks. He starts to win over the people of Israel. Then, he goes off into a secluded place, and starts to gather people to himself; some know what's going on, and some don't.

They blow the trumpets, and he proclaims himself king. David's back in Jerusalem, ignorant of what is going on. Absalom, with this growing group of followers, is threatening a coup. Whew, I think we got through that pretty unscathed.

CHAPTER 7: DAVID DOES NOT SEEK HIS OWN

David Flees

In 2 Samuel 15:13, a messenger comes to David saying,

> "The hearts of the men of Israel are with Absalom."
> So David said to all his servants who were with him at Jerusalem, "Arise, and let us flee, or we shall not escape from Absalom. Make haste to depart, lest he overtake us suddenly and bring disaster upon us, and strike the city with the edge of the sword."
> And the king's servants said to the king, "We are your servants, ready to do whatever my lord the king commands." Then the king went out with all his household after him. But the king left ten women, concubines, to keep the house. And the king went out with all the people after him, and stopped at the outskirts. Then all his servants passed before him; and all the Cherethites, all the Pelethites, and all the Gittites, six hundred men who had followed him from Gath, passed before the king. (2 Samuel 15:13–18)

On down now to verse 24:

> There was Zadok also, and all the Levites with him, bearing the ark of the covenant of God. And they set down the ark of God, and Abiathar went up until all the people had finished crossing over from the city. Then the king said to Zadok, "Carry the ark of God back into the city. If I find favor in the eyes of the LORD, He will bring me back and show me both it and His dwelling place. But if He says thus: 'I have no delight in you,' here I am, let Him do to me as seems good to Him." (2 Samuel 15:24–26)

As an aside, there's a really great book called *The Tale of Three Kings* by Gene Edwards. His most famous book is *The Divine Romance*; he's an incredible writer, buy his books now. *The Tale of Three Kings* is about Saul, David, and Absalom; and he goes into depth about these couple of verses here, describing David's attitude in this situation. I want to pause and emphasize this verse where David didn't want trouble for the city. Saul, David, and Absalom have completely different characters all resulting from their relationship with God. Their love of God or lack thereof dictates their thought process, their choices, and their actions.

LOVE PERSONIFIED

Just as David, when he was escaping from Saul, cared about his parents, here he is, Absalom and his forces bearing down on him, and where are his thoughts? For the people in the city. They don't need a civil war; the civilians don't need to be caught up in a fight between Absalom and David. Even then, he says, "Perhaps God is done with me. Perhaps I need to go. Maybe God has chosen Absalom to rule at this point. I'm not going to fight against God. I'm going to go." And he leaves.

Perhaps God Has Told Him To

Chapter 16 tells a somewhat comical little story of a descendant of Saul throwing rocks at David. His soldiers, his mighty men, are walking along beside him saying, "Let's go chop this guy's head off; he's just one guy throwing rocks at us—really?"

And David says, "Let him curse. Perhaps God has told him to curse me. Perhaps this cursing will later turn and be a blessing to me." He just takes it, instead of taking selfish action. David has returned to this attitude of love for others, saying, "I'm not going to take what I deserve. I'm not going to do what's best for me. Perhaps this is God's plan. Let him curse."

We know the rest of the tragedy of the story, but it's Absalom's, so we'll skip through it quickly—there's a whole bunch of intrigue and so on with advisers before Absalom's army goes out to attack David, and in the midst of the battle, Absalom gets hanged by his own hair in a tree and is killed. David is restored as king. But not without some mild conflict with his own army who were loyal to him. He sucks it up, stops mourning for Absalom, and thanks those who fought for him. Still a little struggle thinking of others first.

There's one other failing of David that I don't think we'll take too much ink to go over, and that's in 1 Chronicles 21; it's the census he takes. Chronicles says that he is tempted by the devil to count the people to see his power. Selfishly, arrogantly, he does this, and then God judges. God gives David the option of three years of famine, three months of being conquered by enemies, or three days of plague. He chooses to throw himself on the mercy of God. These two epic selfish acts, first Bathsheba and now this census, cause so much harm and shame to others around him. His selfish acts cause cataclysmic destruction.

CHAPTER 7: DAVID DOES NOT SEEK HIS OWN

David's Life: A Study of Contrasts

The contrast in David's life shows us what happens when we, as Christ's disciples, either love God first and obey, and love others by considering them; or when we just say, "I'm just going to take advantage; it's for my own pleasure. No one has the right to tell me what I can do or can't do." And we see selfishness's destructive power.

I've tried to be encouraging with the first several stories that there's always this blessing when we follow these examples, when we submit to the Holy Spirit's leading, and we love in this way, with purpose and choice, no matter the situation.

But this one is a warning for us: when we act selfishly, when we are self-seeking, it causes destruction. What I said right off at the top of the chapter about marriage: we've had a good twenty-five years, but it's been up and down. And I look at it and think, "Yeah, that one was my fault. Yeah, that one was my fault, too. Shouldn't have said that; shouldn't have done that." And that's just a small fallout, in my own family. Think about how bad the effects can be in your sphere of influence, if you're a leader in your church, if you're a leader in business.

Preparing for Others

Let's wrap up our study by looking at the last little part of David's life, so let's skip ahead to 1 Chronicles 17. David wants to build a temple for God. He's thinking about others. He says, "I'm living in this wonderful palace, but the Ark of the Covenant is in a tent. We need to build something for God." He's thinking again about somebody else. It's taken a while to get back to this attitude after making a mess of things for a few years. It's ironic that now that he's thinking of others, God says, "No, not you, David. Someone else will build My temple."

But in 1 Chronicles 28 and 29, we have this wonderful, detailed account of David preparing for Solomon to build the temple for the worship of God to be expanded, for the worship of God to be raised up higher in prominence in the people's eyes in Israel. He's thinking again about others. He's on his deathbed at this point, and he's gathering the gold and the silver and everything else for other people; he's planning ahead for other people. I just think that's a nice little picture for us, to see that even on his deathbed, he is thinking of others.

LOVE PERSONIFIED

This is love, and this is why this is not a little child's "Jesus loves me" kind of thing. Love is the mark of a true disciple of Jesus Christ. And it is hard. This is hard! It is so easy, as David did, to slip into selfish behaviour. "One little indulgence, what's it going to harm? It's not gonna hurt anybody." But it does: our actions have consequences. Selfishness destroys, but love that does not seek its own gives life.

Homework

Remember don't just jump to the next chapter thinking, *Oh, what a nice story*. It's time to apply what we have learned. Maybe take a few days before reading on, and really work on this characteristic of love. Start your day in prayer asking for the Holy Spirit to control your urges, to remove temptation. Ask Him to increase your faith, knowing that God will supply all your needs. You don't need to strive; you don't need to look out for yourself.

Prepare ahead of time. As David found out, selfishness can sneak up and grab you out of nowhere. Then, throughout your day, when you are faced with the choice to serve yourself, pause before every sentence you say or choice you make, asking yourself, "Am I doing this for me or for others?" and "What will be the consequences of my words and actions?" Slow down and think; don't be impulsive.

Love thinks of others first.

Chapter 8

Stephen Is Not Provoked

Ever consider the idea of being provoked? If someone is provoking you, they are either doing something to incite a reaction or, in their ignorance, acting in a way that is annoying, bothersome, or hurtful. You are likely more familiar with the second instance. The co-worker who always seems to say the most inappropriate things, the roommate who always leaves a mess, the customer speaking down to you.

The principle that love is not provoked applies to both types of circumstances. We're going to focus on someone who demonstrates love by maintaining their composure, their level-headedness, even though they are being attacked.

Whose example can we follow to replicate this character trait of love? The person we are going to study does not react, even to the point of death. They don't lash out, they don't fight back; they are not provoked. They continue to love under the most severe circumstances. Who is our example? It's Stephen, the first martyr of the church. There are other examples of this characteristic of love, but I always come back to Stephen as being the best.

More than any of the other characteristics that we've come across in 1 Corinthians 13, this is the one that I think proves the most that we're not talking about emotion. This is not a feeling; this is not infatuation or attraction. This is a choice, an act of the will, a character trait. And this is what we've been trying to reclaim with this whole study about love: that we need to make a purposeful decision to love.

Albert Barnes, in the 1830s, commented,

> If you have the love of God, you are calm, serious, patient, sober-minded. And though you may be injured, you control your passions. You restrain your temper and subdue your feelings.

That is the love that we're trying to reclaim—the love that actually subdues feelings, the love that God calls us to. Barnes adds,

> If we are under the influence of benevolence or Christian love, we shall not give way to sudden bursts of feeling. We shall look kindly on the other's actions, put the best construction on their motives, deem it possible that we have mistaken the nature or the reasons of their conduct, seek or desire explanation, wait until we can look at the case in all its bearings; and suppose it possible that they may be influenced by good motives, and that their conduct will admit of a satisfactory explanation.

Love is not provoked; it waits, it pauses, it thinks things through, and reacts in a measured, sober-minded, reasonable way.

Stephen, Full of the Holy Spirit

Acts 6 is where we're introduced to Stephen:

> In those days, when the number of the disciples was multiplying, there arose a complaint against the Hebrews by the Hellenists, because their widows were neglected in the daily distribution. Then the twelve summoned the multitude of the disciples and said, "It is not desirable that we should leave the word of God and serve tables. Therefore, brethren, seek out from among you seven men of good reputation, full of the Holy Spirit and wisdom, whom we may appoint over this business; but we will give ourselves continually to prayer and to the ministry of the word."
>
> And the saying pleased the whole multitude. And they chose Stephen, a man full of faith and the Holy Spirit, and Philip, Prochorus, Nicanor, Timon, Parmenas, and Nicolas, a proselyte from Antioch, whom they set before the apostles; and when they had prayed, they laid hands on them.
>
> Then the word of God spread, and the number of the disciples multiplied greatly in Jerusalem, and a great many of the priests were obedient to the faith.
>
> And Stephen, full of faith and power, did great wonders and signs among the people. Then there arose some from what is called the Synagogue of the Freedmen (Cyrenians,

CHAPTER 8: STEPHEN IS NOT PROVOKED

Alexandrians, and those from Cilicia and Asia), disputing with Stephen. And they were not able to resist the wisdom and the Spirit by which he spoke. Then they secretly induced men to say, "We have heard him speak blasphemous words against Moses and God." And they stirred up the people, the elders, and the scribes; and they came upon him, seized him, and brought him to the council. They also set up false witnesses who said, "This man does not cease to speak blasphemous words against this holy place and the law; for we have heard him say that this Jesus of Nazareth will destroy this place and change the customs which Moses delivered to us." And all who sat in the council, looking steadfastly at him, saw his face as the face of an angel. (Act 6:1–15)

Before we go any further, I want to emphasize again how Stephen is described: "full of the Holy Spirit" in verse 3. "A man full of faith and the Holy Spirit" in verse 5. Verse 10: "They could not resist the wisdom and the Spirit." In the NJKV, there is a capital "S" for Spirit. It's not Stephen's spirit, it's the Holy Spirit.

Stephen's Defense

Stephen's life, his thinking, and his actions are governed by the Holy Spirit.

In chapter 7, Stephen goes into the entire history of Israel as he defends what Jesus claimed, and explains what Jesus said about the temple being destroyed and raised up again in three days. And he starts at the very beginning. He recites an entire overview of the Jewish history, starting from Abraham. He goes through Isaac, Jacob, Joseph, and others and finally comes to Jesus. Everyone is tracking along, nobody interrupting, everything is fine. Let's get to where the action starts and read from Acts 7:51 on to the end:

"You stiff-necked and uncircumcised in heart and ears! You always resist the Holy Spirit; as your fathers did, so do you. Which of the prophets did your fathers not persecute? And they killed those who foretold the coming of the Just One, of whom you now have become the betrayers and murderers, who have received the law by the direction of angels and have not kept it."

When they heard these things they were cut to the heart, and they gnashed at him with their teeth. But he, being full of the Holy Spirit, gazed into heaven and saw the glory of God, and Jesus standing at the right hand of God, and said, "Look! I see the heavens opened and the Son of Man standing at the right hand of God!"

Then they cried out with a loud voice, stopped their ears, and ran at him with one accord; and they cast him out of the city and stoned him. And the witnesses laid down their clothes at the feet of a young man named Saul. And they stoned Stephen as he was calling on God and saying, "Lord Jesus, receive my spirit." Then he knelt down and cried out with a loud voice, "Lord, do not charge them with this sin." And when he had said this, he fell asleep. (Acts 7:51–60)

The Contrast Is Startling

That is the entire history of Stephen, just two chapters in the Acts of the Apostles. But what we get from so short a story is a contrast which helps us understand clearly what it means to have a love that is not provoked. Our last character study was on David, and we saw the contrast there was that when he loved others, things went well; when he acted selfishly, it was a disaster. Fortunately, with Stephen, we don't have the contrast in his own behaviour, but we have his conduct contrasted to that of the Sanhedrin, who gnash their teeth, stop up their ears, and charge at him in a passion and a rage. Whereas Stephen, even while he is being stoned to death, calls out, "Lord, forgive them for this act."

This is incredible self-control. They could not provoke him to any type of behaviour or action outside of love, even for them, his murderers. Stephen gives this whole long testimony to try to convince them that everything was leading up to Jesus Christ—Jesus's death and resurrection was necessary for the Messiah. But they won't hear it. They are stiff-necked and uncircumcised in heart, and he pleads with them.

What is the cause of such a stark contrast? Over and over again, Stephen is described as someone full of the Holy Spirit, but in verse 51 he says to the Sanhedrin, "You resist the Holy Spirit." The difference is the Holy Spirit.

But How Do We Stop Being Provoked?

Recently, I was chatting with a friend about how, for some people, it might be easier to show love through certain of these characteristics. Some people just seem predisposed to be kind, others have a humble personality. But as we discussed Stephen, it became obvious the ability to love as God calls to love is not something that we generate in ourselves or work up towards.

This characteristic of love that we're called to show, not being provoked, is not something we can achieve. It is something that is guided by the Holy Spirit. It's accomplished by yielding to the control of the Holy Spirit. Let me give you an example; and if you want the whole context, read C. S. Lewis's book, *The Four Loves.*

You may remember in John chapter 21, after Jesus has risen again, He's on the beach in Galilee. There's a group of His disciples, out on the water fishing. Jesus calls out to them, and Peter realizes it's Jesus causing him to jump from the boat and swim ashore. They have perhaps the greatest breakfast together ever. A time of quiet and reconnecting and answered questions. Then, Jesus takes Peter aside and says, "Peter, do you love me?"

And Peter says, "Of course I love you."

Jesus responds, "Feed my lambs. Do you love me?" This goes on a few times. Now, in English, we miss something here. There are four Greek words that we translate, or that all of our English versions of the Bible translate, simply as "love", which I think causes a lot of the confusion. Throughout this book, I've been saying this: Love is not affection.

Here is where C. S. Lewis's book really helps us. The Greek word for affection is *storge*. It's that instinctive love that a mother has for her child. If you wonder, "What does that mean?" Think about a woman who's just been through twenty hours of labor; when the baby comes out, she doesn't say, "Look what you did to me!" She says, "Oh, my baby!" Holds it close to her breast, kisses its slimy head, and weeps with joy. It's instinctive, it's *storge*, it's affection. It's what you have for your grandkids, your family. It's familial, it's animal; it is natural.

The next one is *eros:* that's attraction, infatuation—where we get the word "erotic" from. That kind of love is obviously not what we're talking about. Let's move on.

Philia versus Agape

Then we get back to the story of Jesus and Peter, because they are using different words. Jesus says, "Peter, do you *agape* me?" And this is the word that we've been studying. When Jesus was asked, "What's the greatest commandment?" The word that's used there in Mark is *agape*. "Love the Lord your God with all your heart, with all your mind, and with all your strength, and love your neighbor as yourself"—*agape*. When Jesus says, "Love your enemy," he uses *agape*. In 1 Corinthians 13, when Paul is trying to explain love, he is talking about *agape*. This is the word that's used here by Jesus.

But when Peter is asked, "Peter, do you *agape* me?" he responds, "You know, Lord, that I *philia* you." Philadelphia, the City of Brotherly Love—it's brotherly love. If you are a war-movie fan you will have seen *Saving Private Ryan*, or maybe the TV show *Band of Brothers*. This is the concept: the love that you have for your people, your team, your guys, is a bond that's so strong that you would risk your life for your brothers.

This is only my opinion, and I'm happy to be corrected. Many people think that when Jesus says, "Peter, do you *agape* me?" and Peter replies, "Lord, you know that I *philia* you," it's because he isn't able to say, "Lord, I *agape* you." His love hasn't reached that level. But I think Peter replies that way because he thinks *philia* is stronger. He's saying, "Jesus, I just went and cut a guy's ear off for you. I was ready to fight for you. Come on, you know that I *philia* you. Isn't that better?"

And Jesus says again, "Peter, do you *agape* me?" See, *philia*, although it's strong and you're willing to die for someone, it's exclusive. It's only for me and my guys. It's just for me and my team or my unit, or these people that identify with me. But *agape* has no barriers. That's why it's so important. Jesus commands us: love your enemy. I don't know if I have any enemies that I would have to struggle to love. Maybe you do. I just haven't been in those types of bad situations, I guess. But I know that I don't love my neighbours as I should. This lifestyle, this character trait of love, is ready to respond to anyone no matter the situation. But I think sometimes we have trouble understanding what it means to love unconditionally—regardless of how they treat you, where they come from, what they believe, and how they act. You see, love isn't about the recipient; it's about our heart.

How Stephen Did It

And that's why I like this example of Stephen, because it says *how* he did it. He sat there and he took the abuse, the false accusations, as they tried him and told lies about him. And never once in this court case does he say, "That's not true. You guys are lying!" He never fights back. He just preaches the gospel to them and tries to convince them of the truth of Jesus Christ. And when they murder him, he says, "Lord, forgive them." He's never provoked. That's the extent of the love that we're called to act on.

We know the end of the story between Peter and Jesus: it ends where Jesus says, "Peter, do you *philia* me?"

And Peter says, "Yes, Lord, you know I do."

And Jesus says, "Feed my sheep."

Of course, before this, he denied Christ three times and then ran away. But later on, in Acts, we see him boldly standing in front of everyone in the temple proclaiming Christ, tried and beaten by the Sanhedrin for continuing to preach, travelling everywhere and risking his life to tell people of Christ. Church history tells us (not the Bible, but church history) that he was even crucified upside down for his faith and for his identity in Christ.

What happened in Peter's life, between his life up to this encounter at the beach—a life that denied Jesus, fled, and wouldn't say, "Lord, I *agape* you"— between what happened here and what happened later in the Acts of the Apostles? The answer is the Holy Spirit. The truth of this comes through, I think, more in this passage with Stephen not being provoked than any of the other people I talk about.

This is the lesson for all of us: we're not going to be able to work ourselves up, or study ourselves up, to love like this. It comes only by submission to the Holy Spirit.

How are we controlled by the Holy Spirit? Ephesians 2:1 says that we're dead in our trespasses and sins, so the very first step is that we must be born again (John 3). If you have not accepted Jesus Christ as your Savior and Lord, you do not have the Holy Spirit. In Romans 7:14–25, Paul goes through that whole series of "What I want to do I don't do." This is the battle between the natural, sinful nature and the control of the Holy Spirit. What's the answer? The answer is feeding the spiritual nature.

The Fight of the White Dog and the Black Dog

There's an old story Billy Graham used to tell:

> An Eskimo fisherman came to town every Saturday afternoon. He always brought his two dogs with him. One was white and the other was black. He had taught them to fight on command. Every Saturday afternoon in the town square, the people would gather and these two dogs would fight and the fisherman would take bets. On one Saturday, the black dog would win; another Saturday, the white dog would win but the fisherman always won! His friend began to ask him how he did it. He said, "I starve one and feed the other. The one I feed always wins because he is stronger." This story about the two dogs tells us something about the inner *warfare* that comes into the life of a person who is born again. We have two natures within us, both struggling for mastery. Which one will dominate us? It depends on which one we feed.[1]

When my children were younger, we would often talk about the kind of music they listened to or the stuff they were watching on TV or consuming on the Internet. And I would say, "You're feeding the black dog, instead of the white dog." You have these natures; one is good, and one is bad, and if you keep on feeding the evil nature, guess what you're going to do. You're going to do evil. You've got to feed the good nature with the spiritual. It is a daily battle to be controlled by the spirit and not the flesh.

The Secret Formula

Now this may blow your mind. You may have never heard this before. The best way to be filled with the Holy Spirit? It's to read your Bible and pray every day. That's the best I've got! The Christian life isn't complicated; it's hard, but it's pretty simple. We fill our souls with God's Word, the Holy Spirit–indwelt, empowered Word. We spend time in prayer, giving ourselves over to the control of the Spirit, so that, when we get in a situation such as Stephen was in, we can love. We are not provoked; we have yielded ourselves to the control of the Holy Spirit. That is the only way we will ever achieve this kind of love.

That's the end of the story of Stephen; the end of the lesson on "Love is not provoked." I've been giving homework in some chapters; I've been saying that something is going to happen in your life where you're going to be abused. How are we going to respond? There's going to be a situation where you can choose your own comfort and ignore things, or you can be kind. There's going

---

1. Billy Graham, *The Holy Spirit* (Dallas: Word Publishing, 1988), 92–93.

to be a time when something great is going to happen to somebody else; you can envy, or you can celebrate what God is doing in their life. There's going to be a time where that good thing will happen to you, and you can either boast about it, or you can point people to Jesus Christ. There's going to be a time when someone's going to do something infuriating to you, even this week; will you love, or will you be provoked? The key in all these situations is to be prepared, to be controlled by the Holy Spirit.

The Christian life is simple, not easy but simple. There's an old Sunday school song we used to sing when we were little. "Read your Bible, pray every day, and you'll grow, grow, grow." Hopefully, you just found yourself doing the actions. If you can't place it, it's the last verse of "I Will Make You Fishers of Men." Being Spirit-led is about yielding to the Holy Spirit by daily feeding the spiritual nature. So, start your day tomorrow in God's Word and prayer. Then end it with reading God's Word and praying. And maybe play some good worship music for the car ride to work. There's no quick fix, no secret formula or silver bullet. Feed that white dog daily!

Chapter 9
Jacob *Keeps* a Record of Wrongs

Before our next character study, we need to look at I Corinthians 13:5 in various translations to better understand the phrase used.

> New King James Version: "Does not behave rudely, does not seek its own, is not provoked, thinks no evil."

> New International Version: "It does not dishonor others, it is not self-seeking. It is not easily angered. It keeps no record of wrongs."

> American Standard Version: "Doth not behave itself unseemly, seeketh not its own, is not provoked, taketh not account of evil."

> Revised Standard Version: "It is not arrogant or rude. Love does not insist on its own way; it is not irritable or resentful."

> The Darby Translation: "Does not behave in an unseemly manner, does not seek what is its own, is not quickly provoked, does not impute evil."

> New Living Translation: "Or rude. It does not demand its own way. It is not irritable, and it keeps no record of being wronged."

> New Century Version: "Love is not rude, is not selfish, and does not get upset with others. Love does not count up wrongs that have been done."

In our study of characters as examples to us for our benefit, we have been trying to learn how to love others in different situations—again, putting ourselves in somebody else's shoes (or better, putting them in our shoes) to see how we should love when certain things are happening to us and around us.

Several times I've had to spend a lot of time with word studies to try to identify what exactly we're talking about. And so, in my defense, in this tiny little phrase, there's a whole bunch of professional groups of translators that have come up with multiple different renderings of this phrase. Like really different!

I'm trying to focus on stories because they are easier to learn from than theory (remember my physics story?) But you've got to cut me some slack on the fact that we have to identify these differences and clearly define what is being said. Again, we go to the Greek. I encourage you to find resources that provide an interlinear Greek New Testament. Several can be found online to enhance your personal study.

We want to look at what are called the semantic fields of meaning. How are these Greek words used in other passages of Scripture? Then, we look at context to get the best meaning for the situation. By investigating, we can get an understanding of what Paul probably means in this context. In this verse, if we translate word for word in order from the Greek it says, "not it keeps account of wrongs." The word here for "keeps account" is *logizetai*.

It's used forty-one times in the New Testament. It means to calculate, to take into account, to consider, to reckon. When we look at the context in 1 Corinthians, this word probably means to "keep a record of" or "keep an account of." The New King James Version translates it as "thinks."

We start in this phrase with *logizetai*—bookkeeping, keeping a record. The other important word in this passage is *kakon*. It's used fifty-one times, almost always translated into English as "evil". A couple of times, in English, it is translated as "harm". So, we have these two words here.

It's definitely about keeping a record, or an account, or a rendering of something. I'm pretty confident that we've got to look at a different way of interpreting this. It is translated to mean, "Love does not keep an account of evil done to it or done to the person," just by the way those two Greek words are used in the New Testament over and over again.

What's being said is this: wrong is going to be done to you. People are going to be nasty. What are you going to do about it?

CHAPTER 9: JACOB *KEEPS* A RECORD OF WRONGS

What Are You Going to Do About It?

Are you going to keep score? Are you going to hold a grudge? Are you going to cling to something that somebody does to you and say, "I'm going to get them back"? I would postulate that Paul wants us to understand this meaning about our love for others, and I guess, really in this case, love for our enemies is all about not keeping track, not keeping score.

So, who then is a good example for us who doesn't keep score when wrongs keep on adding up? Well, we've already used Joseph. I'd love to have used him again in this instance because of all the wrongs that were done to him by his brothers. And of course, he doesn't hold a grudge. And when they meet him at the end of the story, he forgives his brothers and says, "What you intended for evil, God intended for good."

That's a perfect example of love. It does not keep a record of wrongs, does not keep an account of evil done to it. There are a couple of other really good examples of love that we're going to use in this context, but I don't want to spoil them because they're going to come up in later chapters.

Who's a good example for someone who doesn't keep a record of evil done to them? Well, this is the halfway point of our study on love, and I think maybe it's time to shake things up a bit; maybe we're getting caught in a bit of a rut. So, I'm going to go "Bizarro Superman" here and let's study someone who's the exact opposite of a love that does not keep a record of wrongs.

To Learn What Something Is, Look at What it's Not

And hey, it's beneficial sometimes when learning what something is, if you're having trouble understanding it, to look at what it's not. My favourite example of this is Proverbs 3:5–6: "Trust in the Lord with all your heart." What does it mean to trust in the Lord with all your heart? Well, we have a really good contrast right next to it: "And lean not on your own understanding." So, what does it mean to trust in God? It means not leaning on your own understanding, and not trusting yourself in your own perspective, your knowledge, or your experience. You trust in what God says in His Word.

So, in this case, what does it mean to not keep a record of wrongs? What does it mean to just love somebody, no matter what? Let's look at someone who doesn't, so we can learn what *not* to do. Who's the best example of someone in Scripture who's constantly keeping score, holding a grudge? Jacob. If you've got a Bible handy, turn to Genesis 25:21–26. Let's pick up the story right at the very beginning.

> Isaac pleaded with the LORD for his wife, because she was barren; and the LORD granted his plea, and Rebekah his wife conceived. But the children struggled together within her; and she said, "If all is well, why am I like this?" So she went to inquire of the LORD.
> And the LORD said to her:
> "Two nations are in your womb,
> Two peoples shall be separated from your body;
> One people shall be stronger than the other,
> And the older shall serve the younger."
> So when her days were fulfilled for her to give birth, indeed there were twins in her womb. And the first came out red. He was like a hairy garment all over; so they called his name Esau. Afterward his brother came out, and his hand took hold of Esau's heel; so his name was called Jacob. Isaac was sixty years old when she bore them. (Genesis 25:21–26)

Now, let's look at Jacob. His very name means "supplanter" or "deceiver". And what's great about Jacob's stories? We get a little glimpse of God's sovereignty in them. He has a plan before birth, at conception. God has a plan for Jacob and Esau. Before Jacob can make a conscious choice about anything, he's already grabbing at his brother's heel, trying to take things into his own hands, perhaps using his brother as leverage to get out. Or maybe he's trying to pull him back in. He's trying to get ahead. Now, I'm using a little bit of poetic license here. Of course, these are infants, but God's already declared something here about their character and their future.

Jacob Won't Let God's Plan Unfold

And here is this glimpse into God's sovereignty: "The older will serve the younger." God has a plan for Jacob—a really good plan, a plan to fulfill the promises that he gave to Abraham and Isaac. A huge covenant, blessings, and he's going to give them to the younger, to Jacob. Now, let's remember, "Love does not envy"; we learned we have to discover whether we are content with the plan that God has for our life and willing to celebrate what God has for somebody else.

CHAPTER 9: JACOB *KEEPS* A RECORD OF WRONGS

We looked at Jonathan, crown prince of Israel, someone who had the right to be the ruler, who, by his character, by popular demand, should have been the king of Israel but never envied, never desired someone else's standing, someone else's plan that God had for them.

Well, in this case, Jacob is the one who has the plan for his life, and who is going to receive the blessing. But he can't leave well enough alone. He's conniving right from the beginning, and this is going to cause all sorts of hurt and broken relationships. A broken relationship can be resolved with love, but he just can't do it. It's funny here, this picture that the writer of Genesis gives us, of sibling rivalry in the womb, and the picture of Jacob grabbing at the heel of his brother.

It's telling us a whole lot without having to explain all of their youth. Jacob suffers from a severe case of sibling envy, almost blaming Esau for being the first. Let's jump ahead to their adulthood; really, we have no choice because there's not much written about their youth. In verse 27:

> So the boys grew. And Esau was a skillful hunter, a man of the field; but Jacob was a mild man, dwelling in tents. And Isaac loved Esau because he ate of his game, but Rebekah loved Jacob.
> Now Jacob cooked a stew; and Esau came in from the field, and he was weary. And Esau said to Jacob, "Please feed me with that same red stew, for I am weary." Therefore his name was called Edom.
> But Jacob said, "Sell me your birthright as of this day." (Genesis 25:27–31)

Well, as the kids say, that escalated quickly. Now, perhaps you've heard the story too many times in Sunday school; but really, your brother comes home hungry, and you go directly to "sell me your birthright"?

How Does Levitical Law Apply?

We had to do this previously in the "Love Is Kind" chapter: a little bit of Levitical law review, so we understand the context here. Deuteronomy 21 talks about the inheritance laws, and this is basically how it goes. The oldest son got a double portion of the inheritance, and everybody else got one piece. Say you have five sons. The estate, all the property, was divided into six; the oldest got a double portion, and everybody else got one.

LOVE PERSONIFIED

In this case, with two sons, you split it into three. The older son, Esau, would get two, and Jacob would get one. What Jacob is saying here is, "When Dad dies, I want the double portion, the birthright, the right of the oldest son, and you get my one portion." That is one expensive bowl of stew! Remember, God has already promised that the older would serve the younger and that there was something special about the younger one. Because of this, all the promises for Abraham, these covenant blessing promises, were going to come to Jacob. God has already said this, but Jacob couldn't rest in it. As I said, this escalated quickly.

Or maybe not. Maybe Jacob has been waiting for the opportune moment when he could step in and try to get back at Esau for being the oldest instead of just trusting God to handle the situation. Now, I tried to wrap my mind around this. I mean, there are just two in my family, me and my older sister, and I'm trying to put myself into Jacob's sandals.

I can't find any way that I would jump to "Give me your portion of the estate when Mom and Dad die for this bowl of soup." You know, at my best, at my most holy, godly self, I would show compassion and care and say, "Oh, definitely, you're tired. You're worn out. Here is some food for you. I love you, Jodi."

At my worst—my very worst—I could honestly see myself harassing her, mocking her for some bad planning, teasing her in her weak condition, maybe charging her something: "Oh, it's going to cost you twenty bucks." You know, just something to stick it to her. But two-thirds of the estate, her rightful share? That's just diabolical.

Jacob Scores One

Now, I have a few copies of the Bible, in different versions, and I have the following heading above this section, no matter what version it is. Maybe everyone just copied the first person who wrote headings. I'm sure you know that headings in the Bible are not part of the canon. Somebody else added them in for study purposes, and they all say, "Esau Despises His Birthright," which is a phrase from verse 34. But really, I think we need to focus on Jacob's behaviour here, not Esau's. In verse 32,

> Esau said, "Look, I am about to die; so what is this birthright to me?"
> Then Jacob said, "Swear to me as of this day."

> So he swore to him, and sold his birthright to Jacob. And Jacob gave Esau bread and stew of lentils; then he ate and drank, arose, and went his way. Thus Esau despised his birthright. (Genesis 25:32–34)

I mean, come on! He didn't mean it.

Now again, Esau is thinking he's going to die. What's an inheritance going to do for him if he's dead? Jacob's going to get the whole thing. But again, this is evil, to demand this, to make him swear to give over two-thirds of the estate.

So, one point for Jacob; he's keeping score. Remember, love *doesn't* keep score. It keeps no record of wrongs, but Jacob's keeping score. Esau was one up on him by being born first. Now Jacob has got back at him, and he's got the birthright. He now has the financial and legal birthright, even though he was born second. But oh no, that's not enough.

The Power of Blessing

There's a great book by a pastor near where I live named Terry Bone, and it's been revolutionary for my family. It's called *The Power of Blessing*. And there's a follow-up, *The Blessing Handbook*. In it, Pastor Bone takes you through Scripture, demonstrating how important it is to speak blessing out loud over your children. He goes through all the blessings spoken in the life of Christ: at His conception, the angel Gabriel; while in the womb, Elizabeth; at birth, angels and shepherds; at his naming at the temple, Simeon and Anna; when He's aged three, wise men; aged twelve, in the temple; at His baptism, the voice of God Himself declares blessing. All these people speaking blessings over Jesus. Pastor Bone likens it to stopping at different ports to get needed supplies before heading out to sea on your adult voyage.

Every step Jesus takes is blessed, and that extends into adulthood. All that to say, as Terry Bone points out in his book, I am a father who has the spiritual authority that God gives him to speak blessings over his children. Today, if you're a Christian and a parent, you have the right and authority, the privilege, and the honour to speak blessings over your children, and God will honour that practice.

We've lost the idea of just how valuable and practical a blessing is, but you're about to see how much it's valued in Bible times. Back to our story: Isaac is dying, and he wants to speak a blessing over his sons. The firstborn son would get the first blessing, but before this important blessing ceremony, Isaac wants to commemorate it with a special meal for him and his son. Chapter 27:

> It came to pass, when Isaac was old and his eyes were so dim that he could not see, that he called Esau his older son and said to him, "My son."
> And he answered him, "Here I am."
> Then he said, "Behold now, I am old. I do not know the day of my death. Now therefore, please take your weapons, your quiver and your bow, and go out to the field and hunt game for me. And make me savory food, such as I love, and bring it to me that I may eat, that my soul may bless you before I die." (Genesis 27:1–4)

The power of blessing. This is a huge event—the blessing of the father on his sons before he dies. Isaac is taking this seriously. Esau understands the significance, but so do Rebekah and Jacob, who overhear this conversation. Again, if you've gone to Sunday school, you know what happens next: a goat gets killed, its skin gets put on Jacob, and Rebekah makes the meal—the big deception.

Jacob is taking things into his own hands again. Remember, God promised blessing, but Jacob can't wait for God's plan to unfold. Instead, Jacob is keeping score. It's a contest for him. He's going to take things into his own hands. Isaac is deceived by Jacob, who leaves just as Esau gets back, and the ruse is revealed. Isaac has given the specially prepared blessing to Jacob.

Esau Realizes His Loss

Isaac can't give it to Esau as well. If you've wondered how important blessings are, the mighty hunter Esau weeps when he misses out:

> When Esau heard the words of his father, he cried with an exceedingly great and bitter cry, and said to his father, "Bless me—me also, O my father!"
> But he said, "Your brother came with deceit and has taken away your blessing."
> And Esau said, "Is he not rightly named Jacob? For he has supplanted me these two times. He took away my birthright, and now look, he has taken away my blessing!" And he said, "Have you not reserved a blessing for me?" ... So

CHAPTER 9: JACOB *KEEPS* A RECORD OF WRONGS

> Esau hated Jacob because of the blessing with which his father blessed him, and Esau said in his heart, "The days of mourning for my father are at hand; then I will kill my brother Jacob."
>
> And the words of Esau her older son were told to Rebekah. So she sent and called Jacob her younger son, and said to him, "Surely your brother Esau comforts himself concerning you by intending to kill you. Now therefore, my son, obey my voice: arise, flee to my brother Laban in Haran. And stay with him a few days, until your brother's fury turns away, until your brother's anger turns away from you, and he forgets what you have done to him; then I will send and bring you from there. Why should I be bereaved also of you both in one day?" (Genesis 27:34–36, 41–45)

Jacob has wronged Esau twice.

Now Esau is keeping score, and so is Jacob, as we'll find out later. Jacob runs away to Rebekah's homeland, to her brother Laban. So yes, we're studying Jacob, but we've got Esau in the story here too; everybody's keeping score of the wrongs. Jacob blames Esau for being first and is going to get back at him, so he steals the birthright with the stew and steals the blessing through deception.

Esau's keeping score, and he's going to enact revenge on Jacob when he gets a chance. You can't have love if you're acting like this; there's no relationship here because everyone's keeping a record of wrongs. Chapter 28:

> Isaac called Jacob and blessed him, and charged him, and said to him: "You shall not take a wife from the daughters of Canaan. Arise, go to Padan Aram, to the house of Bethuel your mother's father; and take yourself a wife from there of the daughters of Laban your mother's brother.
> > "May God Almighty bless you,
> > And make you fruitful and multiply you,
> > That you may be an assembly of peoples;
> > And give you the blessing of Abraham,
> > To you and your descendants with you,
> > That you may inherit the land
> > In which you are a stranger,
> > Which God gave to Abraham."

> So Isaac sent Jacob away, and he went to Padan Aram, to Laban the son of Bethuel the Syrian, the brother of Rebekah, the mother of Jacob and Esau. (Genesis 28:1–5)

What an incredible blessing, and we know it all comes true. There's power in speaking blessings, but that's a different book, Terry's book—go buy that one, too.

God Continues to Show His Grace

On his way, Jacob stops to rest in a spot, and puts a little rock up for a pillow—I guess he left so quickly he didn't bring a whole lot with him. And he starts to have a dream, a dream of a stairway to heaven. Cue the music!

> Behold, the Lord stood above it and said: "I am the Lord God of Abraham your father and the God of Isaac; the land on which you lie I will give to you and your descendants. Also your descendants shall be as the dust of the earth; you shall spread abroad to the west and the east, to the north and the south; and in you and in your seed all the families of the earth shall be blessed. Behold, I am with you and will keep you wherever you go, and will bring you back to this land; for I will not leave you until I have done what I have spoken to you."
>
> Then Jacob awoke from his sleep and said, "Surely the Lord is in this place, and I did not know it." And he was afraid and said, "How awesome is this place! This is none other than the house of God, and this is the gate of heaven!"
>
> Then Jacob rose early in the morning, and took the stone that he had put at his head, set it up as a pillar, and poured oil on top of it. And he called the name of that place Bethel; but the name of that city had been Luz previously. Then Jacob made a vow, saying, "If God will be with me, and keep me in this way that I am going, and give me bread to eat and clothing to put on, so that I come back to my father's house in peace, then the Lord shall be my God. And this stone which I have set as a pillar shall be God's house, and of all that You give me I will surely give a tenth to You." (Genesis 28:13–22)

CHAPTER 9: JACOB *KEEPS* A RECORD OF WRONGS

What a great promise from God! This is the promise God made at Jacob's birth. He reiterates it here directly to Jacob personally. Now, look carefully at Jacob's response. It's in verse 20. Jacob makes a vow, saying, "*If* God will be with me and keep me in this way that I am going, and give me bread to eat and clothing to put on, so that I come back to my father's house in peace, *then* the Lord shall be my God."

If?

If God does the following five things: be with me, go with me, give me bread, give me clothing, and bring me back safe—if? That's hardly love for God. If God does these things, then the Lord shall be his God? Back in our introduction, we looked at John 15 where God says, "If you love Me, you will keep My commandments."

There are no conditions here. He is God! We love Him and demonstrate it through our obedience, no matter what. Imagine if some of the people we've looked at already had this attitude. Joseph would have escaped jail or committed adultery with his master's wife because things weren't going right for him. He would have shaken his fist at God and said, "I'm going to take matters into my own hands. I'm not going to obey You."

Saul's son Jonathan might have teamed up with his father and tried to murder David once it was revealed to him that things weren't going to work out his way, that God wasn't going to give Jonathan the kingdom.

Love doesn't keep score. Love doesn't have conditions. Truly bad things are going to happen to us if we start keeping score and say, "God, You let this bad thing and that bad thing happen to me, so I'm not going to follow You."

We will get ourselves into all sorts of trouble. Love says, "God, no matter what happens to me, no matter what evil befalls me, I choose to love You." And loving God means obeying His commandments. As an aside, God's plan will always work out better than anything we could plan, and any evil that befalls us will, as with Joseph, ultimately work for our good.

Well, let's pick up the pace. Jacob gets to Haran and meets Rachel at the well, and she takes him home to her father, Laban. After being there just a month, Jacob and Laban strike a deal: if Jacob works for Laban for seven years, he will earn Rachel as a bride. Seven years go by—all in verse 20—and they hold a wedding feast. That was quick! In the end, Laban sends Leah, Rachel's older sister, in to Jacob to consummate the marriage. The next morning, Jacob wakes up and realizes he has been deceived.

How did he not know? Was he really, really drunk? And was it really, really dark? Did the sisters actually look and sound a lot alike? Just a reminder, the Bible is not a children's book, so this next section is a tough one to teach in Sunday school. The last time I went through it at my Awana Sparks group, aged five to seven, I just said the old "things were different back then, and Jacob married four women" and moved right along. So, let's just move along; nothing to see here.

Laban excuses his behaviour, saying that the culture they live in demands that the oldest daughter gets married first. They strike a new deal for seven more years of work for Rachel. At least this time, Jacob gets Rachel on credit, and he can pay for her over the next seven years of working, instead of having to wait for seven years, like he did for Leah.

The Scorekeeping Continues

Speaking of keeping score, how about the rivalry between Leah and Rachel? Look at how they name their children in chapter 29, starting in verse 32.

> Leah conceived and bore a son, and she called his name Reuben; for she said, "The Lord has surely looked on my affliction. Now therefore, my husband will love me." Then she conceived again and bore a son, and said, "Because the Lord has heard that I am unloved, He has therefore given me this son also." And she called his name Simeon. She conceived again and bore a son, and said, "Now this time my husband will become attached to me, because I have borne him three sons." Therefore his name was called Levi. (Genesis 29:32–34)

Leah's reasons for her first three sons' names are all because of how she sees herself in this complex family relationship. Now Rachel picks up this naming game with the two sons that Rachel's maid Bilhah bears for Jacob in chapter 30:5.

> Bilhah conceived and bore Jacob a son. Rachel said, "God has judged my case; and He has also heard my voice and given me a son." Therefore she called his name Dan. And Rachel's maid Bilhah conceived again and bore Jacob a sec-

ond son. Then Rachel said, "With great wrestlings I have wrestled with my sister, and indeed I have prevailed." So she called his name Naphtali. (Genesis 30:6–8.)

Sorry, we're supposed to be studying the life of Jacob. We've seen how Esau gets into this trap of keeping score. Then Leah gets caught in the trap of keeping score. Now, Rachel; everybody's keeping score. Everybody's looking at others with suspicion. Everybody's looking at what people are doing to them. There's certainly no love lost here between the siblings, Rachel and Leah or Jacob and Esau. Back to Jacob, who eventually has eleven sons and wants to leave Laban.

The New Deal with Laban

They strike a new deal, as Jacob owns nothing; all his work has been to enrich his father-in-law, Laban. He's been there now for more than fourteen years, the price for his two brides. So, they agree on a deal for Jacob to have some possessions. They agree on spotted, speckled, and brown sheep and goats being separated from the pure white flocks of Laban, and these will be Jacob's wages. After all these years, neither Jacob nor Laban trust each other, so they need a very clear and obvious way to know who owns what. Keeping score leads to suspicion.

Jacob sends his flocks off to be cared for by his sons at a distance and stays with Laban to tend his property. So, obviously, some more time has passed because his sons have got to be a little bit more than just children.

Now, I'm not a farmer. I've never raised animals. We don't have any pets at home, and I don't know how to properly care for a sheep or a goat. I have no idea what's happening in chapter 30, verses 37 to 43. Jacob places green poplar, almond, and chestnut rods, peeled to reveal white strips and exposed to the livestock in their water troughs. Somehow this increases Jacob's flocks and decreases Laban's flocks. All the spotted, speckled, and brown sheep produce offspring that are healthy and strong, while all the pure white ones are sickly and don't breed. In Genesis 31:6, Jacob is talking to his wives, and he says,

> "You know that with all my might I have served your father. Yet your father has deceived me and changed my wages ten times, but God did not allow him to hurt me. If he said thus: 'The speckled shall be your wages,' then all the flocks bore

> speckled. And if he said thus: 'The streaked shall be your wages,' then all the flocks bore streaked. So God has taken away the livestock of your father and given them to me." (Genesis 31:6–9)

Now, I don't know if this is hyperbole about his wages being changed ten times, or if there is a part of the story that is skipped over because it was long; we're talking about decades here. But either way, Jacob has been keeping track of the wrongs Laban has committed against him. Every time Laban changes something, Jacob is keeping track. It may not be ten, but he says it's happened two, three, four times, always keeping score of the wrongs done to him—always keeping score, not loving.

Who Does Unforgiveness Hurt?

Something interesting happens to us when we start keeping score of what other people do to us. When we react, take revenge, and do something back, we project onto others the feelings that we would have in response to that same treatment. And so, somebody wrongs me. Somebody does something to me. I keep track of it. I want to get back at them because I feel a certain way. I do something to somebody else, and I assume and project onto them that they feel the same way about me.

I've heard it said, "Unforgiveness only hurts the person who doesn't forgive." It's like a cancer inside. The other person's oblivious, and yet you're hanging on to this hurt and this animosity, and this happens in Jacob's life. We see after this conversation Jacob's having with Rachel and Leah that he has a plan to escape. Later in the chapter, we find out that Jacob steals away from Laban because he thinks that Laban is also keeping score, that Laban's out to get revenge. And so, he takes off.

Alternatively, if there had been love between Jacob and Laban, he would have gone to him and said, "Hey, I need to go back to my home, to my inheritance. Can you send me with your blessing? Let's talk about this. Let's have some sort of relationship here." But no, it's been a contest and keeping score all along, wrongs back and forth, conniving and underhandedness.

Jacob Thinks He Needs to Escape

And so, Jacob takes his family, and they all steal away. Three days later, Laban finds out that they've left. He then thinks something's up, and it says in verse

23 that he takes all his brothers with him, pursues them for seven days, and overtakes Jacob in the mountains of Gilead.

But here again, we are reminded of the promise that God gave Jacob. It says in verse 24 that God comes to Laban in a dream by night, and says, "Be careful that you speak to Jacob neither good nor bad." Remember the promise that God gave Jacob: to bless him, to give him the land, to watch over and care for him. Again, we see God intervening. Jacob doesn't need to have run away like a thief, taking everything; he could have spoken to Laban, and God would have shown favour. The day before, Jacob could have gone to tell Laban politely, kindly, in love, "It's time for me to move back to my family."

Laban overtakes Jacob and confronts him:

> Laban said to Jacob: "What have you done, that you have stolen away unknown to me, and carried away my daughters like captives taken with the sword? Why did you flee away secretly, and steal away from me, and not tell me; for I might have sent you away with joy and songs, with timbrel and harp? And you did not allow me to kiss my sons and my daughters. Now you have done foolishly in so doing." (Genesis 31:26–28)

Note verse 29:

> "It is in my power to do you harm, but the God of your father spoke to me last night, saying, 'Be careful that you speak to Jacob neither good nor bad.'" (Genesis 31:29)

There's a little side detail about Rachel stealing some of the household gods, but that's somebody else's story.

Again, God has promised blessing to Jacob. He didn't have to act this way. He didn't have to load onto Laban the same feelings of harm and distrust that he has, that he's carrying and harboring. I think Laban here is quite hurt and honest. "I wanted to kiss my daughters goodbye. These are my grandsons; let me kiss them goodbye. Okay, you've got your stuff. Fine. I've been blessed while you've been here."

It says earlier that everything that Laban has, Jacob is taking away. I think Laban is okay, though. It looks like he's still got enough to go back to.

LOVE PERSONIFIED

Love does not keep a record of wrongs. If we keep a record of wrongs, it's hurting ourselves. Jacob, in fear, runs from Laban; in fear, he acts out and steals away. We don't have to act this way. We don't need to take our hurts and feelings and project them onto others.

At the end of this chapter, we have a covenant promise between Laban and Jacob after the whole issue of Rachel and the idols. There are accusations back and forth and strong words, but Laban makes Jacob gather stones and set up a monument. "This heap is a witness to you and me this day," it says in verse 48, "May the Lord watch between you and me when we are absent one from another."

God Is Witness

This is a really interesting little phrase from Laban to Jacob in verse 50 that I don't want to skip: "If you afflict my daughters, or if you take other wives besides my daughters, although no man is with us—see, God is witness between you and me!" Yeah, there's some distrust here. Jacob's actions have made Laban not trust him, but there's still love and concern. And like I said, Laban probably would have sent him away with a blessing.

In fact, they stay up all night, have a sacrifice and a meal together, and in the morning, Laban rises, kisses his daughters and grandsons goodbye, and blesses them. And Laban departs and returns to his place.

Yes, Laban is a conniver. Often in Sunday school stories I've read, people talk about Jacob meeting his match in Laban. But it didn't have to be this way. God promised to bless Jacob. Laban would have blessed his family and sent them on their way. But remember, Jacob keeps score, and again, this only hurts *him*.

Remember what I said about projecting your feelings onto others?

The Return of Esau

In Genesis 32, it has been more than twenty years since Jacob left his brother Esau. Yet, when he hears that Esau is coming with a troop of men, Jacob starts to frantically scheme because he assumes that Esau is planning violence and revenge. After all, that's where Jacob's mind is. He hasn't forgotten; he's kept score. So, he divides his family into two, thinking, "Well, if he attacks one, the other half will get away."

What? What kind of thinking is this? He's going to willfully sacrifice some of his wives and children for his own escape! He gives instructions to his servants and his family that they are supposed to split into these groups. And when they reach Esau and his men, they're supposed to give him gifts. Jacob tells them, when he asks, "What is all this?" to say, "They are your servant Jacob's. [Sorry? Not 'brother'—'servant.'] It is a present sent to my lord Esau; and behold, he also is behind us" (Genesis 32:18).

The idea was that Jacob was kind of asking them to report back to him. "If Esau sees the gift, what's his attitude towards it? Oh, and by the way, I'm staying back here on the other side of the river while everybody else moves on ahead to test the waters with my brother."

I'm sure we're familiar with the story back here on the other side of the river, where Jacob wrestles with the angel of God, or perhaps with God Himself. But Jacob won't let go until he receives a blessing, and God changes his name. We've talked about blessing before. God blesses Jacob and changes his name to Israel, the one who wrestles with God.

Then, finally, the next morning, after this encounter with God, Jacob leaves. In the meantime, Jacob's family has been meeting up with Esau and his four hundred men, with Jacob's children divided among Leah, Rachel, and the maidservants. Jacob, in fear, thinking that Esau still remembers the wrongs he had committed against him years ago, looks up, and Esau runs to meet Jacob and embraces him, falls on his neck, kisses him, and weeps. Esau sees the women and children, and says, "Who are these with you?"

Jacob says, "The children whom God has graciously given your servant." He has all his family bow down to Esau, with the maidservants and children first, then Leah and her children bow down. Afterward, Joseph and Rachel come near, and they bow down. Esau asks, "What do you mean by sending all those people ahead?" Jacob answers, "These were to find favor in the sight of my lord."

Esau says, "I have enough, my brother; keep what you have for yourself" (Genesis 33:5–9).

God Still Found a Way to Bless Esau

Something happened in Esau's heart that we don't hear in this story. We don't really focus on this, ever. But somewhere in the last twenty years, Esau has forgotten Jacob's wrongs. As he says, "I have enough. God has blessed me." There is a blessing that Esau received; he has what he needs. He's probably been living at peace, sleeping well at night for decades.

All the while, Jacob has been wrestling with what Esau will do to him when he sees him. In this big plan of sending herds and flocks ahead to appease him, to somehow buy some sort of kindness or forgiveness, splitting up his family just in case Esau takes revenge, Jacob is projecting all these things onto him. Because this is the way Jacob is.

He is always keeping score, keeping count of all the wrongs done to him. He can't believe that someone would forgive him and not remember what he had done to them. Esau is a beautiful picture of forgiveness, peace of mind, and love that Jacob just can't understand. Hopefully, at this point in his life, Jacob finally begins to understand that he can trust God and not fight and strive and keep score.

Love does not keep a record of wrongs. Jacob risks his family, offering all these gifts, calling himself a servant and Esau his lord to try to appease him, while missing the point all along about what love is, missing that God has promised to meet all his needs and take care of him. He didn't have to do all this stuff in his own strength.

Homework

So, here's the lesson for us today: people will wrong you; you're probably going to wrong other people. Number one, keep short accounts. Go and ask for forgiveness when you've done something wrong. When someone wrongs you, let them know. Say, "You've hurt me. Can we make this right?" And even if they don't apologize, don't harbour anger.

Don't keep score—you're only hurting yourself. They've forgotten about it—Esau has forgiven it all. Laban's gone his way; he just wants to kiss his daughters goodbye. Jacob's the only one who's been causing himself heartache, stress, and ulcers in this. Be willing to forgive. Don't keep track.

And lastly, trust that God is in control, no matter what the actions of others are, no matter how they treat you. Allow God to bless you, keep you, and take care of you, and not take things into your own hands.

Chapter 10
Paul Does Not Rejoice in Iniquity, but Rejoices in the Truth

In this study, we're trying to recapture the real, true definition of love, when Jesus said, "Love the Lord your God and love your neighbour," through studying the stories of people in the Bible to whom we can relate. We're also trying to recapture the full meaning of the word *love*, and that it's not an emotion, not infatuation, or an attraction.

As we study the next phrase in 1 Corinthians 13—love "does not rejoice in iniquity, but rejoices in the truth"—we deal with both phrases together. Let's look closely at the definitions of the key words and be as faithful as possible to what the words mean in the original Greek.

A Few Useful Tools

I've had some incredible pastors and teachers in my life who have guided my understanding of the Bible. But we are all encouraged to study them for ourselves, like the Bereans in Acts 17:11. We've talked about word studies a few times now, and I want to encourage you to keep digging

One thing that my seminary professors drilled into my head is something called semantic fields of meaning. This is the study of context, how the word is used in different parts of the New Testament. It gives us an idea of what Paul is trying to get at when he uses certain phrases in this love poem in 1 Corinthians 13. Greek and Hebrew words can be variously translated into English. It's important to understand what Paul is talking about.

When we study the phrase *does not rejoice in iniquity, but rejoices in the truth*, we have to investigate the words Paul uses: *iniquity* and *truth*. We need to know what he's talking about to know how we should behave in love to others and to God. And then we get to the fun part of reading the story of a biblical character and the important part of modelling their behaviour so we can be better disciples.

That's how I'm coming at this. If you don't have the time to take seminary training in Greek and Hebrew, if you're not in the pulpit every Sunday, I think this is a good way for a layperson to study—an accountant, or maybe like you—working in an office, factory, farm, shop or mine (that covers most people in my family). It is in-depth, and I highly recommend it.

Iniquity and Truth—Are They Opposites?

First, let's talk about iniquity and truth. And then we're going to find someone who really exemplifies this for us and how we live it out in love. And what an odd little phrase to be talking about when you're talking about love!

This one is particularly tricky because at first look, iniquity and truth aren't opposites that can be easily compared. Why didn't Paul choose lying versus truth, or iniquity versus righteousness? You know, I don't think I've said this before, but this is a poem, eight *love is*es and eight *love isn't*s. It's not meant to be a comprehensive list. Now Paul was an exceptional writer, giving us all sorts of doctrine and instruction, but he wasn't the greatest poet. I think this was his only attempt.

Back to the task at hand. What do we do with this definition of love that does not rejoice in iniquity but rejoices in the truth? As I've been explaining, here's how I begin to understand the words better.

Let's look at iniquity. Iniquity is defined as being wicked or immoral in nature or character. It's not an action, but the character of an action and is distinguished from sin or trespasses. So, this is why we have a verse like Psalm 32:5, where David says, "The iniquity of my sin." Iniquity can be described as the essence of wrongdoing or evil, while sin is the thought or character practiced in the real world.

Speaking of Psalm 32, if you're clever, you would have realized that the Psalms were not written in Greek. So, all this conversation about what the Greek word is—if you're smart and you caught me here, you'd say, "Tim, that is a Hebrew part of the Scriptures, way back in Psalms. So now you're not dealing with the same words as 1 Corinthians 13."

CHAPTER 10: PAUL DOES NOT REJOICE IN INIQUITY

True! But we do have the Septuagint, the ancient Greek translation of the Old Testament.

Many Words for Sin

In this passage, Psalm 32, and even better, in Psalm 51—the Old Testament translators chose the same word in the Greek that Paul uses. So we know we're on the right track and talking about what Paul also was talking about.

Let's read some of Psalm 51, which addresses sin. Psalm 51 says, "Have mercy upon me, O God, according to Your lovingkindness; according to the multitude of Your tender mercies, blot out my transgressions." The word *transgressions* is translated from the Hebrew *pesha*, which can also mean to rebel. You've purposefully broken a law.

The psalm continues: "Wash me thoroughly from my iniquity." The Hebrew word here translated as "iniquity" is *avon*. This includes the attitude, the character trait, so to speak, of evil. Psalm 51 also states: "Cleanse me from my sin." The Hebrew word for "sin" is *chatta'ah*. So here we have three words we need to consider.

Let's keep reading:

> For I acknowledge my transgressions [*pesha*],
> And my sin [*chatta'ah*] is always before me.
> Against You, You only, have I sinned [*chatta'ah*],
> And done this evil in Your sight—
> That You may be found just when You speak,
> And blameless when You judge.
> Behold, I was brought forth in iniquity [*avon*],
> And in sin [*chatta'ah*] my mother conceived me. (Psalm 51:3–5)

Transgression has been translated as purposely breaking God's law. Sin is us being human; you're "hangry", you say something nasty, you do something wrong, you miss the mark. Just like in archery: you try but you miss. Sin is when we act out of a condition that we have, that we've had since we were born, and that condition is that we have iniquity in us. We are evil. We have a fallen nature that is selfish, lazy, lustful, and arrogant. And this pours out of us as sin. Iniquity, left unchecked, takes us to the point of intentional sin with no fear of God, transgression.

So, when we're talking about love—loving the Lord your God with all your heart, soul, mind, and strength—you can't love the Lord your God with all your heart, soul, mind, and strength if you are *rejoicing* in this evil nature; if you are purposefully acting out, transgressing against God, intentionally sinning, doing evil things, letting those mistakes run rampant, and being unrepentant. That shows that you don't love God.

Here's our connection: love does not rejoice in iniquity; it doesn't wallow in this evilness of character but wants something better. And what is that better? That better is truth.

A Little About Truth

Now, when I think about truth and love, I go to Ephesians 4:15, where we're told to speak the truth in love. But I don't think this is what Paul is getting at because we're supposed to rejoice in the truth. And again, I think this is in our relationship with God. If we love what is true, then we will act a certain way towards God. Now, this word *truth* is one of the easier ones to explore because it's used 109 times in the New Testament: *alētheia*.

Just as iniquity is the nature of evil, truth is not just about not lying when we talk; it's the very nature of truth. In John 14:6, Jesus uses this word when He says, "I am the truth." He is the embodiment of truth, He is truth personified (don't worry, there won't be a sequel). God wants us to embrace the truth, to have this truthful nature inside of us. To believe in His truth, Jesus, as well as the truth of the whole gospel, because then we understand Him better and we love Him. Truth and love: there's a marriage here.

There's something I hear sometimes that bothers me. I hear people say, "How could a loving God ever send someone to eternity in hell?" Or they'll say something like "My God would never do that." Well, he's not your God; He's *the* God. And He's just, and so He must work in truth, He must do things properly. He has this essence of rightness, of truth.

And when love and truth are married together, there's this wonderful peace and lack of conflict. Not just inner peace with God that allows you to persevere when things are going bad; when there's truth and love present, you're also at peace with your neighbour, at peace in society. But when truth and love are separated, you have problems.

CHAPTER 10: PAUL DOES NOT REJOICE IN INIQUITY

I remember years ago working at a Christian kids camp and taking a survey of some youth leaders on whether there was such a thing as absolute truth. Most of the kids said yes, and I was very encouraged by the fact that the younger generation still believed that there is truth, real objective truth, in this postmodern society. But one young man said, "Well, I've been thinking about that."

And I said, "Have you?"

And this fifteen-year-old kid says, "Yeah. You know the story of Corrie ten Boom? Her family hid Jews in their home in secret rooms and compartments and then lied to the Nazis who were looking for the Jews. So, was there absolute right and wrong here? Is there an absolute truth? They lied, but if they had told the truth, it would have caused harm."

I was impressed and had no response.

We live in this broken world, where telling the truth and loving others sometimes come into conflict; that's how flawed our world is. What do you tell children, if they ask you where babies come from? Well, perhaps they're too young for the full biological explanation. You can tell them the whole truth, or you can withhold something in love. There's this tension between truth and love.

It's not until God's kingdom is fulfilled that we will have this perfect marriage again of truth and love. There won't be this tension where if I tell the truth, I might harm someone, and that's not loving. Or if I want to act in love, then I need to withhold the truth from that child, for example. So that's just to add a layer of complexity to the ideas of iniquity and truth, because it's not a matter of truth and lying. It's the essence of truth, the essence of love, and the essence of iniquity that Paul is talking about here.

We can wallow in iniquity, rejecting God, sinning as much as we want, or we can embrace the truth—the truth of God's existence, the truth of the gospel, the truth that is the person of Jesus Christ. And then we can fully express love toward God and others.

Who Embodies Both Iniquity and Truth?

This is probably the longest introduction ever given before getting to the actual story!

LOVE PERSONIFIED

Let's get to our story now. The person who fits this the best, because of the contrasts in his life, is the apostle Paul. Paul's story intersects with one that we've already looked at, and that's Stephen. Let's go to Acts 7; we've looked at this passage before, but this time we're going to look at it not from Stephen's perspective but from Saul's. This passage begins after Stephen enrages the council by claiming to see Jesus standing by the right hand of God.

> They [the council] cried out with a loud voice, stopped their ears, and ran at him with one accord; and they cast him out of the city and stoned him. And the witnesses laid down their clothes at the feet of a young man named Saul. And they stoned Stephen as he was calling on God and saying, "Lord Jesus, receive my spirit." Then he knelt down and cried out with a loud voice, "Lord, do not charge them with this sin." And when he had said this, he fell asleep.
> Now Saul was consenting to his death.
> At that time a great persecution arose against the church which was at Jerusalem; and they were all scattered throughout the regions of Judea and Samaria, except the apostles. And devout men carried Stephen to his burial, and made great lamentation over him.
> As for Saul, he made havoc of the church, entering every house, and dragging off men and women, committing them to prison. (Acts 7:57–8:3)

Remember all that discussion about Greek and Hebrew? Here's something else: I want to clarify a mistake that you might have been taught in Sunday school. Saul didn't change his name to Paul. *Saul* is the Hebrew form of the Greek name *Paul*. He simply used different names depending on the context he was in: when he's in Jerusalem, Saul; when he goes out to the Gentiles, Paul.

Iniquity Personified

Clearly, this young zealot, Saul, a Pharisee, is missing something in his life. He's missing love for others to the point where he is rejoicing in iniquity, in this evil; he is vindictive. He is murderous! He's creating havoc in the church, going from house to house, dragging off men and women and committing them to prison. This fearmongering, this violence, all of his evil nature, this iniquity that's inside of all of us—he's reveling in it. He's causing so much damage. Let's get out of here; we need to fast-forward to Acts 9.

CHAPTER 10: PAUL DOES NOT REJOICE IN INIQUITY

> Saul, still breathing threats and murder against the disciples of the Lord, went to the high priest and asked letters from him to the synagogues of Damascus, so that if he found any who were of the Way, whether men or women, he might bring them bound to Jerusalem.
>
> As he journeyed he came near Damascus, and suddenly a light shone around him from heaven. Then he fell to the ground, and heard a voice saying to him, "Saul, Saul, why are you persecuting Me?"
>
> And he said, "Who are You, Lord?"
>
> Then the Lord said, "I am Jesus, whom you are persecuting. It is hard for you to kick against the goads."
>
> So he, trembling and astonished, said, "Lord, what do You want me to do?"
>
> Then the Lord said to him, "Arise and go into the city, and you will be told what you must do." (Acts 9:1–6)

This is the great story of Saul's conversion; but as he heads into it, he is still breathing threats and murder against the disciples. Now, I've heard a lot of sermons about how he was misguided. You know, he was a Pharisee; he was trying to keep the Jewish faith pure. Christianity was this sect that was breaking off, that wasn't obeying the Law, and he was trying, with all the right motives, to protect it.

I don't get that from the Scripture here. Earlier on, the word *havoc* was used, "dragging" men and women, still breathing "threats and murder". There's nothing about justice here; there's nothing about doing what's right. This is a violent, evil man who, I argue, is using the guise of religious purity of Judaism to harm people, to destroy people and families; he is rejoicing in iniquity. But Jesus Christ gets ahold of him, confronts not only his sin but his sin nature, and starts a process of changing him.

To summarize the rest of Acts chapter 9, Saul is stricken blind and taken into Damascus. A disciple called Ananias is told to go to him and to pray for the healing of his eyes. Ananias is concerned about Saul getting his sight back. He says, "Lord, haven't You heard about this guy? How much harm he has done? How many bad things he has done to Your saints in Jerusalem?"

But Jesus says to Ananias, "Don't worry, I have a special use for this man." Paul receives his sight immediately.

In verse 20, Paul goes and preaches in the synagogues that Jesus is the Son of God. Everyone is amazed that suddenly he's changed his whole demeanor; he's changed his whole message. "What's going on with this guy? What has happened that he's now not this evil, murderous, violent person? He's now proclaiming the truth of Jesus Christ."

The author of Acts, Dr. Luke, goes back and forth between Paul and Peter for a few chapters here, so we need to skip ahead to chapter 11 to follow Paul. We're told that some of the disciples, after the persecution of Stephen, have travelled far away to Antioch, preaching the word of Jesus Christ, and people are coming to faith. The council of Jerusalem sends Barnabas to go and see what's going on. When he gets to Antioch, he sees their faith and encourages them (this is in verse 23), but then he goes to Tarsus to meet Saul.

Wow! Here we have this murderous, evil person who, once converted, starts to preach, and now Barnabas goes and seeks him out to come with him to minister in Antioch. At the end of chapter 11, we're told that a prophet comes by and says there's going to be a famine in Jerusalem and Judea, so the people gather money and resources, and they send it back to Jerusalem by the hands of Barnabas and Saul. There is a great transformation and a great story here. We're seeing this person who was rejoicing in iniquity now rejoicing in the truth—a person who now, by nature, embraces right, embraces truth, and does things properly.

We don't get to hear about Paul again until the end of chapter 12:

> Barnabas and Saul returned from Jerusalem when they had fulfilled their ministry, and they also took with them John whose surname was Mark.
> Now in the church that was at Antioch there were certain prophets and teachers: Barnabas, Simeon who was called Niger, Lucius of Cyrene, Manaen who had been brought up with Herod the Tetrarch, and Saul. As they ministered to the Lord and fasted, the Holy Spirit said, "Now separate to Me Barnabas and Saul for the work to which I have called them." Then, having fasted and prayed, and laid hands on them, they sent them away. (Acts 12:25–13:3)

The First Missionary Journey

We have the incredible stories of the rest of the book of Acts following Paul's missionary journeys. And what is a missionary? A sent-out one, some-

CHAPTER 10: PAUL DOES NOT REJOICE IN INIQUITY

one who goes to other places to declare the truth, someone rejoicing in the truth that there is a God, that He's the Creator. Humanity has fallen into sin; the punishment for sin is eternal separation from God in hell; the only rescue from this sin is to put faith in Jesus Christ, who paid the punishment of death for our sins and was raised again, showing that He has the power to give us eternal life.

That's the truth; missionary work is rejoicing in the truth. For the rest of this book, we have this incredible account of Paul (his Greek name) going from town to town sharing truth. It starts right away in Acts 13:4:

> Being sent out by the Holy Spirit, they went down to Seleucia, and from there they sailed to Cyprus. And when they arrived in Salamis, they preached the word of God in the synagogues of the Jews. They also had John [Mark] as their assistant.
>
> Now when they had gone through the island to Paphos, they found a certain sorcerer, a false prophet, a Jew whose name was Bar-Jesus, who was with the proconsul, Sergius Paulus, an intelligent man. This man called for Barnabas and Saul and sought to hear the word of God. But Elymas the sorcerer (for so his name is translated) withstood them, seeking to turn the proconsul away from the faith. Then Saul, who also is called Paul, filled with the Holy Spirit, looked intently at him and said, "O full of all deceit and all fraud, you son of the devil, you enemy of all righteousness, will you not cease perverting the straight ways of the Lord? And now, indeed, the hand of the Lord is upon you, and you shall be blind, not seeing the sun for a time."
>
> And immediately a dark mist fell on him, and he went around seeking someone to lead him by the hand. Then the proconsul believed, when he saw what had been done, being astonished at the teaching of the Lord. (Acts 13:4–12)

I love this story because it's a great example of not rejoicing in iniquity: a sorcerer involved in the occult, casting spells, doing harm, versus Paul, rejoicing in the truth of Jesus Christ, calling out his deceit and his fraud, relying on the strength of the truth of who God is and who His son Jesus Christ is. Also, there is the irony that Paul called down blindness on him, which was Paul's own punishment until his conversion.

Paul then goes to Perga and then to Pisidian Antioch. They preach there; they have success and then are kicked out of the city. In chapter 14, they go to Iconium. The pattern is repeated: they proclaim the truth, and those who rejoice in evil confront them and attack them, persecute them, and stone them. Paul is miraculously saved by the power of God.

They go from Iconium to Lystra, where they heal a lame man, and the crowd starts to shout out, "The gods have come down to us in the likeness of men!" They're deified, and the people want to worship them by making a sacrifice to them.

Paul and Barnabas stop them, shouting out, "No, no, we're men like you." What's the result? Jews come from another town and stone them, and they get kicked out.

There's this constant cycle in the first missionary journey of opposing evil and standing for the truth. Some people accept it, and then those who revel in evil and rejoice in it, who are consumed by their evil nature, violently attack them. Now, I probably would have given up being a missionary at this point. But even on the return trip back to their home base of Antioch in Syria, they continue ministering all the way.

The Work of the Judaizers

Meanwhile, during their absence, some Judaizers have infiltrated the church at Antioch. They are telling the believers that they need to be circumcised and that they need to obey the laws of Moses.

What I find ironic in Paul's story is that he started as a Pharisee, murdering and imprisoning Christians, the Jews who converted to this sect following Jesus Christ. He was demanding obedience to the Law (as I said before, I don't think that was his true motive; I think he was an evil person). Now he's confronted with people demanding peacefully—I don't think anyone is getting arrested or stoned here—that Gentile believers in Jesus Christ must now obey the laws that Paul had been defending back in chapter 7.

Paul now sides with the truth. What is the truth? Jesus is the truth: the person and work of Jesus Christ on the cross. He stands up and debates these Judaizers to the point where they end up going back to the council in Jerusalem, to Peter and James and the other leaders of the church, to give evidence of what God has done among the Gentile believers outside of the Jewish law. Peter

CHAPTER 10: PAUL DOES NOT REJOICE IN INIQUITY

himself says in Acts 15:11, to affirm Paul's defense of his holding to the truth, "We believe that through the grace of the Lord Jesus Christ we shall be saved in the same manner as they." The "we" are the Jews; the "they" are the Gentiles. We're all saved by the work and person of Jesus Christ.

It's not the keeping of the law—that Paul held to before his conversion, before Jesus Christ transformed him—that saves. Paul is now defending and fighting for the truth. He's risked his life in Iconium and Lystra, and on and on during his journey. He gets back to his base in Antioch, and he fights within the church for truth.

The Second Missionary Journey

After this defense, Paul heads back out on another missionary journey, this time with Silas. They meet Timothy in Lystra, head to Macedonia, and meet Lydia. They cast out demons. There's a wonderful story here that I want to pause and read. They've been preaching in Philippi:

> The multitude rose up together against them; and the magistrates tore off their clothes and commanded them to be beaten with rods. And when they had laid many stripes on them, they threw them into prison, commanding the jailer to keep them securely. Having received such a charge, he put them into the inner prison and fastened their feet in the stocks.
> But at midnight Paul and Silas were praying and singing hymns to God, and the prisoners were listening to them. Suddenly there was a great earthquake, so that the foundations of the prison were shaken; and immediately all the doors were opened and everyone's chains were loosed. And the keeper of the prison, awaking from sleep and seeing the prison doors open, supposing the prisoners had fled, drew his sword and was about to kill himself. But Paul called with a loud voice, saying, "Do yourself no harm, for we are all here."
> Then he called for a light, ran in, and fell down trembling before Paul and Silas. And he brought them out and said, "Sirs, what must I do to be saved?"
> So they said, "Believe on the Lord Jesus Christ, and you will be saved, you and your household." (Acts 16:22–31)

The Character of Truth

Again, when we're talking about rejoicing in the truth, we're not talking about lies versus truth. We're talking about the essence, the character of truth, versus the character of iniquity. Paul and Silas should not have been jailed. We later learn that they are Roman citizens and that they should not have been beaten, and they could have demanded quite a bit of retribution against those who did this to them.

They do get some justice for themselves later on in the chapter. But the point that I want to linger on here is this: unjustly beaten, unjustly jailed, somehow deep inside them—no grumbling, no revenge—they are worshipping God. There's a character change here, something that's consuming them. And as we look at our 1 Corinthians 13 passage, it's the truth, this essence of knowing God, trusting in God, having peace with God—they are confident that God has this under control, whether they're beaten in jail or whether they're free and preaching. They don't fall back into iniquity, this old nature of wanting revenge. And when it gets to the point when they are freed miraculously by God in this earthquake, they, and also all the other prisoners, stay. Why? Because if they leave, the jailer will be executed.

There's mass chaos, there's havoc because of the earthquake; but there's something incredible in the soul and heart of Paul and Silas here that causes truth to reign, love to reign.

There's a kindness and a consideration of others. And because of this, a whole household is saved. Not rejoicing in iniquity but rejoicing in the truth changes our behaviour in situations. It changes our outlook, our perspective. I would have bolted out of that jail; I'm positive I would have! They stay. There's something special inside that they're rejoicing in: the truth. They know that God has it under control.

We can go on for pages looking at chapter 17. Paul and Silas go to Thessalonica, they start preaching there, and they turn the world upside down. From there, they go to Berea, where they meet with Jews who study the scriptures. The Bereans want the truth. They want to see the truth about Jesus Christ in the Old Testament. This is instructive for us, so we are encouraged to be like the Bereans and find the truth.

CHAPTER 10: PAUL DOES NOT REJOICE IN INIQUITY

The Truth About the Unknown God

Paul goes on to Athens, to Mars Hill, and in this incredible passage, he walks by and sees the statue dedicated to the unknown god. Paul says,

> "The One whom you worship without knowing, Him I proclaim to you: God, who made the world and everything in it, since He is Lord of heaven and earth, does not dwell in temples made with hands. Nor is He worshiped with men's hands, as though He needed anything, since He gives to all life, breath, and all things. And He has made from one blood every nation of men to dwell on all the face of the earth, and has determined their preappointed times and the boundaries of their dwellings, so that they should seek the Lord, in the hope that they might grope for Him and find Him, though He is not far from each one of us; for in Him we live and move and have our being, as also some of your own poets have said, 'For we are also His offspring.' Therefore, since we are the offspring of God, we ought not to think that the Divine Nature is like gold or silver or stone, something shaped by art and man's devising. Truly, these times of ignorance God overlooked, but now commands all men everywhere to repent, because He has appointed a day on which He will judge the world in righteousness by the Man whom He has ordained. He has given assurance of this to all by raising Him from the dead." (Acts 17:23–31)

"Truly" Paul is consumed with the truth. He goes to an area where there's worship of all manner of gods, idols, and spirits, and he has to speak for the truth. It's not long since he's been released from jail, and he's already preaching the truth.

The Tables Are Turned

Paul moves on to Corinth. He meets some good coworkers in Aquila and Priscilla and goes to the synagogue. The Jews oppose the truth so much that he leaves, shakes the dust out of his garments, and moves on. But Gentiles are converted. We have an amusing account here in chapter 18 where Paul spends a year and a half preaching in the synagogues in the area around Corinth.

LOVE PERSONIFIED

The Jews are upset about this; opposing the truth, they go to the proconsul, a man named Gallio. He listens to their argument and says, "This is not something that I need to be dealing with. There's no wrongdoing or wicked crimes; it's just your words and your definitions and your own law." He kicks them all out of court.

The Greeks then take the ruler of the synagogue, the one that is rejecting Paul, and they beat him. And it's like an endorsement of Paul. Here is Paul, steadfastly holding to the truth; he's been persecuted everywhere he goes, and suddenly he gets to Corinth, and we see the irony of the Jews being persecuted, being punished for opposing the truth. We start to see what happens when you rejoice in the truth, when you steadfastly hold to the message of Jesus Christ.

Paul returns to Antioch leaving workers behind in the places he visited. It's an incredible transformation of the world, as Paul travels on these missionary journeys preaching the truth, rejoicing in the truth, standing up against iniquity, standing up against evil, and then God does His saving work in people's lives.

What Motivates Paul?

He really is motivated by love. Why else would Paul endure all this? In 1 Corinthians, there's a list of his trials: the shipwrecks and dangers in the city, dangers in the country, and dangers among his countrymen, the whippings and beatings. In all that he does, he's continually pressed; but he must declare the truth. Love rejoices in the truth.

He can't contain himself from declaring this good news of Jesus Christ. And it transforms not only what he says but how he does it and how he perseveres through everything. And there's so much more. I mean, we have Paul preaching so long in Ephesus that a young man, Eutychus, falls out of a window and dies and is brought back to life!

There are all sorts of wonderful stories of Paul's ministry that we're skipping over, but I want to come to one last story. Paul has returned to Jerusalem. The Jews there, knowing the impact of what's happening because he's been rejoicing in the truth, find a cause to arrest him. They accuse him of bringing Gentiles into the temple area where a Gentile could not be. Again, these are false accusations. But Paul doesn't fight this so much as use it as an opportuni-

CHAPTER 10: PAUL DOES NOT REJOICE IN INIQUITY

ty. He is not worried about revenge, fighting, or even justice. He's rejoicing in the truth. I mean, this was prophesied—Agabus in chapter 21 prophesied that he would be tied up, bound in Jerusalem, and arrested. And he goes willingly, because Paul has a love for God and a trust that God has his best interests in mind. Paul will go, whether he's in jail, arrested, or out on the streets; he's going to rejoice in the truth and declare it.

Paul Is Tried by Felix

So, Paul is arrested, and there's a plot to kill him. He's moved from Jerusalem to Caesarea, and he's tried there a couple of times by different governors, and even Herod comes and questions him. In chapter 24, we have the first case of Paul being tried in front of a governor named Felix. Paul defends his actions in Jerusalem, but right away can't help but turn it into an opportunity to share about God.

After defending himself against some of the accusations, he says,

> "This I confess to you, that according to the Way which they call a sect, so I worship the God of my fathers, believing all things which are written in the Law and in the Prophets ... Unless it is for this one statement which I cried out, standing among them, 'Concerning the resurrection of the dead I am being judged by you this day.'" (Acts 24:14, 21)

He gets right to the heart of the matter—who is God, what does God demand, and what hope do we have for the next life?

> After some days, when Felix came with his wife Drusilla, who was Jewish, he sent for Paul and heard him concerning the faith in Christ. Now as he reasoned about righteousness, self-control, and the judgment to come, Felix was afraid and answered, "Go away for now; when I have a convenient time I will call for you." (Acts 24:24–25)

Paul, it seems, was quite content to stay in jail (he had some freedom under Felix) because he saw an opportunity God was giving him to share the truth. Two years go by; Felix is replaced by a new governor named Porcius Festus, and the whole series happens again.

Paul Is Tried by Festus

Festus brings out Paul to judge him; and Paul, as his defense, preaches the gospel. In chapter 25, Luke records during this trial between Paul and his accusers that Paul has appealed to Caesar. So Festus says, "You have appealed to Caesar? To Caesar you shall go!" But he still has no real charge to cite as a cause for judgment. He brings in King Agrippa to see if they can come to some agreement on a pretext for sending him to Caesar. Festus says, "I thought that was all going to be about some sort of criminal issue. But,

> When the accusers stood up, they brought no accusation against him of such things as I supposed, but had some questions against him about their own religion and about a certain Jesus, who had died, whom Paul affirmed to be alive. (Acts 25:18–19)

So, in this summary of Paul's case that Festus relays to Agrippa, he's recounting the gospel. Paul can't help himself but talk about Jesus. No matter what the case is, no matter how he defends himself, it's always about Jesus. Paul is then put on a ship and sent to Rome—there's the incredible story of a shipwreck and the miracles that happen, and God again comes through.

Paul Shows Us Truth

Paul witnesses in Malta, proclaiming the truth there, all the way to Rome. Now, we could go and study Paul's epistles, where he tells more stories, and there are more hints at the way he behaved and what he did. But we know that he spent years in jail in Rome, and what did he do? He wrote those epistles. He sent the truth to all these churches, and he was constantly driven by love for God and love for others to declare the person and work of Jesus Christ, Jesus Christ the Truth.

We've rushed through Paul's story a bit, but here's the point I want to make. We have a sinful nature; we are born in iniquity, and iniquity unchecked results in sin—missing the mark. Unrepented sin results in transgression, boldly thumbing our nose at God and disobeying Him. That is not love. Love does not rejoice in iniquity. Not only does iniquity thumb its nose at God, but also, it is destructive to our neighbours, the people we are called to love in the Great Commandment.

CHAPTER 10: PAUL DOES NOT REJOICE IN INIQUITY

Saul before his redemption, causing havoc, murder, imprisonment; frothing at the mouth with evil, rejoicing in iniquity, causes all sorts of harm. You cannot love God or love others if you are consumed with this evil, unrepentant, unchecked nature.

But when we rejoice in the truth, when it becomes our focus to share the person and work of Jesus Christ the Truth, it changes all our behaviour. We can stand up under all amounts of persecution, as Paul does. He stands for the truth—beatings, stonings, imprisonment, it doesn't matter. When he is tried before Festus, Felix, Agrippa, and maybe even before Caesar (we don't know), all he ever speaks about is Jesus. He barely defends his actions, saying, "Yeah, yeah, yeah, I was in the temple, but I wasn't causing any problems. By the way, let me tell you about Jesus."

Treating others with love changes the way we make decisions. With the Philippian jailer, Paul stayed there, waiting. Why? Because his actions impacted others. Paul trusted God to take care of the situation; he did that in the jail, and he did that with all these court cases. He was happy to wait in prison because his circumstances didn't matter. He rejoiced in the truth. This gave him an opportunity to be clear about Jesus Christ.

What Is Our Motivation?

Our homework on this chapter is for us to do some soul-searching. What is our motivation? Is it from our sinful nature, for our pleasure, do we even care when we sin? Do we want to make it right with God? If so, when we sin, we need to make sure we correct it right away. We don't want to rejoice in this evil, in this iniquity.

We want to rejoice in the truth. Trust God with our circumstances; trust God with the outcomes. Rejoice in Him, in His way, in His person, declaring the good news of Jesus Christ wherever we go, regardless of the circumstances. So, the next time it comes up and there's a debate, stand for truth. And you might get persecuted!

The founder of Galcom International Canada (where I work), Allan McGuirl, was always ready to talk to the server every time I ate out with him. "You know the Lord?" On an airplane, speaking to the person beside him, "Do you know the Lord?" Rejoicing in the truth; he was consumed by the gospel of Jesus Christ, the good news that Jesus came to seek and to save that which was lost. If we are consumed by that, if we rejoice in that, it will change our behaviour.

LOVE PERSONIFIED

This is perhaps the most "missionary" of all the characteristics of love. And it fits that Paul is our example, because it drove him to tell others all over the world, no matter the circumstances, no matter the hardship, no matter the danger. Rejoice in the truth. Why? Because He loves us.

Chapter 11
Daniel, Hananiah, Mishael, and Azariah Bear All Things

We've looked at "love suffers long" in the story of Joseph, "love is kind" in Ruth, and so on. Now we're at "love bears all things." If you've gotten this far in one sitting, please stop. This book is meant to be read in small bites. Even just one chapter per week. The goal in discipleship is to take the things Jesus says and apply them to our lives. Like the parable of the wise and foolish builders. We need to listen and do.

You've taken a break? Honest? Then let's get back to our study. Love bears all things. Another reference to the term *bear* is in Galatians 6, where we are to "bear" one another's burdens. And each one of us will bear our own burdens. The teaching is that bad things happen to us, and we are supposed to respond in a certain way: with love.

Do you have anyone in mind who had a lot of bad things happen, they had to bear a lot of trouble, burdens, and problems, and they were still able to love? It's a rare quality. We do have an excellent example in Scripture of one who bears all things in love.

What Daniel Had to Bear

Daniel is the personification of love bearing all things. We're told to take up our cross and bear it: this idea that the Christian life brings heaviness, brings a burden, brings a beat-down, and we've got to bear it. Most of the examples, most of the stories that I've been sharing, surround the idea of love for each other. We're supposed to love our neighbour as ourselves. We're supposed to love our enemies. Love is to be the identity of the church. "Love one another. By this all will know that you are My disciples, if you have love for one another" (John 13:34–35).

LOVE PERSONIFIED

It's Easier to Understand How to Love a Person than How to Love God

For me, I probably defaulted to these stories because I understand relationship with another human being better than I understand my relationship with God. I know what it means to love my wife in the context of *agape* love, not just *eros*.

I'd been married for about twenty years when my pastor at the time was single at about fifty years of age, and he met a woman, and he was falling in love. That's *eros,* as we mentioned before, attraction. He was in new territory and trying to work things out. He knew the theory but not the practice, so he asked, "Tim, do you love your wife?"

And I said, "I have to." He was very concerned for my marriage! And I explained, "You don't understand truly loving someone. Yes, you're attracted to your wife. And there are those moments where feelings and emotions come through. But biblically, for husbands, when Paul says, 'Husbands, love your wife,' the word there is *agape.* You choose to love your wife in such a way that no matter what, you love." The command is to love as Christ loved the church and gave Himself up for her. That goes way beyond attraction.

Later, after he got married, he came to me and said, "Tim, now I understand."

I said, "Yes, you're living together now. The rough edges are still there." I understand the marriage relationship. But I think this characteristic that love bears all things is the best example to understand the command to love God.

What Does It Mean to Love God?

In Matthew 22, when Jesus is asked what the greatest commandment is, He doesn't start with "Love your neighbor as yourself." The first and greatest commandment is to "Love the Lord your God with all your heart, soul, mind, and strength." I can understand loving people, but how do I love God? How do I demonstrate it in my day-to-day life, with each passing moment? Love for God seems like an abstract idea.

Jesus also says to his disciples, "If you love Me, keep My commandments" (John 14:15). This means that if we are to love God, and love bears all things, then no matter the situation, the trial, the burden, or the pressure, we obey. We do things God's way.

CHAPTER 11: DANIEL, HANANIAH, MISHAEL, AND AZARIAH

So, let's take a look at Daniel 1:

> In the third year of the reign of Jehoiakim king of Judah, Nebuchadnezzar king of Babylon came to Jerusalem and besieged it. And the Lord gave Jehoiakim king of Judah into his hand, with some of the articles of the house of God, which he carried into the land of Shinar to the house of his god; and he brought the articles into the treasure house of his god.
> Then the king instructed Ashpenaz, the master of his eunuchs, to bring some of the children of Israel and some of the king's descendants and some of the nobles, young men in whom there was no blemish, but good-looking, gifted in all wisdom, possessing knowledge and quick to understand, who had ability to serve in the king's palace, and whom they might teach the language and literature of the Chaldeans. (Daniel 1:1–4)

Let's pause here for a second. The word *youth* that is used here is the same word that's used in the story of the boys who came out of the village and started shouting at Elisha, "Hey, you, bald head!" and the bears came out and ate them (see 2 Kings 2:23). So, you get the idea that these youths are not mature; they're not eighteen or nineteen. These are probably like twelve- or thirteen-year-old boys, by the word that is used.

Losing Everything at Age Thirteen

So here is a twelve- or thirteen -year-old boy who's taken as a prisoner of war away from his family, from his mom and dad. I have a thirteen-year-old, so I'm imagining him as maybe a year or two older, being taken from his family. Can he care for himself? He knows how to fry an egg now, so maybe he could make it on his own. But taken as a prisoner of war? He's taken from everything he knows, from all his comforts and safety.

And here's something I don't want us to miss: in verse 3, the king instructs "Ashpenaz, the master of his eunuchs". Do we understand what this is implying? That these young men are now under the charge of the master of the eunuchs. They have been, or will be, castrated. This is a teenage boy, hormones firing everywhere. Emasculated.

Picking it up again at verse 5:

> The king appointed for them a daily provision of the king's delicacies and of the wine which he drank, and three years of training for them, so that at the end of that time they might serve before the king. Now from among those of the sons of Judah were Daniel, Hananiah, Mishael, and Azariah. To them the chief of the eunuchs gave names: he gave Daniel the name Belteshazzar; to Hananiah, Shadrach; to Mishael, Meshach; and to Azariah, Abed-Nego. (Daniel 1:5–6)

Naming something is important; it gives an identity to something, and no more so than in Hebrew culture.

What's in a Name?

When you name your child in Hebrew, you're pronouncing a blessing over them—you're pronouncing their identity over them. It's why it's so important that when God changes somebody's name, like Abram to Abraham, this is significant. When God changes Jacob's name to Israel, it is significant. Names mean something in our culture, too. My wife and I negotiated for nine months for each of the names of our five kids. If it was a boy, it was going to be named one thing, and if a girl, we had an alternative. Interestingly, we never ended up using the boy names we had picked out when our first daughter was born or the girl names after our sons were born. We went the whole way to the day before they were born before we agreed on a name. The names mean something.

Our youngest son is named Tobias. It means "God is good," because my wife almost died during pregnancy. She developed a blood-clotting disorder and suffered from pulmonary embolisms. Then in the hospital she caught *Clostridium difficile* and lost about twenty pounds right when she should have been packing on weight. Then she developed a kidney disorder, which means that her body continually makes kidney stones. And so, when the baby was born, the doctor turned to Melody and said, "Mrs. Whitehead, you're lucky to be alive."

Her response was "God is good!" Tobias.

What does Daniel mean? Daniel means "God is my judge." What does Belteshazzar mean? "Beltes protect the king." Beltes was the queen of the Babylonian gods.

CHAPTER 11: DANIEL, HANANIAH, MISHAEL, AND AZARIAH

Hananiah means "Yahweh is gracious." What a great name—He is always gracious. What does Shadrach mean? "Commanded by the moon god".

Mishael: "Who is equal to Elohim?" Meshach: "Who is like Aku?"—the Babylonian moon god. Just a little twist in the name is a big attack on his identity.

Azariah means "Yahweh has helped." What does Abed-Nego mean? Abed-Nego means "Slave of the god Nergal". Nergal was the Babylonian god of death.

So, they've taken these boys, emasculated them, and then renamed them, mocking their God, mocking their religion, mocking their culture every time their names are said now in Babylon. It's a slap in the face of who they are and where they've come from.

That is a burden, a beat-down. How do you stand up to this kind of beating? Well, read verse 8:

> Daniel purposed in his heart that he would not defile himself with the portion of the king's delicacies, nor with the wine which he drank; therefore he requested of the chief of the eunuchs that he might not defile himself. Now God had brought Daniel into the favor and goodwill of the chief of the eunuchs. And the chief of the eunuchs said to Daniel, "I fear my lord the king, who has appointed your food and drink. For why should he see your faces looking worse than the young men who are your age? Then you would endanger my head before the king."
>
> So Daniel said to the steward whom the chief of the eunuchs had set over Daniel, Hananiah, Mishael, and Azariah, "Please test your servants for ten days, and let them give us vegetables to eat and water to drink. Then let our appearance be examined before you, and the appearance of the young men who eat the portion of the king's delicacies; and as you see fit, so deal with your servants." So he consented with them in this matter, and tested them ten days.
>
> And at the end of ten days their features appeared better and fatter in flesh than all the young men who ate the portion of the king's delicacies. (Daniel 1:8–15)

LOVE PERSONIFIED

Faithful with Little

How does Daniel respond to being pressed in this meat grinder, to the burden, to the heaviness, to the oppression? He purposes in his heart to obey God. We all know in Leviticus there is a long section about the diet laws for the Jews, what they could eat and what they could not eat. He purposes in his heart that no matter what, he is going to obey God.

Now it seems obvious to us that of course you're going to look healthier and better if you eat vegetables and drink water than if you have cake and alcohol all day. This is common sense to us!

But this is a matter of obedience and a matter of faithfulness. I want to highlight verse 17: "As for these four young men, God gave them knowledge and skill in all literature and wisdom; and Daniel had understanding in all visions and dreams" (Daniel 1:17).

There's a great parable in Matthew 25, the Parable of the Talents. As each of the faithful servants comes in, they bring their talents to the king. He says, "Well done, good and faithful servant; you were faithful over a few things, I will make you ruler over many things" (vs. 21).

Daniel and his friends have been faithful in the little things, in the diet laws. God then grants them wisdom, knowledge, and skill, and the ability to interpret dreams. He's giving them more responsibility; He says, "You've been faithful here. Let me give you more."

> At the end of the days, when the king had said that they should be brought in, the chief of the eunuchs brought them in before Nebuchadnezzar. Then the king interviewed them, and among them all none was found like Daniel, Hananiah, Mishael, and Azariah; therefore they served before the king. And in all matters of wisdom and understanding about which the king examined them, he found them ten times better than all the magicians and astrologers who were in all his realm. Thus Daniel continued until the first year of King Cyrus. (Daniel 1:18–21)

They were faithful. God blessed them.

CHAPTER 11: DANIEL, HANANIAH, MISHAEL, AND AZARIAH

Rewarded with Much

In chapter 2, we read about Nebuchadnezzar's famous dream, which he won't tell the astrologers and magicians. "I know you are just going to make something up, so I want you to first tell me what my dream is, and then interpret it," he says.

"No one has ever asked that! We can't do that!" they say.

The king replies, "I am going to kill you all if you can't do this." Daniel's response? He goes away, and he fasts and prays, seeking God for an answer. And in verse 19:

> Then the secret was revealed to Daniel in a night vision. So Daniel blessed the God of heaven.
> Daniel answered and said:
> "Blessed be the name of God forever and ever,
> For wisdom and might are His.
> And He changes the times and the seasons;
> He removes kings and raises up kings;
> He gives wisdom to the wise
> And knowledge to those who have understanding.
> He reveals deep and secret things;
> He knows what is in the darkness,
> And light dwells with Him.
> I thank You and praise You,
> O God of my fathers;
> You have given me wisdom and might,
> And have now made known to me what we asked of You,
> For You have made known to us the king's demand."
> (Daniel 2:19–23)

Daniel is brought before the king, and in verse 26,

> The king answered and said to Daniel, whose name was Belteshazzar, "Are you able to make known to me the dream which I have seen, and its interpretation?"
> Daniel answered in the presence of the king, and said, "The secret which the king has demanded, the wise men, the astrologers, the magicians, and the soothsayers cannot

declare to the king. But there is a God in heaven who reveals secrets, and He has made known to King Nebuchadnezzar what will be in the latter days." (Daniel 2:26–28)

In terms of what we've already learned about not boasting, I think this is a pretty good example of *not* doing that. Daniel stands there and says, "No astrologer or soothsayer is going to be able to do what you ask, but there's a God who can." Through this situation, God is glorified because of Daniel's love for God, bearing with this oppression and the threat of execution. He goes to God and does things God's way, and he comes back, and he declares that God knows the answers, and the result is that God is glorified.

The Statue Goes to Nebuchadnezzar's Head

We have the interpretation of the dream, but we'll leave that where it is, and move on to chapter 3, where Nebuchadnezzar has had the dream about the statue of many materials interpreted by Daniel, and somehow he gets to thinking, "I need to build my own statue!"—where we Sunday school kids know this famous story of Daniel and his friends. But let's examine it more closely in light of our topic of loving God.

Starting at verse 8, we have Hananiah, Mishael, and Azariah (we're going to honour them by using their real names) refusing to bow to Nebuchadnezzar's gold statue.

> At that time certain Chaldeans came forward and accused the Jews. They spoke and said to King Nebuchadnezzar, "O king, live forever! You, O king, have made a decree that everyone who hears the sound of the horn, flute, harp, lyre, and psaltery, in symphony with all kinds of music, shall fall down and worship the gold image; and whoever does not fall down and worship shall be cast into the midst of a burning fiery furnace. There are certain Jews whom you have set over the affairs of the province of Babylon: Shadrach, Meshach, and Abed-Nego; these men, O king, have not paid due regard to you. They do not serve your gods or worship the gold image which you have set up."
> Then Nebuchadnezzar, in rage and fury, gave the command to bring Shadrach, Meshach, and Abed-Nego. So they brought these men before the king. Nebuchadnezzar spoke, saying to them, "Is it true, Shadrach, Meshach, and Abed-Ne-

CHAPTER 11: DANIEL, HANANIAH, MISHAEL, AND AZARIAH

> go, that you do not serve my gods or worship the gold image which I have set up? Now if you are ready at the time you hear the sound of the horn, flute, harp, lyre, and psaltery, in symphony with all kinds of music, and you fall down and worship the image which I have made, good! But if you do not worship, you shall be cast immediately into the midst of a burning fiery furnace. And who is the god who will deliver you from my hands?" (Daniel 3:8–15)

I like that line. Remember, all their names were about God, worship of God, or God being good. Nebuchadnezzar has renamed them, stealing their identities. And here he is mocking them again. "Your god is going to save you? Really?"

> Shadrach, Meshach, and Abed-Nego answered and said to the king, "O Nebuchadnezzar, we have no need to answer you in this matter. If that is the case, our God whom we serve is able to deliver us from the burning fiery furnace, and He will deliver us from your hand, O king. But if not, let it be known to you, O king, that we do not serve your gods, nor will we worship the gold image which you have set up." (Daniel 3:16–18)

This is love for God. "We will not compromise, even if it means our death."

We know the Ten Commandments: "You will have no other gods before me. You will not bow down and worship any graven image" (see Exodus 20:1–5). Never mind all the other laws that are in Leviticus. This is the Big Ten. They know you don't cross this line.

They refuse, even under the burden of torture, of being burned to death. They say, in effect, "Even if God doesn't save us, we will not bow. We will not compromise. Our love for God is so important and all consuming, we will bear anything."

> Then Nebuchadnezzar was full of fury, and the expression on his face changed toward Shadrach, Meshach, and Abed-Nego. He spoke and commanded that they heat the furnace seven times more than it was usually heated. And he commanded certain mighty men of valor who were in his army to bind Shadrach, Meshach, and Abed-Nego, and cast them into the burning fiery furnace. Then these men were bound in their

coats, their trousers, their turbans, and their other garments, and were cast into the midst of the burning fiery furnace.

Therefore, because the king's command was urgent, and the furnace exceedingly hot, the flame of the fire killed those men who took up Shadrach, Meshach, and Abed-Nego. And these three men, Shadrach, Meshach, and Abed-Nego, fell down bound into the midst of the burning fiery furnace.

Then King Nebuchadnezzar was astonished; and he rose in haste and spoke, saying to his counselors, "Did we not cast three men bound into the midst of the fire?"

They answered and said to the king, "True, O king."

"Look!" he answered, "I see four men loose, walking in the midst of the fire; and they are not hurt, and the form of the fourth is like the Son of God."

Then Nebuchadnezzar went near the mouth of the burning fiery furnace and spoke, saying, "Shadrach, Meshach, and Abed-Nego, servants of the Most High God, come out, and come here." Then Shadrach, Meshach, and Abed-Nego came from the midst of the fire. And the satraps, administrators, governors, and the king's counselors gathered together, and they saw these men on whose bodies the fire had no power; the hair of their head was not singed nor were their garments affected, and the smell of fire was not on them.

Nebuchadnezzar spoke, saying, "Blessed be the God of Shadrach, Meshach, and Abed-Nego, who sent His Angel and delivered His servants who trusted in Him, and they have frustrated the king's word, and yielded their bodies, that they should not serve nor worship any god except their own God! Therefore I make a decree that any people, nation, or language which speaks anything amiss against the God of Shadrach, Meshach, and Abed-Nego shall be cut in pieces, and their houses shall be made an ash heap; because there is no other God who can deliver like this." (Daniel 3:19–29)

Quite a turnaround from just a few verses before! "What god can save you from my hand?" What is the result of their love for God in their obedience? God is glorified once again. God was glorified when they didn't eat the food, and then they were given miraculous abilities, wisdom, and skill to interpret dreams. The result? God is glorified.

They don't bow down and worship; they bear this punishment, they bear being burned to death. What's the result? God is glorified. Chapter 4 has

CHAPTER 11: DANIEL, HANANIAH, MISHAEL, AND AZARIAH

this wonderful proclamation from Nebuchadnezzar demanding that everyone worship the God of Hananiah, Mishael, and Azariah. God is glorified.

We then move ahead, three chapters and three kings, to Daniel 6. A lot of people think, because this happens in short order, that Daniel is still a young man; however, at this point, he's probably seventy or eighty years old. He is still serving, but he's on his third king and his second nation.

> It pleased Darius to set over the kingdom one hundred and twenty satraps, to be over the whole kingdom; and over these, three governors, of whom Daniel was one, that the satraps might give account to them, so that the king would suffer no loss. Then this Daniel distinguished himself above the governors and satraps, because an excellent spirit was in him; and the king gave thought to setting him over the whole realm. (Daniel 6:1–3)

The Evil Jealousy Brings

Even if you've not been to Sunday school, I'm sure you've heard this next story. The other governors and satraps envy Daniel; he is going to get the job as prime minister, second in command. They want this power and influence, so they set up a plan. Knowing that Daniel has such integrity, they realize that they will never be able to find fault with him, except if they catch him in something about his God. So, they come to Darius and suggest that, for a certain period of time, no one should pray except to him, knowing that Daniel prays to his God, to Elohim, to Yahweh.

Let's pick up the story at 6:12, just after they have caught Daniel praying:

> They went before the king, and spoke concerning the king's decree: "Have you not signed a decree that every man who petitions any god or man within thirty days, except you, O king, shall be cast into the den of lions?"
> The king answered and said, "The thing is true, according to the law of the Medes and Persians, which does not alter."
> So they answered and said before the king, "That Daniel, who is one of the captives from Judah, does not show due regard for you, O king, or for the decree that you have signed, but makes his petition three times a day."

And the king, when he heard these words, was greatly displeased with himself, and set his heart on Daniel to deliver him; and he labored till the going down of the sun to deliver him. Then these men approached the king, and said to the king, "Know, O king, that it is the law of the Medes and Persians that no decree or statute which the king establishes may be changed."

So the king gave the command, and they brought Daniel and cast him into the den of lions. But the king spoke, saying to Daniel, "Your God, whom you serve continually, He will deliver you." Then a stone was brought and laid on the mouth of the den, and the king sealed it with his own signet ring and with the signets of his lords, that the purpose concerning Daniel might not be changed.

Now the king went to his palace and spent the night fasting; and no musicians were brought before him. Also his sleep went from him. Then the king arose very early in the morning and went in haste to the den of lions. And when he came to the den, he cried out with a lamenting voice to Daniel. The king spoke, saying to Daniel, "Daniel, servant of the living God, has your God, whom you serve continually, been able to deliver you from the lions?"

Then Daniel said to the king, "O king, live forever! My God sent His angel and shut the lions' mouths, so that they have not hurt me, because I was found innocent before Him; and also, O king, I have done no wrong before you."

Now the king was exceedingly glad for him, and commanded that they should take Daniel up out of the den. So Daniel was taken up out of the den, and no injury whatever was found on him, because he believed in his God.

And the king gave the command, and they brought those men who had accused Daniel, and they cast them into the den of lions—them, their children, and their wives; and the lions overpowered them, and broke all their bones in pieces before they ever came to the bottom of the den.

Then King Darius wrote:
> To all peoples, nations, and languages that dwell in all the earth:
> Peace be multiplied to you.
> I make a decree that in every dominion of my kingdom men must tremble and fear before the God of Daniel.

CHAPTER 11: DANIEL, HANANIAH, MISHAEL, AND AZARIAH

> For He is the living God,
> And steadfast forever;
> His kingdom is the one which shall not be destroyed,
> And His dominion shall endure to the end.
> He delivers and rescues,
> And He works signs and wonders
> In heaven and on earth,
> Who has delivered Daniel from the power of the lions. (Daniel 6:12–27)

And God Is Glorified

The result of Daniel's obedience and love for God is that God is glorified once again. The love we are commanded to as Christians is not an emotion; it's not a feeling, it should not come and go. It is a purposeful choice to determine in our hearts to submit to the leading of the Holy Spirit, so that He has control of our lives in all situations. And when we come across these situations where we have a heavy burden to bear, when we are oppressed and beat down, and it seems that all of society is against us, we say, "No matter what, I will love God, and I will show that by obeying His commands."

Jesus said, "If you love Me, you will keep My commandments."

The best way that I can show my love for God is to look at His Word and say, "What does God tell me to do in this situation?" And I do it.

I said to my kids all the time as they were growing up, "No matter what anybody else does—" and if they were here, they would all recite together, "You do what's right." We drilled this into them. You do what's right. You obey God. That is how you show your love for God. It's not infatuation, it's not an attraction, it's not affection; it's a choice.

We Obey God, Period

Sometime in your life you will be oppressed, if you work in a secular workplace. The pressure will be on to fudge the numbers, to cut the corners, to say certain things or go along with certain jokes at a party. Society around us is saying certain things about the value of life, and we as Bible-believing Christians often fear stepping on minefields about gender and sexuality. The Bible gives us clear instructions: no matter what happens to us, we obey God; we do things God's way. As they said in Daniel 3:16–18, "Our God is able to deliver us. But even if He doesn't, we will not bow down." We obey God, period; even to our detriment, even to our death. We obey God; that's what it means to love God. I told you, this love talk is not elementary, not 'milk'; this is high-level discipleship "meat".

Pray this little prayer:

> Father, I recognize that love is beyond human, natural ability to attain. I am selfish, arrogant, lazy, vindictive, and, Lord, fearful. I confess I don't like bearing burdens. I want comfort and ease and the easy way out. But Lord, love for others and love for You demands more.
>
> I pray that today You will help me to be prepared by being filled by Your Holy Spirit, by spending time in Your Word, knowing what it commands me to do. Help me to spend time in prayer, listening to You, not just speaking and asking. Help me to spend time in worship, humbling myself before You, giving You the sacrifice of praise. So that, Lord, I can respond to any burden, any persecution, any challenge with a love for You that bears up under it, no matter what. Lord, I need Your help desperately to do this, so I ask this in Jesus's name. Amen.

Chapter 12
Barnabas Believes All Things

Let's stop for a moment and look again at 1 Corinthians 13:

> Love suffers long and is kind; love does not envy; love does not parade itself, is not puffed up; does not behave rudely, does not seek its own, is not provoked, thinks no evil; does not rejoice in iniquity, but rejoices in the truth; bears all things, believes all things, hopes all things, endures all things. Love never fails. (1 Corinthians 13:4–8)

Love believes all things. You may be thinking, "That doesn't sound good at all." Someone who believes all things we would call gullible, which isn't in the dictionary, by the way. You've heard that joke before, right? Proverbs 14:15 says, "The simple believes every word." It's like the proverb is telling us, "Don't believe everything you hear." So, what do we do with this little phrase in the midst of this love section that says, "Love believes all things"?

Wisdom or Gullibility?

Here are a few helpful quotes from some dusty old commentaries I own. The first is from Barnes to start our discussion.

> It cannot mean, that the man who is under the influence of love is a man of "universal credulity;" that he makes no discrimination in regard to things to be believed; and is as prone to believe a falsehood as the truth; or that he is at no pains to inquire what is true and what is false, what is right and what is wrong.

So, we're not talking about abandoning wisdom and prudence and good thinking. We don't just go gullibly along with everything. That's not what we're saying.

LOVE PERSONIFIED

Do you know who St. Basil is? The big, colourful church in Red Square in Moscow with the really colourful onion-shaped domes, that's St. Basil's Cathedral. He cared for the poor and the underprivileged. Here's what he says about love believing all things. And this is getting us closer to where I want to head with this.

> If you see your neighbor in sin, don't look only at this, but also think about what he has done or does that is good. And, in frequently trying this, in general, while not partially judging, you will find that he is better than you.

Here's another one from Barnes; "It will go to the uttermost lengths, trusting and believing in the better elements of human nature, before it is reluctantly forced to some other conclusion." That's a quote from an old commentary I got from my grandfather that I dusted off. When you look at someone, you don't try to find something wrong with them; you don't suspect them of ill intent; you don't think that they're a bad person. You give them the benefit of the doubt. You believe them to be good.

John Calvin states,

> Not that a Christian should knowingly and willingly suffer himself to be imposed upon; not that he should deprive himself of prudence and judgment, so that he may be the more easily deceived; but that he should esteem it better to be deceived by his kindness and gentleness of heart, than to injure his brother by needless suspicion.

As you are reading these quotes, is it starting to hit home?

Tim Does Not "Believe All Things"

Let me tell you a story to illustrate. I'm naturally skeptical and was trained as an accountant, so I don't trust things until I see them and can measure them and evaluate them. My wife, however, is a wonderful person, full of grace.

Years ago, we had a family in our church that was troubled. It was a second marriage for the wife, and she had a daughter from the previous marriage who didn't get along with the stepdad or the other two kids from that marriage, and there were constant fights. The older daughter was getting in trouble at school and eventually was expelled.

CHAPTER 12: BARNABAS BELIEVES ALL THINGS

We were newly married, probably not five years, already with an infant and a toddler. We were just trying to figure out this marriage thing for ourselves, and I was trying to work and scratch out a living. My wife says to this family, "I'll tell you what; I want to help you out. Send your daughter to our house every day. I'll help her with her homework, and she can help me around the house."

So, our lives become entwined with this other family, and … I resent it. I work hard every day, and I come home and just want to unwind and play with my kids, but this other person is always there. I don't trust them; I feel taken advantage of, and I don't think we are going to make any positive difference in their lives. I had already given up on them.

I hope this story illustrates the difference between "love believes all things" and a person who is selfish and sceptical, unforgiving, and suspicious. One day, I come home, open the door, and say, "Honey, I'm home!"

And my wife meets me at the door and says, "I was talking to the mother today …"

"Enough! I've had enough! They can go to hell for all I care." As the words leave my mouth, I realize what I have said. Do you know the look your father gives you when he's disappointed but sorry for you as well?

I could feel like God was looking at me in that moment. "Tim, you just don't get it. You're not understanding. I love them!" This was a low point in my Christian life, but this is the point about love believing all things.

We can look at someone and think, *They're hopeless, they're beyond redemption.* But love says, "I believe that God can redeem you. I believe you're worth something. I believe you're valuable. I believe you at face value. And unless you absolutely prove you are bad, I'm going to believe in you." That's what we have when we're told that love believes all things.

Barnabas Believes

So, it's not gullible. It's not just nodding our head at everything, but we give the benefit of the doubt. We believe in the person. And a great example of this in the Bible is Barnabas. In Acts chapter 4, we have the beginning of the church, where we meet Barnabas for the first time. Let's start at verse 32.

> The multitude of those who believed were of one heart and one soul; neither did anyone say that any of the things he possessed was his own, but they had all things in common. And with great power the apostles gave witness to the resurrection of the Lord Jesus. And great grace was upon them all. Nor was there anyone among them who lacked; for all who were possessors of lands or houses sold them, and brought the proceeds of the things that were sold, and laid them at the apostles' feet; and they distributed to each as anyone had need.
>
> And Joses, who was also named Barnabas by the apostles (which is translated Son of Encouragement), a Levite of the country of Cyprus, having land, sold it, and brought the money and laid it at the apostles' feet. (Acts 4:32–37)

I think we're all more familiar with the next chapter, which is the really exciting one with Ananias and Sapphira doing the same thing, but lying about the proceeds and keeping back some for themselves. And so, it's a great, exciting story—lots of action, people are dying—but I would say that just as dramatic is Barnabas's act, who just sold his assets, his livelihood, his security, and gave them to the church. He believed in the integrity of the apostles who were distributing to those who had need. He believed in the cause of the church, and gave the leaders the benefit of the doubt and gave them everything he had. Barnabas believed; love believes all things.

We don't hear much from Barnabas again until Acts 9. This is the story of Saul—Paul's conversion on the road to Damascus.

This is the part we know about in chapter 9—the big, dramatic part we're skipping again. Light from the heavens. The Lord speaks, Saul responds, "Who are you?" Jesus answers, "It's hard for you to kick against the goads—you're going to be blind." We all know that part, right?

For contrast to Barnabas's love, let's take a quick look at Ananias (a different one, not the one married to Sapphira).

> The Lord said to him, "Arise and go to the street called Straight, and inquire at the house of Judas for one called Saul of Tarsus, for behold, he is praying. And in a vision he has seen a man named Ananias coming in and putting his hand on him, so that he might receive his sight."

CHAPTER 12: BARNABAS BELIEVES ALL THINGS

> Then Ananias answered, "Lord, I have heard from many about this man, how much harm he has done to Your saints in Jerusalem. And here he has authority from the chief priests to bind all who call on Your name."
> But the Lord said to him, "Go, for he is a chosen vessel of Mine to bear My name before Gentiles, kings, and the children of Israel." (Acts 9:11–15)

Should We Believe in Saul?

I can almost imagine Ananias thinking, "Wait a minute, God, I don't think that's safe. I don't think I should go anywhere near Saul of Tarsus; You know that he's been killing people, right? You know he's got papers to put us in jail? I don't think I should go." Even with God's endorsement, Ananias does not believe in Saul.

Contrast that to a little bit later in the chapter. Ananias does go, and he does pray for Saul. Immediately, Saul starts preaching. The people try to kill him, but the disciples get Saul out of there. And then, in verse 26:

> When Saul had come to Jerusalem, he tried to join the disciples; but they were all afraid of him, and did not believe that he was a disciple. But Barnabas took him and brought him to the apostles. And he declared to them how he had seen the Lord on the road, and that He had spoken to him, and how he had preached boldly at Damascus in the name of Jesus. (Acts 9:26–27)

Barnabas! Barnabas believes Paul is authentic in his conversion. Ananias has his doubts; the disciples in Jerusalem don't even let him in the door. They want nothing to do with him. But Barnabas believes in Paul. Love believes all things. Would you let a known murderer into your church meeting? How about something worse: a government official with power and authority and the law on his side who is actively executing and jailing your friends?

Before we jump ahead again, we have this great story in chapter 10, which is pertinent to what we're going to read about later. It's the account of Peter and his vision of the sheet from heaven filled with unclean animals. God says to Peter, "What I have called clean, don't call unclean." He then sends him to Cornelius, a Roman soldier, and the gospel is preached to the Gentiles for the first time. Up to this point, the church is pretty much all Jews, so God is now opening the door to the Gentiles.

Peter goes to the Gentiles, and there's a wonderful conversion story of Cornelius and his whole household. With that context, let's get back to Barnabas and move ahead to Acts 11:19:

> Those who were scattered after the persecution that arose over Stephen traveled as far as Phoenicia, Cyprus, and Antioch, preaching the word to no one but the Jews only. But some of them were men from Cyprus and Cyrene, who, when they had come to Antioch, spoke to the Hellenists, preaching the Lord Jesus. And the hand of the Lord was with them, and a great number believed and turned to the Lord.
> Then news of these things came to the ears of the church in Jerusalem, and they sent out Barnabas to go as far as Antioch. When he came and had seen the grace of God, he was glad, and encouraged them all that with purpose of heart they should continue with the Lord. For he was a good man, full of the Holy Spirit and of faith. And a great many people were added to the Lord.
> Then Barnabas departed for Tarsus to seek Saul. And when he had found him, he brought him to Antioch. So it was that for a whole year they assembled with the church and taught a great many people. And the disciples were first called Christians in Antioch.
> And in these days prophets came from Jerusalem to Antioch. Then one of them, named Agabus, stood up and showed by the Spirit that there was going to be a great famine throughout all the world, which also happened in the days of Claudius Caesar. Then the disciples, each according to his ability, determined to send relief to the brethren dwelling in Judea. This they also did, and sent it to the elders by the hands of Barnabas and Saul. (Acts 11:19–30)

Barnabas Believes Again

So here's Barnabas, going to the Gentiles. And you've got to remember, this is a new thing, this idea of the gospel being for Gentiles. "Are we sure they are believing? Barnabas, you go check it out. Go check out if they're really Christians or not, these crazy Gentile dogs." Barnabas goes and believes them; he

CHAPTER 12: BARNABAS BELIEVES ALL THINGS

encourages them. He believes their conversion is true and encourages them in the faith. He gets Saul to come too, and they teach them for a year, discipling them. Love believes all things.

Back to the action in chapter 12. Paul and Barnabas go to Jerusalem, they deliver the food, they report on what's going on, and then return to Antioch. Reading verse 25, "Barnabas and Saul returned from Jerusalem when they had fulfilled their ministry, and they also took with them John whose surname was Mark." (Acts 12:25) We are now introduced to John Mark. He's an important part of the story later on.

> In the church that was at Antioch there were certain prophets and teachers: Barnabas, Simeon who was called Niger, Lucius of Cyrene, Manaen who had been brought up with Herod the tetrarch, and Saul. As they ministered to the Lord and fasted, the Holy Spirit said, "Now separate to Me Barnabas and Saul for the work to which I have called them." Then, having fasted and prayed, and laid hands on them, they sent them away. (Acts 13:1–3)

[This is actually where we get the word "missionary"—"sent-out ones", in Acts 13:3. But that's a different book for a different time.]

> So, being sent out by the Holy Spirit, they went down to Seleucia, and from there they sailed to Cyprus. And when they arrived in Salamis, they preached the word of God in the synagogues of the Jews. They also had John as their assistant. (Acts 13:4–5)

There is another great story here involving a sorcerer called Bar-Jesus, but we will skip over that too. Something much less exciting but important for us: "When Paul and his party set sail from Paphos, they came to Perga in Pamphylia; and John, departing from them, returned to Jerusalem." (Acts 13:13)

Like previous people in our study, they are not the main characters in the story. This really is Paul's story; Barnabas is a supporting character. Paul and Barnabas continued their journey, preaching. Just to give Barnabas as much ink as we can, let's include this short account of a different aspect of love that he demonstrates: love is not puffed up. We pick up the action just after they get kicked out of Iconium and arrive in Lystra, starting at Acts 14:7:

LOVE PERSONIFIED

> They were preaching the gospel there.
>
> And in Lystra a certain man without strength in his feet was sitting, a cripple from his mother's womb, who had never walked. This man heard Paul speaking. Paul, observing him intently and seeing that he had faith to be healed, said with a loud voice, "Stand up straight on your feet!" And he leaped and walked. Now when the people saw what Paul had done, they raised their voices, saying in the Lycaonian language, "The gods have come down to us in the likeness of men!" And Barnabas they called Zeus, and Paul, Hermes, because he was the chief speaker. Then the priest of Zeus, whose temple was in front of their city, brought oxen and garlands to the gates, intending to sacrifice with the multitudes.
>
> But when the apostles Barnabas and Paul heard this, they tore their clothes and ran in among the multitude, crying out and saying, "Men, why are you doing these things? We also are men with the same nature as you, and preach to you that you should turn from these useless things to the living God, who made the heaven, the earth, the sea, and all things that are in them, who in bygone generations allowed all nations to walk in their own ways. Nevertheless He did not leave Himself without witness, in that He did good, gave us rain from heaven and fruitful seasons, filling our hearts with food and gladness." And with these sayings they could scarcely restrain the multitudes from sacrificing to them. (Acts 14:7–18)

Barnabas refuses to take any credit for what God did. Love for God is not puffed up, does not parade itself, but we've already learned that. Fast-forward again, and the Jews show up; they stone Paul. Paul and Barnabus have to escape, and they do some ministering on the way back, eventually returning safe and sound to Antioch. Paul and Barnabas have been travelling the world, preaching to Jews and encouraging them, evangelising Gentiles and converting them; this is a wonderful time of ministry. But while they were away:

> Certain men came down from Judea and taught the brethren, "Unless you are circumcised according to the custom of Moses, you cannot be saved." Therefore, when Paul and Barnabas had no small dissension and dispute with them, they determined that Paul and Barnabas and certain others of them should go up to Jerusalem, to the apostles and elders, about this question. (Acts 15:1–2)

CHAPTER 12: BARNABAS BELIEVES ALL THINGS

We Get to Eat Bacon!

Paul and Barnabas go back to Jerusalem, and they go in front of Peter and the other church leaders to get a decision on the issue. Once the issue is presented, Peter recounts the vision he had and how God commanded him to go and preach to the Gentiles as well.

"All the multitude kept silent and listened to Barnabas and Paul declaring how many miracles and wonders God had worked through them among the Gentiles" (Acts 15:12). They come to their decision—James and Peter, who are the heads of the church. They write a wonderful letter, making sure that all of us Gentiles who are Christians can still eat bacon. It's wonderful news! Thank you, Barnabas!

> When they were sent off, they came to Antioch; and when they had gathered the multitude together, they delivered the letter. When they had read it, they rejoiced over its encouragement. Now Judas and Silas, themselves being prophets also, exhorted and strengthened the brethren with many words. And after they had stayed there for a time, they were sent back with greetings from the brethren to the apostles.
> However, it seemed good to Silas to remain there. Paul and Barnabas also remained in Antioch, teaching and preaching the word of the Lord, with many others also.
> Then after some days Paul said to Barnabas, "Let us now go back and visit our brethren in every city where we have preached the word of the Lord, and see how they are doing." Now Barnabas was determined to take with them John called Mark. But Paul insisted that they should not take with them the one who had departed from them in Pamphylia, and had not gone with them to the work. Then the contention became so sharp that they parted from one another. And so Barnabas took Mark and sailed to Cyprus; but Paul chose Silas and departed, being commended by the brethren to the grace of God. And he went through Syria and Cilicia, strengthening the churches. (Acts 15:30–41)

Barnabas Believes in John Mark

This is the last we hear about Barnabas; Luke, the author of Acts, follows Paul. We don't know about Barnabas's ministry with John Mark.

LOVE PERSONIFIED

We don't know whether they were successful; were they able to preach the gospel to more Gentiles and lead other people to Christ? Johnny Cash sings about Paul ever getting to Spain, maybe Barnabas and John Mark got there. Did they have shipwrecks? Did they perform miracles? What happened? We do have a little clue in 2 Timothy 4:11: Paul is quite aged at this point, and he's writing to Timothy and says, "Get Mark and bring him with you, for he is useful to me for ministry."

At some point not reported in Scripture: John Mark has been restored to Paul. But we do know John Mark has become a useful minister, and it's almost like Paul is apologizing—at least I like to think he is. "I made a mistake. John Mark is useful to me in ministry; send him here to help me." Previously, he was so adamant that Mark was useless that it broke up his friendship with Barnabas, and Paul went off with Silas instead. Something that Barnabas did restored John Mark, gave him his value back, and made him a valuable minister for the gospel. I wish we knew the story. I wish we had some story of Barnabas and John Mark's adventures to see what happened in John Mark's life. But we do know this: Barnabas's real name is Joses, but his nickname *is* "Son of Encouragement".

Love believes all things. Love gives the benefit of the doubt. It looks at someone and says, "Yes, you're doing something bad now, but you're not a bad person."

Let's return to that St. Basil quote: "If you see your neighbor in sin, don't look only at this, but also think about what he has done or does that is good. And, in frequently trying this, in general, while not partially judging, you will find that he is better than you." That's what love does. Love never discounts someone.

If you're thinking, *Tim, maybe you're stretching things a bit, we need to protect ourselves, put up boundaries like Ronald Reagan famously said: "Trust but verify."*

Let's read Matthew 18:21–22. "Peter came to Him and said, 'Lord, how often shall my brother sin against me, and I forgive him? Up to seven times?' Jesus said to him, 'I do not say to you, up to seven times, but up to seventy times seven.'"

Jesus taught in Matthew 5:39, "Whoever slaps you on your right cheek, turn the other to him also." This is utterly counter to what we think; if someone wrongs us, we write them off. They're done. Someone fails us, so we write them off. They're done. "You get only one chance with me."

Fool Me Once ...

What's the saying? "Fool me once, shame on you. Fool me twice, shame on me." That's not biblical.

The biblical one is "Fool me once, shame on you; fool me twice, shame on you; fool me three times, okay, I forgive you seventy times seven."

Love says, "I believe the best in you. You failed, I'm going to forgive you, and I'm going to hope for better. And I'm going to help you and love you. And you're going to fail me again. And I'm going to hope for better, and I'm going to restore you, and you're going to fail me again."

I mentioned my wife and her grace and her mercy towards people. She now leads a ministry in our church to the homeless who live around our church. We're right in downtown Hamilton, Canada, beside the Salvation Army Booth Center, a men's drop-in center.

When COVID started, they limited their services because of COVID restrictions and spacing and all that. All those guys start sleeping on our church steps, and we as a church had to ask, "What do we do with this situation? Do we call the police and kick them off?"

Well, no, we should do something. And so, my wife swept up the garbage and needles off the steps; she washed off the urine and vomit. We started a clothing bank, and she gave out the clothes, and they took advantage of it. Now we feed them on Thursdays along with a brief service, and they try to get the food and get out without listening to the sermon. (They do love singing "I Saw the Light" every week though.)

When she comes home, she has to detox and process her day. I listen to her, and I'm thinking, *I would be done with these guys. You get one chance, and you've had it.* But love believes all things.

Oh, about that family I mentioned, with the daughter who was in our house, and I said, "I don't care if they go to hell!"—guess who showed up on our church steps.

LOVE PERSONIFIED

Twenty Years Later

It's twenty years since I have thought about the daughter. Melody comes home one day and says, "You won't believe who's sleeping on the church steps." Over the next weeks, she proceeds to pour her heart out for that girl to try to get her into the hospital, to get her cleaned up, to get her rehabilitated, to find her family. She has kids of her own now. Things are going along well with the restoration when one day, Melody goes up to the hospital to visit her, and she has already skipped out. And it breaks her heart.

I say to her, "Melody, just stop! Stop caring, stop loving." That's how I would handle it. But no, Melody keeps praying for her. Keeps looking for her.

Months later, she gets a Facebook message. The girl has gone through a rehabilitation in another city, far away from the bad influences that brought her down. She is clean and sober and getting help. Melody reaches out and is trying to help her along in her journey. Love believes in others.

There are heartbreaking stories of people failing as we try to love them, but also, there are success stories. A young guy who was in university had an anxiety attack, ran away, and ended up on the steps of our church. Melody and the pastor start trying to find out who he is and minister to him. They get him to the hospital, get him cleaned up, and find his family. He is now restored to his family. Boy, did I need to hear that good story! I need to hear that love works. That I really do need to believe in others. That no one is beyond God's help.

As Christians, we don't get the option of saying, "I'm done." Jesus doesn't give us that option. How many times are we to forgive? Seventy times seven. What happens when they take advantage of you? They steal your shirt? Give them your cloak, too. They want you to walk a mile? Okay, you walk two. That's what love that believes all things does. We keep loving because we believe they are worth it.

The Absurdity of God's Love

We all know John 3:16: "For God so loved the world that He gave His only begotten Son." That's *agape* love. It sounds nice when we say it, but it's kind of abstract. Listen to this—it sounds absurd to me: "God so loved Adolf Hitler, Saddam Hussein, Osama bin Laden, Jeffrey Dahmer …" I could keep going. Doesn't that sound ridiculous to you, as I name those people? God loved them, believed they were worth dying for. But I just have trouble with this aspect of

CHAPTER 12: BARNABAS BELIEVES ALL THINGS

how we are to love, probably more than any of the other characteristics. I give up on people so quickly.

We don't hear anything more from Barnabas after his break-up with Paul. I like to think (though I have no evidence, just my own personal feelings) that Barnabas wrote Hebrews. People often think it was Paul, but scholars say the vocabulary isn't consistent with his other epistles. It has to be someone close to Paul, because it has some of the same themes. So, if you'll indulge me, I think Barnabas wrote it (or Timothy).

In Hebrews 13:1–3, "Barnabas" writes,

> Let brotherly love continue. Do not forget to entertain strangers, for by so doing some have unwittingly entertained angels. Remember the prisoners as if chained with them—those who are mistreated—since you yourselves are in the body also.

At Galcom, where I work, we partner with a prison ministry to partially fund audio Bibles with their correspondence course lessons. I look at people in jail and think, *They don't deserve it. They're hopeless.* But then I talk to Nadia Zeversenuke, the director of New Life Prison Ministry, and I hear the story of a guy who's in jail in Canada for life. To be jailed in Canada for life, you have to have done something *really* bad, but you know what? He's leading Bible studies now on anger management. God can redeem anyone and everyone. Love believes all things.

In Hebrews 13:15, it says, "Therefore by Him let us continually offer the sacrifice of praise to God, that is, the fruit of our lips, giving thanks to His name." We talked about this before, but the next verse says: "Do not forget to do good and to share, for with such sacrifices God is well pleased" (Hebrews 13:16). Love believes all things. Love is an act of worship.

Believing in That Difficult Person

I don't know if you've got somebody in your life who takes advantage of you, who lets you down. Guess what? God has put them there to refine you, to help you be a better disciple. I've got a couple of them, and I pray, "Lord, do something in their life, because it's killing me, putting up with them!" And that's the wrong attitude. You can see how much I struggle with this. Love believes all things.

LOVE PERSONIFIED

Here's our homework: God has called us to this love, which is such a high level of discipleship. It demands so much of us: giving up of ourselves, our self-seeking ways, our selfishness, and our self-righteousness. It demands that we submit to the guiding and leading of the Holy Spirit.

Someone will fail you this week, may be even betray you. You will need the help of the Holy Spirit. So pray:

> Lord, help me to love; fill me with Your Holy Spirit today. Lord, help me look at others the way You have told us to in the Golden Rule: to not only do unto others as we would have them do unto us, but also to think of others as we would have them think about us. Amen.

Then extend grace; extend mercy; give them a second chance; think well of them until you absolutely can't.

Chapter 13
Abraham Hopes All Things

As we've been going through this study of love and trying to fulfill the commandment of Jesus Christ to love others, to love our neighbours as ourselves, and to love God with all our heart, soul, mind, and strength, we've defined that it's not an emotion. It's not infatuation or attraction. It is a purposeful choice to behave in a certain way in certain situations.

We've been learning from people in different situations how to respond in love. Some of these concepts, like "love is kind," I find simple. I mean, we tell our children when they are toddlers and when they go to kindergarten, "Be kind to other kids," and they know what that means. Don't hit people, don't steal their food, don't say mean things.

Being kind seems to be easily understood. But hope is a little more abstract for me. What does hope *mean*? I think because we live in a society that relies so much on things like the lottery, people hope they win the lottery to solve all of their financial problems and make their lives better, more fulfilled, and happier. But that's more like wishing.

It's the same with love; we've had to learn what Jesus means when he uses the word *love*. Now we need to understand what Paul means when he uses the word *hope* here in 1 Corinthians. Biblically, *hope* is a word that is used throughout the New Testament more than thirty times, and it most often means actively waiting for God's fulfillment of a promise He has made. In the last chapter, we learned what it means to believe all things, or better, to put your faith in someone, that someone is going to come through for you. We learned this through the story of Barnabas.

Hope is similar to belief, or having faith in someone, but it's a little more specific. It's like a subset of faith, as per *Strong's Concordance*, where I always end up going when I need to understand what a word really means. Hope is actively waiting, as I've said, for God's fulfillment. It sounds a lot like faith, and in fact, faith and hope are used almost interchangeably in Scripture and by many people in general.

But there is a subtle difference. "I hope I will be in heaven someday with Christ." Compare that to "I have faith that Christ will one day bring me to heaven to be with Him." Did you catch the subtle difference? The first statement is hope—I hope something will happen. The second is faith—I have faith that Jesus will make it happen.

As we learned from Barnabas, faith is not just hoping *for something*; it's *in someone*. We put our faith in God because of what He has done in the past and who He is in the present. We also put our hope in His promise for the future. Sometimes we can say, "I trust God," meaning the same thing as "I have faith in God."

We can trust in a person in the present time because of what they've done in the past. Hope can be understood as a subset or a segment of trust or faith, but it's always looking to the future. Since we're discussing etymology, we should ensure that when we talk about hope, we're referring to biblical hope, not worldly hope.

Biblical hope is not wishing. It's a confidence that something promised will happen. In Acts 26:7, Paul is defending himself, his actions, and his faith before King Agrippa. He says, "To this promise our twelve tribes, earnestly serving God day and night, hope to attain." Now, that's a short verse, but the context is that he's talking about the Jews' hope of the Messiah, of resurrection. This hope is based on a promise. Biblical hope is always based on a promise, usually a promise right from God Himself. So, you can see why hope and faith are connected. Our hope is always strengthened by the fact that our faith is in God, who has made the promise for which we are hoping. It's a bit of circular thinking, but I hope you catch the point.

Romans 8:24–25 says, "We were saved in this hope, but hope that is seen is not hope; for why does one still hope for what he sees? But if we hope for what we do not see, we eagerly wait for it with perseverance."

Hope Is Always Forward-Looking

Faith can be backward-looking at the person who made the promise, but hope is always forward-looking to what we have not received and cannot see. So, it's a confidence, not a cross-my-fingers wish. Romans 5:5 says, "Hope does

CHAPTER 13: ABRAHAM HOPES ALL THINGS

not disappoint." Why? Because the hope is based on the promises that a faithful God has made.

Because we love God, we believe Him. We've put our faith in Him, and now we look forward, hoping that everything He's promised us will come true. Enough academic talk! Let's get to the story: the story of someone who personifies a love that works itself out in hope, a hope in God's promises.

As we've gone through our studies, some of the characteristics and phrases about love have been very neighbour-focused. "Love your neighbor." Others are very God-focused: "Love the Lord your God with all your heart, soul, mind, and strength." Hope really is all about loving God, and who personifies hope and faith and trust in the Bible? That's Father Abraham. His faith was in God, and so he put his hope in the promises that God gave him … most of the time.

Father Abraham Hoped for the Fulfillment of God's Promises

Let's begin with the introduction to Abraham's story in Genesis 11. We're in the middle of a genealogy that starts right after the story of the Tower of Babel. We are introduced to Abraham and his family, and the chapter ends with Abraham's father, Terah, taking Abram (as he was called at the time), Abram's wife Sarai, and Terah's grandson, Lot, to Haran from Ur of the Chaldeans. The writer of Genesis is setting the stage, highlighting the sinful, rebellious state of humankind.

The Tower of Babel was man's way to make a name for themselves, not loving God, but loving themselves. Ur was a pagan land. The Chaldeans were idolatrous people. In fact, we need to be reminded that at this time in history, there was no codified way for people to relate to or worship God. That came over four hundred years later with Moses. But we have seen evidence of how God wanted His people to interact with Him. We have the stories of Enoch and Noah. There's a relationship that God wants with His creation, and He wants them to act in justice, in righteousness. He expects them to behave in a certain way.

He calls Abraham out of a society that has abandoned any type of relationship with God, any type of love for God, to start something new.

> The Lord had said to Abram:
> "Get out of your country,
> From your family

> And from your father's house,
> To a land that I will show you.
> I will make you a great nation;
> I will bless you
> And make your name great;
> And you shall be a blessing.
> I will bless those who bless you,
> And I will curse him who curses you;
> And in you all the families of the earth shall be blessed." (Genesis 12:1–3)

Successes—and Failures

That's promise number 1. And immediately we have success number one in verse 4: "So Abram departed as the LORD had spoken to him, and Lot went with him. And Abram was seventy-five years old when he departed from Haran."

God makes Abram a promise. We don't know the relationship that Abram has had with God up to this point, but Abram believes and obeys. Chapter 11 says God spoke to Abram and Terah. They left Ur of the Chaldeans, settled in Haran, then, after his father Terah passed away, Abram is called again to leave for another land in chapter 12. Abram has faith in God, so he believes the promise, hopes in the promise, and obeys—success!

Promise number 2: "The LORD appeared to Abram and said, 'To your descendants I will give this land.' And there he built an altar to the LORD, who had appeared to him" (Genesis 12:7).

Abram arrives in Canaan, and God says, "This is the land I'm going to give to you." It's a promise. Abram worships God, gives a sacrifice, and builds an altar there to signify that he hopes in God's promises and believes in Him.

But Abram is like any human, and we're not successful all the time. Like many of the people we've studied, there have been some ups and some downs for Abram. Here's failure number 1:

> There was a famine in the land, and Abram went down to Egypt to dwell there, for the famine was severe in the land. And it came to pass, when he was close to entering Egypt, that he said to Sarai his wife, "Indeed I know that you are a

woman of beautiful countenance. Therefore it will happen, when the Egyptians see you, that they will say, 'This is his wife'; and they will kill me, but they will let you live. Please say you are my sister, that it may be well with me for your sake, and that I may live because of you." (Genesis 12:10–13)

If you went to Sunday school—actually, this may have been skipped over in the younger kids' class, but in an adult class, you may have studied this failure of Abram to hope in God's promises. Suddenly, there's a famine; things turn bad. His trust and his faith in God waver, and he abandons hope in God's promise. He leaves the land, and then he lies about who Sarai is because he's afraid he will be killed.

Well, how could God fulfill any of the promises He's just made to Abram if he is dead?

Love for God has faith in Him and puts its hope in His promises. Consider Proverbs 13:12: "Hope deferred makes the heart sick, but when the desire comes, it is a tree of life."

When Hope Is Deferred

Again, the people that we're studying are human. We want to learn from them, from their successes and failures. How do they respond in certain situations? The hope was deferred; Abram's heart was sick, discouraged, beaten down. The promise wasn't coming. And this is where we need love to take over: a passionate love for God that helps us hold firm to His promises, because He is faithful.

Well, God intervenes. Abram, of course, is saved, Sarai's identity as Abram's wife is revealed, the famine lifts, and Abram returns to Canaan. And we have these indications throughout the story that Abram is increasing in wealth, with flocks and herds, servants, and slaves. In fact, he has so much now that he looks at his nephew Lot and says, "We need to part company because the land here can't support both of us" (see Genesis 13:8–9). Their herdsmen are fighting. Abram, trusting in God and believing and hoping in His promises, says to Lot, "You choose first." He hopes, trusts, and knows God's going to fulfill His promise. Lot chooses the better-looking land, and Abram chooses what's left. God then reiterates the promise to supply everything that he's going to need. So, that's success number 2 for Abram's life.

Mysterious Melchizedek

Genesis 14 is a great story! It was one of my favourites growing up. I love this idea of a mysterious Melchizedek who appears and then disappears, this mystical being that some even think may have been what's called a Christophany, but that's another topic entirely!

Lot is living near Sodom, and some kings from another land come in and attack the area, taking the king, the citizens, and yes, Lot captive. Abram, having become so wealthy and powerful, sets out to rescue them. And he's incredibly successful. He trusts God that God is going to preserve him. God has made these promises of land, descendants, and blessing. So, Abram risks his life to rescue Lot. After the battle, this mysterious Melchizedek arrives.

> Then Melchizedek king of Salem brought out bread and wine; he was the priest of God Most High. And he blessed him and said:
> "Blessed be Abram of God Most High,
> Possessor of heaven and earth;
> And blessed be God Most High,
> Who has delivered your enemies into your hand."
> And he gave him a tithe of all. (Genesis 14:18–20)

Tithing Before There Was Tithing

Now, tithing hasn't been codified yet; that's part of the Mosaic Law that comes after the days of Abraham. But I believe this is a special covenant relationship that we can have with God. He makes promises throughout His word about giving Him the firstfruits, or the tithe, of our goods, acknowledging that He is God Most High, possessor of heaven and earth.

This is important. Remember back to our study about making a "sacrifice of praise" as a way to express love for God. Let's talk about tithing as an act of love. This is the first introduction of this idea of giving 10 percent of your income to God as an offering, acknowledging Him as the Provider. Leviticus 27 is where it's introduced as law for the Jews, and it talks about giving a tenth of everything, whether it's the produce of the land, fruit of the tree, herds, or flocks.

It's always the best tenth and the first tenth. It's often referred to as the firstfruits. This was an act of worship. Oftentimes in churches, we pass the offering plate and think we're donating to the work of the church. That's not the right perspective to have. Giving the tithe is an act of love and worship of God, acknowledging that He is the Provider and that He will continue to provide. This law is reiterated in Numbers. It's reiterated in Deuteronomy. It comes up in Nehemiah, this idea that we ought to be tithing, giving our firstfruits, and our best 10 percent to God. It comes up in 2 Chronicles: the people had stopped giving a tithe, and God commands the people to bring back the 10 percent.

But here's why tithing goes beyond the Law. If you're a New Testament Christian, we're taught through Galatians that we don't have to abide by the Jewish Law—that we are to abide in a relationship with Jesus Christ through His death and resurrection in faith, through the Holy Spirit, to walk in the Spirit, to have freedom from the Law because we can't fulfill it anyway.

Now, Abraham lived four hundred years before the Law was written, and we have promises like this in Proverbs 3:9–10:

> Honor the LORD with your possessions,
> And with the firstfruits of all your increase;
> So your barns will be filled with plenty,
> And your vats will overflow with new wine.

How do they get filled and bursting if we're giving it away? This is the covenant relationship with God. This is a promise that God gives us when we worship Him through our giving. Malachi 3:8–9 says,

> "Will a man rob God?
> Yet you have robbed Me!
> But you say,
> 'In what way have we robbed You?'
> In tithes and offerings.
> You are cursed with a curse,
> For you have robbed Me,
> Even this whole nation."

God is warning people that if they don't give the tithe, there is a curse. But right after that, Malachi 3:10–12 says,

> "Bring all the tithes into the storehouse,
> That there may be food in My house,

> And try Me now in this,"
> Says the LORD of hosts,
> "If I will not open for you the windows of heaven
> And pour out for you such blessing
> That there will not be room enough to receive it.
> "And I will rebuke the devourer for your sakes,
> So that he will not destroy the fruit of your ground,
> Nor shall the vine fail to bear fruit for you in the field,"
> Says the LORD of hosts;
> "And all nations will call you blessed,
> For you will be a delightful land,"
> Says the LORD of hosts."

Jesus gives a warning in Matthew 23:23 about tithing, "Woe to you, scribes and Pharisees, hypocrites! For you pay tithe of mint and anise and cummin, and have neglected the weightier matters of the law: justice and mercy and faith."

And this is the point that I'm trying to make: this isn't a religious or a legal practice. This is a reliance on a promise that God makes. He will provide for our needs, and He will bless us. Do you have faith in God, and do you hope in His promise? Abram did. Abram was blessed beyond measure because he followed God's commands.

And here's one other warning: "For where your treasure is, there your heart will be also" (Matthew 6:21). If we put our reliance on our money and our goods, or even on our ability to earn, we are not loving God and trusting Him as Provider—money versus God. You cannot serve God and mammon, Jesus warns. I think it's important because so often we love the things of the world; we love money, and it distracts us or blocks us from truly loving God. And part of loving God is hoping in His promises; love hopes all things.

Back to our story: this is success number 3 for Abram. He shows that he trusts God's promises to bless him. He's willing to give away the spoils of war to Melchizedek, the high priest of God, the representative of God.

The Introduction of the Covenant

Moving on, in Genesis 15, we have the reiteration of God's covenant with Abram. A covenant is a special kind of promise; it's a contractual promise. In the ancient Near East, these covenants were binding to the point that if one of

CHAPTER 13: ABRAHAM HOPES ALL THINGS

the parties broke the covenant, they could be subject to execution—to death—for not keeping up their end of the covenant.

This is a serious matter. God reiterates that He will be Abram's shield and exceedingly great reward.

> But Abram said, "Lord GOD, what will You give me, seeing I go childless, and the heir of my house is Eliezer of Damascus?" Then Abram said, "Look, You have given me no offspring; indeed one born in my house is my heir!"
> And behold, the word of the LORD came to him, saying, "This one shall not be your heir, but one who will come from your own body shall be your heir." Then He brought him outside and said, "Look now toward heaven, and count the stars if you are able to number them." And He said to him, "So shall your descendants be." (Genesis 15:2–5)

This is a huge promise. Abram is quite old—more than seventy-five years old, not quite a hundred. And God makes the promise of so many descendants that he won't be able to count them, and listen to this next verse: "he believed in the LORD, and He accounted it to him for righteousness" (Genesis 15:6).

God is faithful. God makes a promise. Abram believes God's promise, and it is accounted to him as righteousness, as doing good, as obeying the Law.

This is where the covenant then comes in, and we see a practice that we don't see anywhere else in Scripture relating to the idea that a covenant is ratified by animals being cut in two; in this case, a three-year-old heifer, a three-year-old female goat, a three-year-old ram, a turtledove, and a pigeon. Tradition indicates that the two members of the covenant promise are to walk together, arm in arm, between the animals, signifying, "If I break this promise, let this happen to me"—being cut in two. But Abram falls asleep, and only the torch representing the presence of God passes between the sacrificed animals.

> It came to pass, when the sun went down and it was dark, that behold, there appeared a smoking oven and a burning torch that passed between those pieces. On the same day the LORD made a covenant with Abram, saying:
> "To your descendants I have given this land, from the river of Egypt to the great river, the River Euphrates—the Kenites, the Kenezzites, the Kadmonites, the Hittites, the

> Perizzites, the Rephaim, the Amorites, the Canaanites, the Girgashites, and the Jebusites." (Genesis 15:17–21)

God goes through this covenant ritual by himself. There is no part for Abram to play in keeping the promise. It is all up to God. That's the promise.

The Hagar Failure

Instead of success number 4, we have failure number 2. In Genesis 16, Abram and Sarai start to falter in their faith in God and their hope in His promise.

They don't see how God can fulfill this promise for a child through Sarai in her old age, so they take matters into their own hands. Sarai convinces Abram to go and "marry" (note the quotes here) her servant, Hagar. Hagar becomes pregnant and starts to disobey Sarai; Sarai retaliates with harsh treatment, so Hagar runs away. God, in love, redeems Hagar. We're skipping over the details to focus on Abram.

We need to know what happens when we step out of hope in God's promise and take matters into our own hands. We just make a mess. The mess gets worse when Hagar's son, Ishmael, is born, and thirteen years later, God fulfills His promise for Sarah to have a child. There's strife in the home and problems.

Loving God means keeping our hope in His promise. Waiting for God to fulfill His promise and not fulfilling it our way is a lesson we have to learn. This is failure number 2 for Abram.

In chapter 17, we have another reiteration of the covenant promise that God has made with Abram; and to solidify it even more, God renames Abram and Sarai to Abraham and Sarah, redefining them based on the promise—Abraham, "father of many nations". God is reiterating His covenant promise at this time. There's a promise for Sarah too, being renamed "princess," indicating that she will give birth to a royal line.

Abraham Shows His Belief in the Promise

At this time, Abraham is ninety-nine years old, and God calls for another act of obedience to show that Abraham believes and hopes in the promise. He says,

> "This is My covenant which you shall keep, between Me and you and your descendants after you: Every male child

among you shall be circumcised; and you shall be circumcised in the flesh of your foreskins, and it shall be a sign of the covenant between Me and you. He who is eight days old among you shall be circumcised, every male child in your generations, he who is born in your house or bought with money from any foreigner who is not your descendant." (Genesis 17:10–12)

The call for circumcision is a radical act that God is asking Abraham to do. There's no evidence that this is common in any other ancient Near Eastern culture. That alone is significant. The bottom line is, Abraham had faith in God, believed Him, hoped in His promise, and obeyed. This is success number 4.

To get us beyond this rather awkward topic, let's jump ahead in the story. Again, love hopes all things; hope is based on promises—for us, promises that are made by God, in whom we can put our faith.

Moving to chapter 18, God is kind and gracious to Abraham, who has been waiting for decades now since the original promise, and we have a beautiful gesture here of God visiting Abraham in some sort of theophany. We have a dialogue that makes it look like it's God himself in human form, talking with Abraham, promising again that Abraham will have a son, that he'll be the father of many nations. God says to him, "I will certainly return to you according to the time of life, and behold, Sarah your wife shall have a son" (Genesis 18:10).

The Promise that Makes Sarah Laugh

Some translations say, "This time next year, Sarah will have a son." Again, just in case Abraham's faith is wavering, God comes face-to-face with him to make a promise. And of course, we have the famous passage where Sarah laughs in the tent, saying,

> "After I have grown old, shall I have pleasure, my lord being old also?"
> And the LORD said to Abraham, "Why did Sarah laugh, saying, 'shall I surely bear a child, since I am old?' Is anything too hard for the LORD? At the appointed time I will return to you, according to the time of life, and Sarah shall have a son." (Genesis 18:12–14)

LOVE PERSONIFIED

I like the little bit where Sarah denies her laughing, and God says, "No, you did laugh." There's a real human touch in the story here—our natural human response to being caught in doubt. And I think God is being gentle in this interaction. But the key part of this is, "Is anything too hard for the LORD?"

Loving God means loving Him in all His fullness. He is the Sovereign Lord of the universe, the all-powerful, mighty God who hung the stars in space. There are all sorts of hymns about His glory, majesty, and power. And yet, we so quickly forget and try to take things into our own hands instead of hoping in His promises. "Is anything too hard for the LORD?" He's worthy of our love, our faith, and our hope in the promises He's made.

The next part of the story diverts away and focuses on Lot. I'm not meaning to ignoring it and it is important to read on your own, but let's follow Abraham and Sarah and keep our focus on learning how to love God by hoping in His promises.

Sarah Is the Sister Again

In chapter 20, we unfortunately read about failure number 3. Isaac hasn't been born yet, and the promise has not been fulfilled.

> Abraham journeyed from there to the South, and dwelt between Kadesh and Shur, and stayed in Gerar. Now Abraham said of Sarah his wife, "She is my sister." And Abimelech king of Gerar sent and took Sarah. (Genesis 20:1–2)

Now, remember, Sarah is probably eighty years old at this point—she must be incredibly beautiful and youthful for another king to claim her as his wife.

> God came to Abimelech in a dream by night, and said to him, "Indeed you are a dead man because of the woman whom you have taken, for she is a man's wife."
> But Abimelech had not come near her; and he said, "Lord, will You slay a righteous nation also? Did he not say to me, 'She is my sister'? And she, even she herself said, 'He is my brother.' In the integrity of my heart and innocence of my hands I have done this." (Genesis 20:3–5)

Once again, Abraham's faith in God and hope in His promises falter; instead of trusting even after God has reiterated this promise face-to-face, instituting

CHAPTER 13: ABRAHAM HOPES ALL THINGS

the covenant of circumcision, and having that incredible experience where God appeared as a flaming torch going through the covenant animals, and on and on.

God makes these promises and shows Himself faithful. But again, Abraham's hope and faith waver. He lies again about Sarah, in fear that he will be killed. In verse 11, Abraham says, "Because I thought, surely the fear of God is not in this place; and they will kill me on account of my wife." Again, there is the fear that somehow something else is going to intervene so that God won't be able to keep His promises.

God steps in to deliver Abraham and Sarah. We have to be patient in God's promises, trusting in His sovereignty and His ability to fulfill them. Love hopes all things.

> The LORD visited Sarah as He had said, and the LORD did for Sarah as He had spoken. For Sarah conceived and bore Abraham a son in his old age, at the set time of which God had spoken to him. And Abraham called the name of his son who was born to him—whom Sarah bore to him—Isaac. Then Abraham circumcised his son Isaac when he was eight days old, as God had commanded him. Now Abraham was one hundred years old when his son Isaac was born to him. And Sarah said, "God has made me laugh, and all who hear will laugh with me." She also said, "Who would have said to Abraham that Sarah would nurse children? For I have borne him a son in his old age." (Genesis 21:1–7)

Laughter at Isaac's Birth

I think this overwhelming joy at the birth of Isaac is their relief. Their faith has been tested; their hope has been stretched. God has delayed this promise until the time He determined was right. Abraham and Sarah tried to intervene in their own abilities with Ishmael, by lying about their relationship, and with all these other little failures. But God, who is faithful, keeps His promises, and we can hope in them. As the apostle Paul said—and we looked at the verse earlier—"Hope does not disappoint." We're not like the heathen, wishing and crossing our fingers; we hope in God's promises, as sure as a concrete foundation.

Now, we need to address the rest of this chapter, which is the fallout caused by Abraham and Sarah's attempt to fulfil God's promise in their own way.

> The child [Isaac] grew and was weaned. And Abraham made a great feast on the same day that Isaac was weaned.
>
> And Sarah saw the son of Hagar the Egyptian, whom she had borne to Abraham, scoffing. Therefore she said to Abraham, "Cast out this bondwoman and her son; for the son of this bondwoman shall not be heir with my son, namely with Isaac." And the matter was very displeasing in Abraham's sight because of his son.
>
> But God said to Abraham, "Do not let it be displeasing in your sight because of the lad or because of your bondwoman. Whatever Sarah has said to you, listen to her voice; for in Isaac your seed shall be called. Yet I will also make a nation of the son of the bondwoman, because he is your seed." (Genesis 21:8–13)

The Love of God for Hagar

And then we have this tragic story of Hagar and Ishmael being cast out. Hagar departs and wanders in the wilderness of Beersheba. Her waterskin is used up. She takes her young teenage boy, puts him under a shrub for some shade, and sits down a little way away from him because she doesn't want to watch him die.

God intervenes again, though. Why? Because He's just made a promise to Abraham that Ishmael would also become a great nation.

> God opened her eyes, and she saw a well of water. And she went and filled the skin with water, and gave the lad a drink. So God was with the lad; and he grew and dwelt in the wilderness, and became an archer. He dwelt in the Wilderness of Paran; and his mother took a wife for him from the land of Egypt. (Genesis 21:19–21)

The emotional damage and trauma caused to Hagar and Ishmael because of Abraham and Sarah stepping out of God's promises and trying to take things into their own hands was significant.

We're often guilty of trying to become our own gods, relying on ourselves instead of relying on God. Loving God means setting aside our desires, our wishes, our timelines, and putting our hope in His promises. When we step outside of what God has promised to us, we cause harm to ourselves, and in this case, terrible harm to two innocent victims in the story, Hagar and Ishmael.

CHAPTER 13: ABRAHAM HOPES ALL THINGS

Well, there are more stories here at the end of Abraham's life to learn from as well. He comes back to Abimelech. There are some disputes over some wells and some land, which are important because, of course, God has promised the land to Abraham. And this time, though, there is no deceit. Abraham makes a sacrifice and a covenant with Abimelech that God honours.

When God Asks for Isaac

In chapter 22 comes the real test of Abraham's faith. Let's take our time to soak it in; perhaps it's familiar to us from our Sunday school days, but it's important to read it carefully again:

> It came to pass after these things that God tested Abraham, and said to him, "Abraham!"
> And he said, "Here I am."
> Then He said, "Take now your son, your only son Isaac, whom you love, and go to the land of Moriah, and offer him there as a burnt offering on one of the mountains of which I shall tell you." (Genesis 22:1–2)

Just stop! Wait a minute! "God, I waited for twenty-five years, from the first time You promised me descendants until Isaac was born. I know I failed in between, but now I've seen your promise come true. And now you're asking me to sacrifice my son?" There is no doubt in the language here what God is asking. There is no doubt that God is asking Abraham to sacrifice, to kill his son as an offering to God.

I wish there was a bit of dialogue here between verses 2 and 3 to give us some insight into the struggle that Abraham might have had. I know I wouldn't have been able to sleep that night, lying awake, tossing and turning. Does he tell Sarah? What does he do now?

We have no insight into what Abraham is thinking. We just have his actions in verse 3, which, quite frankly, demonstrate success number 5 of obedience, and reliance and belief in God and His promises that are incredible.

> Abraham rose early in the morning and saddled his donkey, and took two of his young men with him, and Isaac his son; and he split the wood for the burnt offering, and arose and went to the place of which God had told him. Then on the third day Abraham lifted his eyes and saw the place afar off.

> And Abraham said to his young men, "Stay here with the donkey; the lad and I will go yonder and worship, and we will come back to you."
>
> So Abraham took the wood of the burnt offering and laid it on Isaac his son; and he took the fire in his hand, and a knife, and the two of them went together. But Isaac spoke to Abraham his father and said, "My father!"
>
> And he said, "Here I am, my son."
>
> Then he said, "Look, the fire and the wood, but where is the lamb for a burnt offering?"
>
> And Abraham said, "My son, God will provide for Himself the lamb for a burnt offering." So the two of them went together. (Genesis 22:3–8)

Again, I wish there were some insight into what Abraham is thinking. Does he have complete faith that God is going to provide a lamb? Is he saying, perhaps in a coded way, that Isaac is the lamb, but he just doesn't want to tell him out loud? What can be going through his mind in this situation?

> They came to the place of which God had told him. And Abraham built an altar there and placed the wood in order; and he bound Isaac his son and laid him on the altar, upon the wood. And Abraham stretched out his hand and took the knife to slay his son. (Genesis 22:9–10)

How Could Abraham Bear It?

Again, please, can someone give me some insight? What is Abraham thinking? What is Isaac thinking? We understand he's a young teenager at this point. I can imagine one of my sons lying there, screaming out, pleading, writhing, fighting. I wish we had more indication of what is actually happening here. Is Abraham weeping as he holds up the knife? What is going through everyone's mind here? But whatever it is, his actions show that, somehow, he believes that God will keep His promise—of descendants, of land, of blessing. He's believing God for a miracle.

> The Angel of the LORD called to him from heaven and said, "Abraham, Abraham!"
>
> So he said, "Here I am." [I can just hear the relief in his voice!]

CHAPTER 13: ABRAHAM HOPES ALL THINGS

> And He said, "Do not lay your hand on the lad, or do anything to him; for now I know that you fear God, since you have not withheld your son, your only son, from Me."
>
> Then Abraham lifted his eyes and looked, and there behind him was a ram caught in a thicket by its horns. So Abraham went and took the ram, and offered it up for a burnt offering instead of his son. And Abraham called the name of the place, The-Lord-Will-Provide; as it is said to this day, "In the Mount of the Lord it shall be provided." (Genesis 22:11–14)

And then, once more, God reiterates the promise, the covenant promise.

> The Angel of the Lord called to Abraham a second time out of heaven, and said: "By Myself I have sworn, says the Lord, because you have done this thing, and have not withheld your son, your only son—blessing I will bless you, and multiplying I will multiply your descendants as the stars of the heaven and as the sand which is on the seashore; and your descendants shall possess the gate of their enemies. In your seed all the nations of the earth shall be blessed, because you have obeyed My voice." So Abraham returned to his young men, and they rose and went together to Beersheba; and Abraham dwelt at Beersheba. (Genesis 22:15–19)

The Start of the Promise's Fulfillment

To give Abraham his due, we need to complete the story. Genesis 23 is the account of Sarah's death. We have an interesting incident where Abraham purchases property in the Promised Land. He's been living next to the Canaanites and he wants to buy a burial place. As we see in verse 16, he buys a plot of land that includes a cave for four hundred pieces of silver.

This is the first time Abraham has a solid claim in the Promised Land. It's the beginning of the fulfillment of the promise—he doesn't have to capture it, he doesn't have to fight for it. It is a simple purchase from a man by the name of Ephron—that's just a little bit of Bible trivia for you.

Chapter 24 has another instance where we see Abraham holding on passionately to the promises of God.

> Abraham was old, well advanced in age; and the LORD had blessed Abraham in all things. So Abraham said to the oldest servant of his house, who ruled over all that he had, "Please, put your hand under my thigh, and I will make you swear by the LORD, the God of heaven and the God of the earth, that you will not take a wife for my son from the daughters of the Canaanites, among whom I dwell; but you shall go to my country and to my family, and take a wife for my son Isaac." (Genesis 24:1–4)

One of the promises that God gave Abraham was for descendants. Here's Abraham near the end of his life, thinking about how that promise will be fulfilled. He wants to act this time in a way that honours God, unlike his failures before when he slept with Hagar and had a child through her. Isaac is a son of promise, and this time, Abraham wants to do things right. So, he wants Isaac to go back and get a wife from his family and not from the heathen and pagan cultures around him.

I acknowledge I was happy to talk about tithing but skipped over Abraham's circumcision earlier because it makes me uncomfortable to discuss. Here's another awkward cultural practice that's not found anywhere else in Scripture—the reference to putting a hand under somebody's thigh. All I can say is, if somebody made me do that, I would never forget the promise that I had made!

The servant goes to Abraham's family, Rebekah agrees to marry Isaac, and she returns with the servant. We start to see, just as with the purchase of land in the last chapter, another little step towards the promise being fulfilled.

It's Just the Start

These two promises are not fulfilled for generations. In fact, Abraham's descendants don't number into hundreds of thousands or millions for a long, long time. And we definitely don't get the fulfillment of the promise of land until the Israelites return from four hundred years of captivity in Egypt. But these are the first steps in the covenant that God promised to Abraham, and Abraham is now holding on to these promises. And we're starting to see the beginnings, like a little seed starting to sprout. The final promise that God gives Abraham—that through his descendant, all of the world would be blessed—will not be truly fulfilled until the coming of Jesus Christ.

I mention this because we live in such a "fast-food society". We want the fulfillment of promises made to us right away. We have no endurance. The first characteristic of this love from 1 Corinthians is "Love suffers long." We could have used Abraham for this one! My goodness, he never gets to see the fulfillment of these promises for himself: the promise of land, the promise of descendants, and the promise of a descendant who would bless the whole world. But he hangs on to those promises; we need to learn to hang on to the promises of God. We can look back at the story of Abraham and God's faithfulness to him. God has a plan, and God is in control.

His timeline isn't ours. God is an eternal being; He's the Sovereign LORD of the universe. He's the Alpha and the Omega. We are here for such a small amount of time, just a little breath, so we need to love God enough to trust His promises.

Faith That Counts as Righteousness

Well, let's wrap up Abraham's story. At the age of 175, after taking another wife and having several more sons, Abraham dies. Romans has a great summary of Abraham's life.

> What then shall we say that Abraham our father has found according to the flesh? For if Abraham was justified by works, he has something to boast about, but not before God. For what does the Scripture say? "Abraham believed God, and it was accounted to him for righteousness." Now to him who works, the wages are not counted as grace but as debt.
> But to him who does not work but believes on Him who justifies the ungodly, his faith is accounted for righteousness. (Romans 4:1–5)

I don't want to wander off into soteriology—the study of salvation, faith, and grace. But they're all intertwined here in the life of Abraham. It's his faith in the person of God, his hope in the promises of God, that are counted to him as righteousness, that put him in a right standing with God, that save him. We need to love God, have faith in who He is, and hope in His promises. This is the way of right relationship for salvation: loving God for who He is and what He's done, believing in the promise of resurrection, and the promise of forgiveness of sins. This is the testimony of Abraham, this love for God that allows him to have hope and faith.

Never Give Up on His Promises!

Here's our homework for this chapter: God's Word is full of promises, and maybe you've received a promise from God—perhaps regarding one of your children or a health issue you've had. Someone has spoken a word (I'm not sure where you stand on prophetic things); but, somehow, God has made a promise to you. Don't give up on it, don't take the shortcut, don't skip the line, don't rely on yourself. Hope in His promises. Hope in God does not disappoint, as the apostle Paul said at the beginning of our chapter.

God is able. He is faithful, and He loves us. You can put your faith in Him. Any of the promises that He gives you, you can hope in. This isn't a wish. This is a concrete hope that it will happen. Just have patience.

Chapter 14

Jeremiah Endures All Things

We are almost done. We now come to "love endures all things." This time, there is no long introduction, no etymological study of words; we're going to get right to the story of the weeping prophet, Jeremiah. Jeremiah's life could be summed up, really, in one verse: John 16:33. Jesus says, "These things I have spoken to you, that in Me you may have peace. In the world, you will have tribulation; but be of good cheer, I have overcome the world." Jeremiah had to endure war, persecution, imprisonment, torture, more war, political intrigue, and the oppressive evilness of the society he lived in. He had to endure all of this in order to express love. Love for God endures all things; love for our neighbour endures all things.

The Man Called to Endure

Let's take a look at Jeremiah's life. Who was Jeremiah? He was born to a family of priests, the son of Hilkiah, we're told in Jeremiah 1, in a little town called Anathoth, just outside of Jerusalem. He was born in the days of Josiah, a good king in Judah. But he also served during the slow moral decline of the reigns of Josiah's son, Jehoahaz, and three more kings, all the way until Jerusalem was destroyed, and the people of Judah were carried captive off to Babylon.

I have often heard it said that people wish that they knew their purpose, why they were put on this earth, or that God would tell them clearly what He wants them to do with their life, to know their future. God does this with Jeremiah, but I think it actually brings more stress and strain on him than not knowing.

In verse 5, God says, "Before I formed you in the womb I knew you; before you were born I sanctified you; I ordained you a prophet to the nations." Jeremiah has a very clear, specific, and distinct call on his life. Sounds good so far, but there's more:

> "Behold, I have put My words in your mouth.
> See, I have this day set you over the nations and over the kingdoms,
> To root out and to pull down,
> To destroy and to throw down,
> To build and to plant." (Jeremiah 1:9–10)

This is a huge task, a huge responsibility that God has given to Jeremiah, and Jeremiah's response to all of this is "Who am I? I am but a youth; I can't do these things" (see v. 6). This is a heavy load under which Jeremiah is going to be called to endure. But it gets worse.

> "Behold, I have made you this day
> A fortified city and an iron pillar,
> And bronze walls against the whole land—
> Against the kings of Judah,
> Against its princes,
> Against its priests,
> And against the people of the land.
> They will fight against you,
> But they shall not prevail against you.
> For I am with you," says the LORD, "to deliver you." (Jeremiah 1:18–19)

The Heavy Calling

What a terrible calling on your life—to be told right at the beginning that your destiny is to be constantly fighting against others, constantly calling out evil, standing up for what's right, but no one will listen. This is the battle that Jeremiah is going to have to endure through his whole life. I don't know if you've ever been put in a position where you have to correct other people, but they don't take kindly to it. No one likes having their sins pointed out to them, and no one wants someone constantly being the know-it-all, the goody two-shoes, calling them to change their behaviour. And unfortunately, this is what God calls Jeremiah to do with his whole life.

How does Jeremiah stand up against all this opposition? How does he endure? Well, we need to know more background on him. The first couple of verses in Jeremiah tell us that Jeremiah's first vision comes during the thirteenth year of Josiah. Josiah was a godly king who instituted great sweeping reforms.

CHAPTER 14: JEREMIAH ENDURES ALL THINGS

The Old Testament tells us that Josiah, in the twelfth year of his reign, starts to purify the temple and gets rid of evil idol worship; in the eighteenth year of his reign, he asks for the temple to be repaired. A priest by the name of Hilkiah—sound familiar?—finds the book of the Law in 2 Kings 22:8. There's two interpretations here. Either they don't know what to do with it, which is amazing to me that the high priest Hilkiah and the other priests in the temple don't know God's law. Or, they've been hiding the law, waiting for a worthy king.

We can go on to read how Josiah under Hilkiah's guidance reinstates proper temple worship, tearing down all of the altars and the idols that were spread throughout the country that people were worshipping, all of the images of Baal and Asherah—the sins of the people of Israel which had trickled down into the south. He tears down all these images, throws them into the Kidron Valley, and burns them up.

Serving an Unknown God

What have they been teaching the people? How are they conducting the temple worship and the sacrifices, and just how have things gone this far? So, they read this law, and they respond to it exactly as they should, with great repentance. This is the beginning of Jeremiah's life, seeing these wonderful reforms. And we read that Josiah doesn't just cleanse Jerusalem or Judah; he goes into the other tribal areas, all the way up to Naphtali, where the people have already been taken off into Assyria. The northern kingdom of Israel has already been destroyed. But Josiah institutes these sweeping reforms, calling the people back to celebrate Passover. It's amazing, all these wonderful, godly things happening. This is what Jeremiah is witnessing in the first couple of decades of his ministry calling.

Right after Josiah starts these reforms, God starts to talk to Jeremiah.

As an aside, we'll be jumping around the book of Jeremiah a lot! One difficulty we have is that Jeremiah is not written in chronological order. In fact, in Jeremiah 47 and 48, Jeremiah gives prophecies first against Gaza and then Moab. The first prophecies are fulfilled right here at the beginning of his ministry, after Josiah has started his reforms; then the second perhaps shortly after the king's death, when Josiah interfered with Egypt, going to enact God's judgment on Gaza.

Who Was Jeremiah?

Enough about Josiah, we need to focus on Jeremiah. Josiah dies, and Jeremiah composes funeral songs for Josiah, as it tells us in 2 Chronicles 35:25, and then we have the decline of the nation. Now, one quick aside here: when we're told that Jeremiah is the son of Hilkiah, he could have been the son of this high priest who worked with Josiah on these reforms. In 1 Chronicles 9, we're given a genealogy, and it talks about Azariah, the son of Hilkiah. Later on, the books of Ezra and Nehemiah both mention this Hilkiah, and they mention Azariah; they also mention some other sons. Jeremiah is never mentioned. So, his genealogy is a bit confusing.

I like to think that Jeremiah is the son of Hilkiah, this wonderful priest who finds the law and who's involved in the reforms. But he may not be; there are two other alternatives. One, it could be a different Hilkiah because a couple of different Hilkiahs are mentioned in the Bible. We know this because the same guy couldn't be named in stories three hundred years apart. Or it could be like the way people refer to Jesus as the son of David. I mean, David is the most renowned person in the family, and this way everybody knows Jesus is descended from David. It could be the same thing. Perhaps Hilkiah is a grandfather, a great-grandfather, or an uncle. He could be a descendant in the line of Hilkiah, so he's a "son" of Hilkiah. Instead of naming his biological father whom no one may know, everybody knows Hilkiah.

In summary, we have this wonderful, godly young man who is part of this restoration and reformation of Judah and Jerusalem, related to this godly high priest who restarts the Passover celebration and reinstitutes temple worship under Josiah's rule.

Life Under Josiah

He knows what it means to love God and obey Him and, as a result, he experiences the blessings of God. Now, Jeremiah is wondering, "God, why did You tell me about no one listening to me? How I am going to be this prophet to the nations, and I'm going to have to endure persecution and hardship, and that my life is going to be a fight?"

Well, it looks as though a reprieve intervenes here for almost twenty years while he is built up, seeing what a godly nation looks like. So, he has something rooting him, something to hold on to, something to give him the peace that God promises to give to those that obey as in John 16:33. This is good, because Josiah, in the thirty-first year of his life, dies in battle, his son Jehoahaz becomes king, and now Jeremiah's fight starts.

For context, Israel had been under Assyrian rule for some time but under Josiah gained independence. As we go through the story of Jeremiah, other nations will make appearances, and so will several kings. It will be difficult to keep them all straight. We're now introduced to Jehoahaz (king #2). The only commentary we have on him is in 2 Kings 23:

> He did evil in the sight of the LORD, according to all that his fathers had done. Now Pharaoh Necho put him in prison at Riblah in the land of Hamath, that he might not reign in Jerusalem; and he imposed on the land a tribute of one hundred talents of silver and a talent of gold. Then Pharaoh Necho made Eliakim the son of Josiah king in place of his father Josiah, and changed his name to Jehoiakim. And Pharaoh took Jehoahaz and went to Egypt, and he died there. (2 Kings 23:32–34)

I'd love to hear the intrigue behind all of this. I suspect there's a whole other story here that we're not getting.

But this is the important thing in our study about love, and specifically love for God, as personified by Jeremiah. He's got to endure under evil kings. Remember, love is not an emotion. Love is a choice.

Jehoahaz, the Brief Footnote in History

We're choosing to love God. One thing that can help us in our love for God is to understand that He is sovereign. Clearly, it is God's choice that Jehoahaz is removed after three months. What could he have done in three months that was more evil than any of the kings we will read about, or any previous king? But God is sovereign and has a plan. So, we can learn to trust Him, which helps us choose to love Him, which then helps us obey Him. In John 14:15, Jesus says to his disciples, "If you love Me, keep My commandments." The same principle is here: if we love God, we keep His commandments. But, by knowing that God is sovereign, knowing that God is in control, Jeremiah can love God and obey Him, even amid all the evil in the rule of Jehoahaz.

Jehoiakim, Once Eliakim

Let's move on to the next king, Eliakim. If you look, there's no King Eliakim anywhere else; that's because he gets a name change to Jehoiakim. At twenty-five years old, he becomes king and reigns in Jerusalem for eleven years.

Listen to this: "He did evil in the sight of the Lord" (2 Kings 23:37). This is exactly the same thing that was said about Jehoahaz, his brother, but God keeps him in power for eleven years. Why? Because God is sovereign, He is in control and has a plan. So now Jeremiah needs to endure under Jehoiakim (king #3). So, what is the evil that Jehoiakim does?

Our answer is in Jeremiah 22. God says to Jeremiah,

> "Go down to the house of the king of Judah, and there speak this word, and say, 'Hear the word of the Lord, O king of Judah, you who sit on the throne of David, you and your servants and your people who enter these gates! Thus says the Lord: "Execute judgment and righteousness, and deliver the plundered out of the hand of the oppressor. Do no wrong and do no violence to the stranger, the fatherless, or the widow, nor shed innocent blood in this place. For if you indeed do this thing, then shall enter the gates of this house, riding on horses and in chariots, accompanied by servants and people, kings who sit on the throne of David. But if you will not hear these words, I swear by Myself" says the Lord, "that this house shall become a desolation."'" (Jeremiah 22:1–5)

What Jehoiakim Does

He's murdering the innocent? He's abusing those at risk? Even though Jeremiah brings these warnings to Jehoiakim, they don't resonate. God says, "If you obey me, there will always be a descendant of David sitting on the throne." But he doesn't change, and the palace will indeed be reduced to a pile of rubble.

One thing that's a little confusing in all of Jeremiah's stories is the oppression from the surrounding nations. So, let me flesh out a little more on the comment I made about Assyria. When Jeremiah was born, Judah was actually under Assyrian rule. Assyria had already destroyed the north—Israel—and taken all the people captive; then Judah paid tribute to the kings of Assyria, just to

CHAPTER 14: JEREMIAH ENDURES ALL THINGS

keep some sort of peace. In about 612 BC, Nineveh, the capital of Assyria, is destroyed.

The Babylonians and the Medes conquer Assyria and take over all their land. So, under Josiah, the people have freedom for a time. But shortly after Josiah's death, Egypt attacks, Jehoahaz (king #2) is taken off to Egypt, and Egypt installs Jehoiakim (king #3) in his place. We read in 2 Kings 24 that during Jehoiakim's reign, King Nebuchadnezzar of Babylon conquers Egypt and invades the land of Judah. Jehoiakim surrenders and pays him tribute for three years. He rebels against the Babylonians, and Nebuchadnezzar and his whole army come to besiege the city. This is where most of the action in Jeremiah's life happens.

The people have first had to endure Assyria, then Egypt, and now Babylon. And Jeremiah is in the midst of this, trying to prophesy, trying to bring forth change in the people. We just read the warning given to Jehoiakim: if you change your ways, you'll have a king on the throne. But Jehoiakim refuses, and so God continues to bring His punishment.

Going Against the Flow

And now we reach a difficult part of the story. Jeremiah is a priest and comes from a priestly line, a priestly family. His prophecies are made in full public display, in the temple. God calls him to prophesy the coming judgment on Israel because they will not return to Him. They will not confess their sins. In chapter 4, Jeremiah is told to declare that Jerusalem is going to be besieged and destroyed and that the people will be taken. But this is not what the other prophets or leaders are saying. They tell him to be quiet and to stop prophesying evil and harm to Israel, although he's obeying God and calling people to repentance and holy living.

Doublespeak in Ancient Israel

There's a famous verse in Isaiah 5:20 where God declares "woe" on people who call evil good and good evil, and that is what's happening here. People are allowing sin, debauchery, and evil to continue. And whoever stands up and says, "No more, this is wrong and harmful," is shouted down as being the evil one, out of touch, wrong, mean, and nasty.

I mentioned earlier that there were other prophets in Israel proclaiming peace and prosperity for the people: "Just continue on in your ways."

> The word that came to Jeremiah from the LORD, saying, "Stand in the gate of the LORD's house, and proclaim there this word, and say, 'Hear the word of the LORD, all you of Judah who enter in at these gates to worship the LORD!'" Thus says the LORD of hosts, the God of Israel: "Amend your ways and your doings, and I will cause you to dwell in this place. Do not trust in these lying words, saying, 'The temple of the LORD, the temple of the LORD, the temple of the LORD are these.'" (Jeremiah 7:1-4)

This is what the other prophets were saying: that you can trust in the temple, you can trust in these traditions, even when their hearts were not in it—they were hypocrites.

And though Jeremiah is called to make this proclamation, God says to him, "Therefore, you shall speak all these words to them, but they will not obey you. You shall also call to them, but they will not answer you." (Jeremiah 7:27) They're just rebellious, and he has to endure doing this work for God, knowing it will yield no results—not just no results, but that it will cause persecution and harm to him.

When It Doesn't Matter *What* You Do

As I mentioned before, I have five kids, and as they were growing up, probably from age six through to the age of ten, I would sit with them on their bed each night and read through *The Chronicles of Narnia*; that's actually how I taught them to read.

I'd read a sentence; they'd read a sentence; I'd correct them, and we'd go through the whole series. Now, if you've never read *The Chronicles of Narnia*, put a bookmark on this page, get those books out, and read them. Welcome back, if you didn't read them—spoiler alert—the final installment *The Last Battle* features a wonderful king, Tirian, and his friend Jewel, a unicorn: wonderful, noble leaders with integrity, courage, kindness, and grace.

They fight against an ape who has styled himself as a prophet and dressed up a donkey to be Aslan. He's deceived everyone. When Tirian tries to rescue the nation of Narnia, when the battle looks like it's about to turn and he will be victorious because he has convinced enough Narnians to help him, he's betrayed by a group of dwarves. The dwarves rain arrows down on his soldiers. He is crushed, physically and morally. Even when the heroes of the series, the Pevensies, are called from our world to Narnia to help, they fail too. No matter what the good guys do, inevitably the end comes.

It's actually kind of depressing for a kid's book; Tirian is constantly trying to do what's right, but no matter what he does, things are marching on towards the destruction of Narnia. In his novels, C. S. Lewis powerfully and effectively demonstrates the emotion of what someone like Jeremiah is going through.

Back to Jeremiah: God has declared judgment, and people are going to go into captivity to be punished for their sins and rebellion. Jeremiah is told he's going to stand up and preach, and no one's going to listen to him, no matter what he does. The judgment of Jerusalem, of Judah, is inevitable, and he has to stand there and take it. The end is coming.

This is what boggles my mind. Jeremiah knows that he's not going to win, but his love for God motivates him to endure all of this. The attacks come from both the enemy without and "friends" within.

The Betrayal of Friends and Family

We read these warnings over and over again in the next couple of chapters. Then, in chapter 11, Jeremiah confronts a conspiracy of leaders of Israel who are saying one thing but living another way, in complete rebellion against God's word. Jeremiah speaks here:

> "O Lord of hosts,
> You who judge righteously,
> Testing the mind and the heart,
> Let me see Your vengeance on them,
> For to You I have revealed my cause.
> "Therefore thus says the Lord concerning the men of Anathoth who seek your life, saying, 'Do not prophesy in the name of the Lord, lest you die by our hand'—therefore thus says the Lord of hosts: 'Behold, I will punish them. The young men shall die by the sword, their sons and their daughters shall die by famine; and there shall be no remnant of them, for I will bring catastrophe on the men of Anathoth, even the year of their punishment.'" (Jeremiah 11:20–23)

God has given Jeremiah the task of pronouncing doom against this group of priests, perhaps his very close relatives. In response, they threaten his life.

They scheme to kill him, and Jeremiah appeals to God to bring judgment on them. And God does; God promises to punish them. But can you imagine having this kind of fight with people in your own family, with this group of priests and prophets from your hometown? Everyone is rejecting Jeremiah, and this is just the first time that people plan to kill him.

Was Jeremiah Depressed?

In the next chapters, Jeremiah prophesies judgment on the people of Israel. We get to a verse in Jeremiah 15. Many commentaries suggest that Jeremiah is suffering from depression or other mental issues; but when he is constantly fighting, when God has asked him to stand up for what is right and warned him that no one's going to listen to him, and that he's going to be constantly battered against by the popular views and the sin of the day, his dejection makes sense. He says this:

> "Woe is me, my mother,
> That you have borne me,
> A man of strife and a man of contention to the whole earth!
> I have neither lent for interest,
> Nor have men lent to me for interest.
> Every one of them curses me." (Jeremiah 15:10)

I almost feel like Jeremiah doesn't have a friend in the world. All he sees around him is sin, evil, and disobedience. God keeps calling him to keep on doing what's right, to point out sin, to proclaim His judgment, and to call for repentance. There are more calls for repentance in Jeremiah than in almost any other book of the Bible, and this does not make Jeremiah a very popular person.

And his enduring hardship doesn't come from the people around him only; God calls him to a difficult life path. "The word of the Lord came to me, saying, 'You shall not take a wife, nor shall you have sons or daughters in this place'" (Jeremiah 16:1–2). The reason why is that God is going to pour out His judgment, and He doesn't want Jeremiah to suffer the loss of his potential family to gruesome deaths like the other people around them. And so, Jeremiah is going to miss out on some of the basic pleasures of life, of being married and having a companion and a family. He's all alone and has to endure all of this by himself.

Pulling Love Out of the Story

There's a great deal we can learn from the book of Jeremiah, from all the prophecies, warnings, and calls to repentance, and much to pull out of the

CHAPTER 14: JEREMIAL ENDURES ALL THINGS

story regarding love: that the greatest command for us as followers of God is to love Him with all our heart, soul, mind, and strength and to love others as ourselves.

And when we look at our focus phrase, "love endures all things," there is no better example than Jeremiah, who is called to such a high level of obedience to God but is constantly beaten down by everyone around him.

Forgive me for jumping over so many chapters, but we need to get to the action of the story. Do take the time to read the prophecies and calls to repentance and hear God's passion for His people. He wants them to be restored; He wants them to change; He wants them to be reconciled to Him, but they simply won't listen. And His messenger, Jeremiah, gets the brunt of the abuse.

> They said, "Come and let us devise plans against Jeremiah; for the law shall not perish from the priest, nor counsel from the wise, nor the word from the prophet. Come and let us attack him with the tongue, and let us not give heed to any of his words."
>
>> Give heed to me, O Lord,
>> And listen to the voice of those who contend with me!
>> Shall evil be repaid for good?
>> For they have dug a pit for my life.
>> Remember that I stood before You
>> To speak good for them,
>> To turn away Your wrath from them.
>> Therefore deliver up their children to the famine,
>> And pour out their blood
>> By the force of the sword;
>> Let their wives become widows
>> And bereaved of their children.
>> Let their men be put to death,
>> Their young men be slain
>> By the sword in battle. (Jeremiah 18:18–21)

Calling Out God's Judgment

Jeremiah, who has been a man interceding on behalf of the people of Israel before God to forgive them, to restore them, has had enough. And he calls out for judgment on them as they attack him with slander. Note this comment here: "Shall evil be repaid for good?"

LOVE PERSONIFIED

If you're a parent, I'm sure you've had your kid come home from school one day, complaining about a bully on the playground who always seems to win. You know the kind: if he doesn't get his way, he takes his ball and goes home, even if it's your ball and not his. And he always seems to get away with it. Or maybe there's a kid in class who can act out and misbehave and talk, and nothing ever happens. And then, if your child turns and whispers to someone, the teacher sends them out to the hall or the principal's office, and there just doesn't seem to be justice. I always tell my kids that no matter what anybody else does, you do what's right. There is injustice; things aren't always going to be fair. My father repeatedly told me, "Life isn't fair." but we're still called to do what's right. To endure ... by obeying God ... out of love.

Jeremiah is trying to do what's right; he's sure he's doing what's right. He's doing what God has called him to do, but it doesn't seem to be working. His good is being repaid with evil, and it seems the evil people are repaid with good, and now they're out to get him, so he calls for justice from God. He's getting to the end of being able to endure all these things, but God is with him, and we'll see how God carries him through as Jeremiah shows his love for God by enduring.

The Price of Obedience

> Jeremiah came from Tophet, where the LORD had sent him to prophesy; and he stood in the court of the Lord's house. (Jeremiah 19:14)

So, he's right in the temple, right around all the people who hate him, and says:

> "Thus says the LORD of hosts, the God of Israel, 'Behold, I will bring on this city and on all her towns all the doom that I have pronounced against it, because they have stiffened their necks that they might not hear My words.'"
> Now Pashhur the son of Immer, the priest who was also chief governor in the house of the LORD, heard that Jeremiah prophesied these things. Then Pashhur struck Jeremiah the prophet, and put him in the stocks that were in the high gate of Benjamin, which was by the house of the LORD. (Jeremiah 19:15–20:2)

What does Jeremiah expect? God has warned him no one will listen, but a priest is so upset with the prophecy of Jeremiah—the prophecy of God's

CHAPTER 14: JEREMIAH ENDURES ALL THINGS

judgment—that he hits him and puts him in the stocks. I don't know if you've ever seen any old medieval-era movies like *Robin Hood,* where people would have their legs, arms, and head put in the stocks and be left outside overnight, hungry, exposed, and uncomfortable. You can't stretch, you can't move, you can't go to the bathroom. This is now the next level of persecution for Jeremiah.

The next day, Pashhur releases Jeremiah from the stocks, and Jeremiah confronts him about his sin and tells him that he's going to be carried off by the king of Babylon, along with his family. Jeremiah accuses Pashhur of prophesying lies. I'm amazed that he has the nerve. Isn't he afraid of more punishment? During Jehoiakim's rule, there's no regard for Jeremiah, not among the king and his nobles, not even among the other priests, his *family!* Remember, Jeremiah is the son of a priest. Pashhur is a relative.

God's Word Is a Burning Fire in Jeremiah

Once released and alone, Jeremiah has this angry outburst against God. Again, the persecution is getting to him; he says to God, "I am in derision daily; everyone mocks me" (Jeremiah 20:7). But he can't hold God's word in.

> I said, "I will not make mention of Him,
> Nor speak anymore in His name."
> But His word was in my heart like a burning fire
> Shut up in my bones;
> I was weary of holding it back,
> And I could not.
> For I heard many mocking:
> "Fear on every side!"
> "Report," they say, "and we will report it!"
> All my acquaintances watched for my stumbling, saying,
> "Perhaps he can be induced;
> Then we will prevail against him,
> And we will take our revenge on him." (Jeremiah 20:9–10)

Jeremiah doesn't want to do this anymore. He's tired of the fight, but he can't hold in God's word; it's like a fire inside of him, even though everyone on every side is mocking him, trying to make him stumble, to make him slip up so that they can take their revenge on him for sinning, for doing something wrong.

LOVE PERSONIFIED

The mental burden on Jeremiah is escalating. The physical persecution is also escalating, but his love for God helps him endure.

Again, Jeremiah is a confusing book in the way it's laid out. When we get to chapter 26, it's a repeat of what's already been told in chapter 15 about the beginning of the reign of Jehoiakim. For context's sake, I'm trying to put this story in order.

Now, God is telling Jeremiah to stand at the gate of the temple and proclaim his judgment on the city and the people (sound familiar?).

> The priests and the prophets and all the people heard Jeremiah speaking these words in the house of the Lord. Now it happened, when Jeremiah had made an end of speaking all that the Lord had commanded him to speak to all the people, that the priests and the prophets and all the people seized him, saying, "You will surely die! Why have you prophesied in the name of the Lord, saying, 'This house shall be like Shiloh, and this city shall be desolate, without an inhabitant'?" And all the people were gathered against Jeremiah in the house of the Lord.
>
> When the princes of Judah heard these things, they came up from the king's house to the house of the Lord and sat down in the entry of the New Gate of the Lord's house. And the priests and the prophets spoke to the princes and all the people, saying, "This man deserves to die! For he has prophesied against this city, as you have heard with your ears."
>
> Then Jeremiah spoke to all the princes and all the people, saying: "The Lord sent me to prophesy against this house and against this city with all the words that you have heard. Now therefore, amend your ways and your doings, and obey the voice of the Lord your God; then the Lord will relent concerning the doom that He has pronounced against you. As for me, here I am, in your hand; do with me as seems good and proper to you. But know for certain that if you put me to death, you will surely bring innocent blood on yourselves, on this city, and on its inhabitants; for truly the Lord has sent me to you to speak all these words in your hearing." (Jeremiah 26:7–15)

CHAPTER 14: JEREMIAL ENDURES ALL THINGS

Jeremiah's Life Is in God's Hands

There's some debate between the princes, the leaders of the people, and the priests, trying to decide what to do with this prophet whose message they don't like.

To get an idea of the severity of the risk that Jeremiah was under, there was another prophet, Urijah, who also prophesied against the city, much like Jeremiah, and he escaped to Egypt because of threats on his life. But Jehoiakim sent men to Egypt to bring him back, and they executed him.

Somehow, Jeremiah is saved by someone called Ahikam, son of Shaphan, who sides with Jeremiah so that the people do not put him to death. If Jeremiah wasn't afraid already, he can see these aren't just empty threats; the people will put someone like him to death.

How Jehoiakim Respects the Word of God

Even though there are prophecies to Zedekiah (king #5) in chapter 21, we need to jump ahead to chapter 36 to go back to another part of the story revolving around Jeremiah and Jehoiakim (king #3). Jeremiah is told by God to write down a list of prophecies on a scroll. He dictates them to a scribe, Baruch, who then takes it to the king. It is read before King Jehoiakim, but every time they read a column from the scroll, the king cuts it off and burns it in the fire. He is completely rejecting God's warnings, not loving God. Loving God means obeying His commandments. Remember, at the beginning, God has told Jeremiah his life's mission: "You're going to be a prophet for me, and no one's going to listen."

It's nice to read that Jeremiah had at least one faithful friend. We're introduced to Baruch as if we should know him; then he leaves the story just as quickly. There's a little ray of sunshine with some lower officials actually reacting with what looks like repentance to Jeremiah's writings and sending them up the ladder to the king.

Jeremiah doesn't see it himself, but he must have heard about the king cutting up his words, burning them with utter disregard. Then, God tells Jeremiah to rewrite the scroll! "Write it again, do it again, stand up for Me again; endure the rejection."

LOVE PERSONIFIED

Daniel's Life Versus Jeremiah's During the Exile to Babylon

A little aside: during Jehoiakim's reign, we have the first exile to Babylon, and Nebuchadnezzar takes some treasures from the temple. This is probably where the story of Daniel crosses the story of Jeremiah. He's one of the young men who are taken with the nobles off to captivity. Meanwhile, Jeremiah is stuck in Jerusalem during an enemy occupation, starving, with evil all around him, and nobody is listening. During this time, there is food rationing. Jeremiah, who is obeying God, has to suffer the consequences along with all those evil people who are disobeying. He's suffering for others' sins. Jeremiah's prophecies continue—wonderful descriptions of God's mercy and judgment.

You might be wondering, "Tim, what about the famous visit to the potter's house, or the story of the linen belt that he buries and how it decays?"

Jeremiah and His Contact with Kings

We're learning how to love God and love others by looking at other people's lives. This isn't a study on prophecy; that's for a different book by a different author. But one thing I have noticed is that the more I read Jeremiah, the more I realize how incomparable my life is with his experiences. Jeremiah is talking to kings, to the high priest, to the nobles; he's right in the middle of it all, speaking at the temple, speaking to big crowds, and we learn later that even Nebuchadnezzar knows his identity.

Everybody knows who Jeremiah is. He has access to these people. I've never met the leader of my country, the prime minister. I've never met our mayor. I could dismiss this lesson by saying, "I don't have this kind of influence. I don't know if I can relate to Jeremiah." But I think the lesson is the same. In our small sphere of influence, we will encounter people who are opposing God's way or opposing us with their lifestyle. How do we stand up to them? How do we endure their persecution, their comments, their ridicule? That's the lesson we're trying to pull out of this.

Back to the life of Jeremiah. He is given several prophecies around this time (but recorded in Jeremiah 50), when the Lord proclaims judgment on Babylon, the ruling nation of the day. They're in control of Judah and Jerusalem. And in the midst of this, God tells Jeremiah to prophesy that there's going to be judgment on the people who are oppressing them and that they will be freed. Again, this takes endurance and a lot of faith. This is a time of judgment, a

CHAPTER 14: JEREMIAL ENDURES ALL THINGS

time of suffering; but there is a coming time of hope. Just endure for now: God is sovereign and just; He will right the wrongs.

Hope to Come

I think this is what allows Jeremiah to continue and endure: no matter how bad it is, there is always hope to come. God has a purpose and a plan for the world, and also for our lives. And we can trust Him and then love Him and obey Him. Remember Abraham? He could hope because he had faith in the One who made the promise.

It's right at the same time that Jeremiah is making these prophecies of judgment on Babylon that King Nebuchadnezzar himself arrives in Jerusalem, besieges the city, takes Jehoiakim captive off to Babylon, and ransacks the temple.

Jehoiachin Takes the Throne

Jehoiakim dies, and his eighteen-year-old son, Jehoiachin, becomes king (that's king #4). Then Nebuchadnezzar besieges Jerusalem again and takes Jehoiachin, the queen mother, and all his princes and officers as prisoners to Babylon, completely loots the temple, and takes everything of value from the land, leaving only the poorest people behind (2 Kings 24:10–14). Jehoiachin is only eighteen years old when he becomes king, but he only reigns in Jerusalem for three months. Second Kings 24:9 states, "He did evil in the sight of the LORD, according to all that his father had done." If you didn't catch it the first time, God is sovereign. For whatever reason, He chooses to let Jehoiakim reign for eleven years, but his son only has three months. God is in charge. He is dictating events.

Zedekiah Is Next

Nebuchadnezzar puts into place someone who's going to obey him, Jehoiachin's uncle, a twenty-one–year-old named Mattaniah, whose name King Nebuchadnezzar changes to Zedekiah (king #5). He's an evil king, like those who had come before him. I'm just glad its not another J.

We have some interesting symmetry here: we go from Jehoahaz ruling for three months, to Jehoiakim for eleven years, to Jehoiachin for three months, and now Zedekiah for eleven years. It sounds like God is really in charge here, even down to the math. That is why we can trust Him and love Him and obey Him.

LOVE PERSONIFIED

This is a terrible time for Jeremiah and the remnant of people left in Jerusalem. There's an interesting start to Zedekiah's career as king. Jeremiah 37:3 states that Zedekiah sends the priest to ask Jeremiah, "Please pray to the Lord our God for us." It says here that Jeremiah was not yet imprisoned, so he could come and go among the people as he pleased.

Interestingly, Zedekiah is asking for prayer, but the Lord gives this message to Jeremiah:

> "Thus you shall say to the king of Judah, who sent you to Me to inquire of Me: 'Behold, Pharaoh's army which has come up to help you will return to Egypt, to their own land. And the Chaldeans shall come back and fight against this city, and take it and burn it with fire.'" Thus says the Lord: "Do not deceive yourselves, saying, 'The Chaldeans will surely depart from us,' for they will not depart. For though you had defeated the whole army of the Chaldeans who fight against you, and there remained only wounded men among them, they would rise up, every man in his tent, and burn the city with fire." (Jeremiah 37:7–10)

Note that Chaldeans and Babylonians are synonymous for our purposes.

Earlier in Jeremiah's story, he has purchased a piece of property on the promise from God that Judah will once again be a free area, and people will be able to come and go in the territory, farming and living normally. However, on his way out to the land of Benjamin, he is arrested and accused of defecting to the Babylonians. They are furious with Jeremiah and have him flogged and imprisoned in the house of Jonathan, the secretary. Jonathan's house has been converted into a prison. Jeremiah is put into a dungeon cell where he remains for many days.

Evil, But Still Wanting Answers

Zedekiah wants answers, so he secretly requests Jeremiah's presence, asking, "Do you have any messages from the Lord?" Zedekiah is a mysterious character in this story, acting in an evil way, still not turning to God, and yet wanting to know what God's messages are.

Zedekiah frees Jeremiah from the dungeon because Jeremiah begs the king not to return him there or he will die. But shortly thereafter, Jeremiah is thrown

CHAPTER 14: JEREMIAH ENDURES ALL THINGS

in a cistern, again accused of being in league with the Babylonians. The officials say to the king, "This man must die. This kind of talk will undermine the morale of the few fighting men we have left."

And Zedekiah agrees: "All right. Do what you like. I can't stop you," and they drop him into a muddy, empty cistern in the prison yard (Jeremiah 38:4–6).

From Prison to the Pit

I don't know how many days he is left down there. But he's wet, cold, muddy, probably with all sorts of insects, slugs, worms, and other slimy things down there; Jeremiah is slowly sinking deeper and deeper into the mud, soon to suffocate to death. Just in time, an Ethiopian official gets some men and pulls him out of the mud. This is worse torture than the stocks. He's stuck so deep in the mud that it takes thirty men to lift him out. How thick is this mud? How deep has he sunk? Do they rescue him from drowning in mud? What a terrible death!

So, if you're keeping score: Jeremiah has endured being whipped and put into stocks, flogged and put in prison, and left to die in a muddy cistern. These physical trials are enough. But I've been emphasizing over and over again just what he goes through as he tries to be a righteous person, loving and obeying God amid a society that is not only in disagreement with him, but opposes him, persecutes him, and fights against him; and he has to stand up and endure.

Zedekiah now rebels against the king of Babylon. On January 15, during the ninth year of Zedekiah's reign, King Nebuchadnezzar of Babylon leads his entire army against Jerusalem, surrounds the city, and builds siege ramps against its walls. Jerusalem is kept under siege until the eleventh year of King Zedekiah's reign. And at the end of that reign, the entire nation is destroyed just as God has prophesied through Jeremiah. So, while Nebuchadnezzar is in the field besieging Jerusalem, we come back to Jeremiah chapter 21:

> The word which came to Jeremiah from the LORD when King Zedekiah sent to him Pashhur the son of Melchiah, and Zephaniah the son of Maaseiah, the priest, saying, "Please inquire of the LORD for us, for Nebuchadnezzar king of Babylon makes war against us. Perhaps the LORD will deal with us according to all His wonderful works, that the king may go away from us."

LOVE PERSONIFIED

> Then Jeremiah said to them, "Thus you shall say to Zedekiah, 'Thus says the LORD God of Israel: "Behold, I will turn back the weapons of war that are in your hands, with which you fight against the king of Babylon and the Chaldeans who besiege you outside the walls; and I will assemble them in the midst of this city. I Myself will fight against you with an outstretched hand and with a strong arm, even in anger and fury and great wrath.""" (Jeremiah 21:1–5)

Jeremiah is enduring, faithfully proclaiming a very unpopular message of judgment from God, right to the end. Remember Pashhur, the priest who struck Jeremiah earlier? We're at the point where no one is accusing Jeremiah of lies. They all know now that he has God's messages.

The Men of War Flee

> The famine had become so severe in the city that there was no food for the people of the land.
> The city wall was broken through, and all the men of war fled at night by way of the gate between two walls, which was by the king's garden, even though the Chaldeans were still encamped all around against the city. And the king went by way of the plain. (2 Kings 25:3-4)

Starvation is at the end of it all. After all that Jeremiah has been through, he endures even more suffering—so that's the physical torture. Now how about the emotional torture?

> In the fifth month, on the seventh day of the month (which was the nineteenth year of King Nebuchadnezzar king of Babylon), Nebuzaradan the captain of the guard, a servant of the king of Babylon, came to Jerusalem. He burned the house of the LORD and the king's house; all the houses of Jerusalem, that is, all the houses of the great, he burned with fire. (2 Kings 25:8–9)

I can't imagine watching everything important to me burned. But the siege is finally over, so perhaps now Jeremiah can live out the last years of his life in peace? No! Shortly after, Zedekiah is taken off into exile, Gedaliah is made governor of Judah, and there's rest in the land for a very brief time. Then a group of rebels—guerrilla fighters—come and attack Gedaliah and kill him; then they take the war-torn remnant of people off to Egypt.

Jeremiah warns them to stay in Judah, where God will protect them and where they will have peace under Babylon. But again, just as it happens during the rest of his life, nobody listens to Jeremiah. He is taken off to Egypt, where, legend tells us, he is persecuted and eventually killed and buried in an unmarked grave.

It's All Greek to Me!

Let's recall 1 Corinthians 13:7, "love endures all things." The word for "endures" is translated as "patience" in James:

> Count it all joy when you fall into various trials, knowing that the testing of your faith produces patience. But let patience have its perfect work, that you may be perfect and complete, lacking nothing. (James 1:2–4)

The New Living Translation renders it:

> When troubles of any kind come your way, consider it an opportunity for great joy. For you know that when your faith is tested, your endurance has a chance to grow. So let it grow, for when your endurance is fully developed, you will be perfect and complete, needing nothing. (James 1:2–4)

This version uses *endurance* instead of *patience*. Skip down to verse 12:

> God blesses those who patiently endure testing and temptation. Afterward they will receive the crown of life that God has promised to those who love him. (James 1:12 NLT)

In the New King James, James 1:12 reads, "Blessed is the man who endures temptation."

Here's the point: Endurance is a characteristic of love; love endures and perseveres through hard times. There's significance in the length of time Jeremiah endures: he lasts through four kings and decades of trouble and trial.

This is the longest chapter of my book on purpose; I'm teaching you to endure.

Endurance Is Indeed a Marathon

Endurance is not a sprint; it is a marathon. This is an agonizing step-after-step, mile-after-mile slog. If you're running a marathon, it is grueling work. Jeremiah's life is a nonstop marathon, running uphill into the wind, enduring war, famine, beatings, torture, and opposition the whole time.

Endurance on its own is a virtue; being able to take abuse and last for the long haul. And I love the idea of your endurance needing a chance to grow. When I was younger, I was a bit of an athlete—honest, I was—although I'm the most average-looking, dad-bod kind of guy right now. I used to run and play all sorts of sports.

When I was younger, I would run longer distances, the 1500m and the 3000m races in spring track season and 3K and 5K in the fall on the cross-country team.

Now, fast-forward a couple of decades of not running, and I'm no longer in any shape for long distances. But we were approached at Galcom, where I work, to participate in a charity race in Hamilton called the Road 2 Hope. They do all the planning and allow charities to raise funds through sponsorships. What a great opportunity to raise some funds and awareness of our work! I wanted to set a good example for our staff by setting the bar high. I would raise a few thousand dollars in sponsorship and run the 10K. The 5K was too easy (and the marathon was way too hard). Now, I hadn't run even a 5K since junior high, so we're talking thirty years later. I started to train for the 10K run, and I started to really learn about endurance.

My Own Personal "Marathon"

I got up one April morning, my first day of training, stretched and went for a run. Now the 10K race wasn't until November, but I knew I had to build up some endurance. I shuffled about halfway around our city block—it's not even four hundred meters—and I thought I was going to have a heart attack. I dragged myself home and said to my wife, "I've got to call my brother-in-law." He'd had a heart attack maybe a year or so before, and I needed to ask him about his symptoms. I was really concerned! With my wife's gentle comforting (read reality check), I got over it. I was okay; it was just a matter of not having run anywhere, at any time, for twenty to thirty years. The next day,

CHAPTER 14: JEREMIAL ENDURES ALL THINGS

I got around the block. The day after that, I went out again and ran a little bit farther. I just kept on pushing myself, "growing" endurance.

Finally, I got up to a kilometer. Yes, just a kilometer; then two, three, four, five kilometers. It was now August, and I still hadn't been able to run ten kilometers. I could not endure that distance. I was speaking at a camp up in Peterborough, Ontario, called Elim Lodge—a little plug here for them! They have been wonderful to the ministry I work for, and they've been great for our family; some of our kids have worked there over the years. Anyway, I commented in one of my Galcom presentations, "I'm running in the 'Road 2 Hope' to raise money for Galcom. And hey, if anyone wants to wake up"—I was being, you know, a little bit macho here—"If anyone wants to get up at six a.m. and run with me, come on out. I'm doing endurance training."

I didn't see any hands taking me up on the offer, which was what I was hoping, but a guy came up to me after the service and said, "Hey, I run. I'd love to meet you at six to run." And I looked him up and down, and I realized this guy was an actual runner.

I am so glad that he ran along with me because he dragged my sorry rear end down the roadway and back, and I finally got to 10K! He ran just a step in front of me, dragging me along, motivating me. "You can do it. Come on, keep up … Don't slow down. We've got to keep our pace." He was a trained runner; he had the fancy watch on; he knew his optimal pace. He knew what he could withstand.

I was exhausted!

It took a lot, but I finally endured the distance. Here's the thing about endurance—by itself, it is a virtue. James says when your endurance is fully developed, you'll be perfect and complete, needing nothing. You see, you've got to train; you've got to build it up. You have to endure trials, tribulations, and temptation, and get through them.

When you get through one, you're stronger. Something harder then comes your way, something more tempting. But you know what? You've already built up some resilience. You're in spiritual shape to endure it; and you reach a level of maturity where even in the worst situations, you can walk through them with confidence in Christ, confidence in God, and a maturity of belief that you can endure just about anything.

LOVE PERSONIFIED

Endurance Has to Grow

It takes time to achieve, as it says in James, so let endurance have a chance to grow. We're motivated by love, and remember godly love is not an emotion that flames up in passion, a short sprint, an affection, a romance; it's nothing like that. It is something that grows and matures and strengthens. Godly, *agape* love for our enemies, for our friends, for God, withstands the worst situations—the plight of Jeremiah in a devolving culture with constant attacks from without and within. Ever read about Corrie ten Boom enduring the concentration camps, or Joni Eareckson Tada enduring a lifetime of paralysis? Read their stories, be inspired. You can endure! Fill in your trial here:

Purpose to endure it, to conquer it, and then move on to the next challenge.

Jeremiah, to the bitter end, endures because that muscle has grown. He is perfect and complete, needing nothing. May God help us to mature, to endure, to grow in endurance, and to strengthen our muscle in this way.

Your homework for this chapter is about the small things; because at first, you're not going to be able to run that spiritual 10K run. You're not going to make it through the toughest times unless you start building up to it, letting that endurance grow your love for God. Choose to love God and choose to love others in a small thing this week. Stick it out; endure some hardship. I've got to warn you what God will reward you with: more hard times, a bigger challenge.

Commit to loving God through it, doing things His way. Buckle down and serve Him during hard times; serve others during hard times. It's going to take effort and mental strain, emotional strain, but endure it. That's just for now. But next week, when next week becomes this week, again commit to enduring through something hard and you'll see the muscle—that spiritual muscle—developing into maturity because God will come through for you.

God will be there to sustain you; He gives you the gift of His Holy Spirit. Put Him to the test, and you will see God come through; you will trust Him more and obey Him more. So, commit to enduring through hard times by living loyally and pleasing God, demonstrating your love for Him.

Chapter 15

Jesus Never Fails

There are sixteen characteristics of love—eight *is*es and eight *isn't*s. Love is patient, it is kind, it rejoices in the truth, bearing all things, believing, hoping, enduring, and never failing. It is not envious, boastful, puffed up, evil-thinking, rude, self-seeking, or provoked, and does not rejoice in iniquity. I don't think this is a comprehensive list; I think Paul could probably have kept on going with more characteristics.

But quite honestly, if any of us mastered two or three of these, our lives would be marked with such love for others that people would seek us out—they would want to find out what this person is all about. And I use that term "mastered" carefully; because, as I've said over and over again, this isn't something that we muster up in ourselves or practice and work at; it comes from submitting to the Holy Spirit. The Christian life is simple—it's not easy, but it is simple: love for God and love for others. And how do we submit to the Holy Spirit? The old Sunday school song says it best: "Read your Bible and pray every day." Being immersed in the Spirit is our only hope for love.

The End Says It All

We've come to the end of our poem, and it's time to examine the climax: "Love never fails." We've been looking at a character in the Bible, someone who exemplifies and personifies the different aspects of love so we can put ourselves in their shoes and say, "How would I respond in love if I submitted to the Holy Spirit in this situation?"

Can you guess who is our example of someone who exemplifies a love that *never* fails? Jesus! As I thought about this, mulling it over, there are two parts of love never failing: there's the desire to love, and the other is the ability to love.

Growing up, I had wonderful, loving parents. They were always there for me and my sister, and they were intentional in guiding us. I don't remember a sporting event or a music competition at which my parents weren't there for us. I also remember the wooden spoons that were broken over my backside.

They were there; they were intentional. They loved us: they corrected us and nurtured us. And so, when my wife and I had kids, I was determined that I was going to be a good parent. I was going to be intentional, attentive, and there for my kids. Nothing wrong was ever going to happen to them; I was going to guide them and protect them.

Desire Doesn't Always Match Ability

On Christmas 2003, my oldest daughter, Georgia, was about three years old, and my daughter Providence was not quite a year old. We are loading up the car to go to my parents' house for Christmas Day. I can still see it: Georgia is outside in the snow in her blue snowsuit with little white dogs on it, with a matching red hat, red scarf, and red mitts with the string between them.

And you know how little kids look all bundled up; they can't move around properly. Arms out at their sides, legs not bending. So, she's toddling around in the driveway, and I'm coming in and out of the house, bringing gifts and food, the baby bag, portable playpen—all the things you've got to bring when you have a little baby. And Georgia's there, wobbling around happy as anything, and I walk out; and I'm not five feet from her, and she falls—thud-thump—right on her face, and I *can't do anything.* I see it happen in slow motion, and I can't get to her or put down the stuff I'm carrying in time. She falls, she's crying. I pick her up, and there's just a little scratch on her cheek. I kiss it better, and she's crying, and I think, *Oh, she was* this far *from me, and I couldn't protect her.*

The Holy Spirit whispered to me, "Tim, I know you want to protect your kids and see that nothing wrong ever happens to them, but you know that you can't always be with them. You're not going to be there to help them all along the way. And even if you're there, you aren't able to protect them. But I can." I have been able to rest in that. I'm glad I learned it when I was quite a young father. I will fail.

What Kind of Love Does God Want From Us?

As a parent, it's taken me years to really understand it. As I reflect and now apply it to our study, I think of the desire to love. We've been talking about how God wants us to love. What does it mean to have Christian love? Recapturing the definition of love; we looked at John 21, where Jesus says to Peter, after they've had breakfast, after the resurrection, "Peter, do you love Me, *agape*?" And Peter responds back, "Lord, I *philia* You." You're part of my band of brothers. I love You. I'd kill for You.

Going back to my story about Georgia, that's the *storge* love we talked about. I'm a dad; that's my daughter. I love her. She's mine. And so, there's this natural instinctive love. And what Peter feels for Jesus here—they have spent three years together through thick and thin, he'd do anything for Him. But Jesus is calling us to *agape*—a love that isn't limited to family or tribe but is for everybody. This is one of our problems: we limit our love, but we're called to love everyone.

Let's do a little word study. In Luke 7, starting at verse 11, it says:

> It happened, the day after, that He went into a city called Nain; and many of His disciples went with Him, and a large crowd. And when He came near the gate of the city, behold, a dead man was being carried out, the only son of his mother; and she was a widow. And a large crowd from the city was with her. When the Lord saw her, He had compassion on her and said to her, "Do not weep." (Luke 7:11–13)

If we move over to Matthew 14, verses 13 and 14, it says:

> When Jesus heard it, He departed from there by boat to a deserted place by Himself. But when the multitudes heard it, they followed Him on foot from the cities. And when Jesus went out He saw a great multitude; and He was moved with compassion for them, and healed their sick.

Mark 8 says:

> In those days, the multitude being very great and having nothing to eat, Jesus called His disciples to Him and said to them, "I have compassion on the multitude, because they have now continued with Me three days and have nothing to eat." (Mark 8:1 2)

LOVE PERSONIFIED

With What Organ Do We Love?

"Compassion" here comes from the same word as "intestine" in the Greek. We talk about loving someone with all our hearts. In ancient times, it was said, "I love you with all my bowels." In the Old Testament, it was always bowels—the deepest part of our being. We care about others from the deepest seat of our soul and our being. Whether it was a widow who lost her son, a group of five thousand Jews on the hillside, or a group of Gentiles in the passage from Mark, Jesus had compassion from the depth of His being. He had the desire to love; He *wanted* to care for them.

We have talked about love being kind and patient, but what about the desire to love? This is what I lack sometimes. I don't always desire to love. It's easy to love my kids—most of the time! It's easy to love people in my group. We protect each other—I got your back. But what about everybody else? Do I love them? Do I have compassion and concern for somebody else from the deepest part of my guts?

There are two aspects: the *desire* to love and the *ability* to love. In the story about Georgia—I just couldn't be there for her. I tell these stories because I want to contrast a weak, failing human with our Lord and Savior, Jesus Christ. He always has the desire *and* the ability to love.

Another story from my experience is when I used to work at Crossroads TV. They have a prayer partner ministry, so a lot of people volunteer to answer the phones because people call in all the time with prayer requests or to seek salvation. And most of the people who volunteer are retired, so they're a little bit older.

I come out of a meeting one day and walk into the hallway, and there's a very elderly lady holding a Kleenex on her head with blood coming down her face. She says, "I fell by my car. Can you help me?" And so, I spring into action. I kind of grab her and move the Kleenex over to where the cut actually is, and it is quite a gruesome cut. I bring her into the reception area, I sit her down on a couch, and I start shouting, "We need some help here! Someone's got to come!" So, people come running, someone calls an ambulance, and others take over.

Then I walk over to a little lunchroom, and I see the blood all over my hands, so I am washing that blood off. And I—vaboom!—faint. I'm absolutely out. I wake up on the floor a couple of hours later and stumble up to my office. My boss, the vice president of finance, says, "Where have you been? Did you hear about the lady that fell, and they had to bring an ambulance? Where have you been this whole time?"

I say, "I've got a splitting headache right now, but let me tell you where I've been! I've been lying on the second-story lunchroom floor!" I learned that I don't have the ability to help in these types of situations.

Now I'm better with this stuff! Just a month ago, I was preaching at a partnering church of Galcom in Stoney Creek, Ontario, Cheyne Presbyterian Church, and after I finished preaching, I was at my little Galcom table, and I was talking to people and handing out newsletters. A lady comes in and says, "My husband fell in the parking lot. Can you help?" And I ran out and didn't faint this time, but it was still touch and go. I was just hanging on at first, but then the other people came, and there wasn't as much blood. I lack the *ability* to love sometimes; even when I want to, I can't always help.

Jesus Has the Desire *and* the Ability

These stories that I read of Jesus—if you notice, I left them all just at the first part. We know the end of the story of the widow of Nain: Jesus walks up to the coffin, puts His hand on it, and says, "Son, arise," and presents the son back to his mother. He is *able* to fulfill that desire and demonstrate love. He feeds the five thousand men plus women and children by multiplying the bread; and in Mark 8, he does it again—four thousand people plus women and children. It doesn't matter who they are—Jews, Gentiles, whoever—He has the desire, the compassion, the love; He desires to love them, and He *can*. Jesus's love never fails.

Here's the thing, with all of the rest of love's characteristics that we've studied: we can submit to the Holy Spirit when we get in a situation and can respond properly. We won't be rude if the Spirit controls. We can demonstrate love; love is not rude. We can be patient, long-suffering, demonstrating love by forgiving, and so on. But I think with this last characteristic, "love never fails," Paul puts it at the end so that we understand how incredible this *agape* love of God is. This is the love that never fails; it's beyond us. There are times no matter how much we want to help, to love, we come up short.

Jesus Shows Us How to Love in Amazing Ways

For this last chapter I want you to grab your Bible to read some stories just so we can bask in the love of Christ—no application here, just a reminder for us of Jesus' desire to love us and His ability to love us—what an amazing Lord and Savior! We've started reading in Matthew 14 about the feeding of the five thousand. Return to the story in verse 22 and read through to verse 32. You may recognize the story when you start to read it—Peter stepping out of the boat unto a stormy sea, then sinking and Jesus calming the storm. But take the time to read it again and notice Jesus's ability.

Later in that chapter, in verse 34:

> When they had crossed over, they came to the land of Gennesaret. And when the men of that place recognized Him, they sent out into all that surrounding region, brought to Him all who were sick, and begged Him that they might only touch the hem of His garment. And as many as touched it were made perfectly well. (Matthew 14:34–36)

In chapter 15, from verse 29:

> Jesus departed from there, skirted the Sea of Galilee, and went up on the mountain and sat down there. Then great multitudes came to Him, having with them the lame, blind, mute, maimed, and many others; and they laid them down at Jesus' feet, and He healed them. So the multitude marveled when they saw the mute speaking, the maimed made whole, the lame walking, and the blind seeing; and they glorified the God of Israel. (Matthew 15:29–31)

Jesus Christ, our Lord and Savior, has all power over nature. There's nothing He cannot do: heal the sick, multiply food, walk on water, calm storms.

Jesus's power extends beyond just the natural realm. Have you still got your Bible at hand? Please turn to Mark 5 and read verses 1 to 13. This may be another familiar story to you; this one stuck with me from childhood since the scene of a few thousand pigs running off a cliff captured my imagination. You may not remember it all, but again take the time to read it. I'll wait here.

Two thousand demons; and at the word of Jesus, they were gone. Not one, but two thousand at the word of Jesus, and He commands them to go.

CHAPTER 15: JESUS NEVER FAILS

Mark 5, a little bit later, starting at verse 21:

> When Jesus had crossed over again by boat to the other side, a great multitude gathered to Him; and He was by the sea. And behold, one of the rulers of the synagogue came, Jairus by name. And when he saw Him, he fell at His feet and begged Him earnestly, saying, "My little daughter lies at the point of death. Come and lay Your hands on her, that she may be healed, and she will live." So Jesus went with him, and a great multitude followed Him and thronged Him. (Mark 5:21–24)

We know that a woman grabs the hem of His garment as He goes by, and she is immediately healed. Just then (from verse 35):

> While He was still speaking, some came from the ruler of the synagogue's house who said, "Your daughter is dead. Why trouble the Teacher any further?"
>
> As soon as Jesus heard the word that was spoken, He said to the ruler of the synagogue, "Do not be afraid; only believe." And He permitted no one to follow Him except Peter, James, and John the brother of James. Then He came to the house of the ruler of the synagogue, and saw a tumult and those who wept and wailed loudly. When He came in, He said to them, "Why make this commotion and weep? The child is not dead, but sleeping."
>
> And they ridiculed Him. But when He had put them all outside, He took the father and the mother of the child, and those who were with Him, and entered where the child was lying. Then He took the child by the hand, and said to her, "*Talitha, cumi,*" which is translated, "Little girl, I say to you, arise." Immediately the girl arose and walked, for she was twelve years of age. And they were overcome with great amazement. (Mark 5:35–42)

Jesus's love never fails. Nothing in nature, in the physical realm, nothing in the spiritual realm—demons, evil spirits—not even death itself can stop Him, stop His love for us. Turn ahead in your Bible to Mark 14:43. Jesus and the disciples have had the Passover meal together. Judas has gone off. They're up in the garden praying. Jesus has sweat drops of blood. He knows what's coming; He

LOVE PERSONIFIED

knows that He's going to be tortured; He knows He's going to be crucified. He knows the pain that He's about to endure. Read from verse 43 to 50.

It Was His Love that Kept Him on the Cross

The disciples failed. Jesus, knowing what was coming, went with the soldiers. It was Jesus's desire to love that led Him to the cross for us. It was His desire to love that held Him on the cross, taking the full measure of God's wrath, the full measure of God's punishment for sin. It was Jesus Christ's love for us, His desire to love us, that kept Him there.

> On the first day of the week, very early in the morning, they, and certain other women with them, came to the tomb bringing the spices which they had prepared. But they found the stone rolled away from the tomb. Then they went in and did not find the body of the Lord Jesus. And it happened, as they were greatly perplexed about this, that behold, two men stood by them in shining garments. Then, as they were afraid and bowed their faces to the earth, they said to them, "Why do you seek the living among the dead? He is not here, but is risen! Remember how He spoke to you when He was still in Galilee, saying, 'The Son of Man must be delivered into the hands of sinful men, and be crucified, and the third day rise again.'" (Luke 24:1–7)

It Was His Love that Raised Him from the Dead

It is Jesus's ability to love that raised Him from the dead. He does not fail us. Death could not hold Him. Sin could not keep Him. There's a hymn that goes like that! He has conquered sin, He has conquered death. Jesus's love never fails; it's His power, His ability to love, that raised Him from the dead. His desire sent Him to the cross; His power, His ability, raised Him. That is why I believe in Jesus. He's the only one who never fails; He's the only one who can save me from my sin, the guilt and shame in this life, and the punishment in the next. He's the only one who can guarantee me eternal life.

I don't have an application or homework for this chapter, only to say how good it is to trust in Jesus. What a wonderful Savior! It makes me think of all the wonderful Easter hymns, and I just want to sing.

CHAPTER 15: JESUS NEVER FAILS

Pray this prayer:

> Lord Jesus, I am amazed and overwhelmed when I stop and reflect on Your love for me; this unfailing, uncompromising love for all humankind, even in our rebellion and sin, while we were enemies with God. You loved me while I was a rebel; while I was still a sinner, Jesus Christ, You died for me. Your love is beyond measure, beyond comprehension. My love is so limited and selfish; I love such a small group of people.
>
> Lord, you want me to love all, as You've loved. Lord, I'm so weak; I fail my family and friends. Even when I want to love, I come up short; and so, I'm so grateful that Your love never comes up short. Fill me with Your Holy Spirit so I can do my best to love others and when I come up short, I would commit those I fail trying to love, to You, Jesus, because You can meet their need, whether it's physical, spiritual, emotional, or relational.
>
> Lord, You never fail; over and over, the Scriptures recount how You never fail; You always come through. Lord, I pray that You would increase my faith and trust; help me to rest in this love, abide in this love; and then fill me with Your Spirit, so that I will be able, as best I can, to submit to the Spirit and love others. In Jesus's name. Amen.

Conclusion

Throughout this study, we focus on narratives that teach us about our theme of love. Let's end by looking at the context of our passage in 1 Corinthians 13. Instead of starting at verse 4, let's start back in chapter 12.

Paul has just explained the different gifts of the spirit. He pauses in the middle to give a brief lecture on unity and valuing the diversity in the body of Christ regardless of the gift or the perceived importance of that gift. It's almost as if he stops short in this teaching when, in verse 31, he says:

> Earnestly desire the best gifts. And yet I show you a more excellent way.
>
> [And yet I show you a more excellent way. Now just hold off on these gifts, everybody; there's something more important to desire. There's a higher priority in being a disciple of Christ then any gift.]
>
> Though I speak with the tongues of men and of angels, but have not love, I have become sounding brass or a clanging cymbal. And though I have the gift of prophecy, and understand all mysteries and all knowledge, and though I have all faith, so that I could remove mountains, but have not love, I am nothing. And though I bestow all my goods to feed the poor, and though I give my body to be burned, but have not love, it profits me nothing.
>
> [Even the best spiritual gift is worthless next to genuine agape love. Even the most developed spiritual gift is nothing compared the power of true agape love.]
>
> Love suffers long and is kind; love does not envy; love does not parade itself, is not puffed up; does not behave rudely, does not seek its own, is not provoked, thinks no evil; does not rejoice in iniquity, but rejoices in the truth; bears all things, believes all things, hopes all things, endures all things.

Love never fails. But whether there are prophecies, they will fail; whether there are tongues, they will cease; whether there is knowledge, it will vanish away. For we know in part and we prophesy in part. But when that which is perfect has come, then that which is in part will be done away.

When I was a child, I spoke as a child, I understood as a child, I thought as a child; but when I became a man, I put away childish things. For now we see in a mirror, dimly, but then face to face. Now I know in part, but then I shall know just as I also am known.

And now abide faith, hope, love, these three; but the greatest of these is love. (1 Corinthians 12:31–13:13)

Even the most miraculous spiritual gifts will fail, cease, or vanish. But love endures. When this life is over and when we enter eternity with Christ, love remains.

Love.

I hope you read through our study of 1 Corinthians 13 slowly, taking small bites. Trying to emulate each one of these biblical "heroes" all at once will suffocate you! If you are able to master even two or three of these characteristics of love, you will look like a radical Christian to anyone you come in contact with. Don't just put this book up on your shelf (or donate it to a thrift store); use it as a guide. Take it out again and again to help you change your behaviour and become more loving. Don't just "listen"—do. This book will not help you unless you try to apply the lessons taught to us by the examples of those who went before. Jesus tells us in Matthew 7 that those who obey Him are like a wise man building his house on a rock; those who just like to listen to the story for entertainment only are like a fool building on sand. Please take these lessons on love seriously. Build your life by loving others as God commands.

The Other Love Chapter

We've made it through the love poem of the "Love Chapter" of the Bible. But what if I told you there was another "Love Chapter"? Look up 1 John 4 in your Bible and give it a quick read through; I'll wait here until you're done.

You may think the apostle John is a bit all over the place, testing spirits, listening to his teaching, having the Spirit within us, acknowledging Jesus as God, and loving others. But it's all about the same thing: John is explaining how we know if we are, or if someone else is, a Christian. One: they must acknowledge that Jesus is God. Also (I purposely didn't write "second" here because it's more of a 1b), "Beloved, let us love one another, for love is of God; and everyone who loves is born of God and knows God. He who does not love does not know God, for God is love" (1 John 4:7–8).

If you don't love others, John is questioning your salvation. If you don't love others, you don't even know God. Did you get the severity of John's statement? He doesn't think you're a Christian if you don't love others. This is the last time I'll say this: Love isn't a Sunday school, baby food topic. This is difficult, high-level discipleship, but it's the essential element to our Christian life.

Back to Paul and the love chapter:

> If I speak in the tongues of men or of angels, but have not love, I have become sounding brass or a clanging cymbal. And though I have the gift of prophecy, and understand all mysteries and all knowledge, and though I have all faith, so that I could remove mountains, but have not love, I am nothing. And though I bestow all my goods to feed the poor, and though I give my body to be burned, but have not love, it profits me nothing. (1 Corinthians 13:1–3)

What Are We Without Love?

Without love, we are nothing. Just a bunch of hot air and noise. We must understand what Jesus is saying when He commands us to love. We must put all our effort into loving God, loving each other, and loving our enemies. Why? Because when we do, everything else falls into place. We will be people of patience and kindness; we won't envy or boast. We'll be encouragers and have self-control, and we'll be able to withstand all sorts of trials and burdens.

I've said it before, and I'll say it again, the Christian life is simple—not easy, but simple. Read your Bible and pray every day. That's the way to fill your heart and mind with the Holy Spirit, and that's the only way to express *agape* love. It's outside our natural ability to love like God loves us, so we need Him to love *through* us.

According to 1 John 4, we know His Spirit is in us and working through us when we love. Start today; in whatever situation you are, ask yourself, "How do I show love to God and to this person in my response?" And if you need some help, think of our friends who have gone before us and set an example. Maybe I need to make myself a pocket guide—I know I need the constant reminder. Until then, don't store this book away; keep coming back to our biblical examples, those who have personified love for us. Work out your salvation in love. Prove your relationship with God through love.

Rest In Love

If it feels like this is just too difficult, just stop and reflect on the love of Christ for you—this unfailing, uncompromising love for all of us, even in our rebellion and sin, while we were enemies with God.

> Lord, You loved us while we were rebels; while we were still sinners, Christ died for us. Your love is beyond measure, beyond comprehension. Our love is so limited and selfish; we love such a small group of people and so conditionally.

Jesus commands us to love all, as He has loved. But we're so weak; we fail our family and friends. Even when we want to love, we come up short. I am so grateful that His love never comes up short. When we do come up short, we should say to those we're trying to love, "I know I have failed you, and I am sorry, but Jesus is here and can meet your need, whether it's physical, spiritual, emotional, or relational."

> Jesus, You never fail; over and over, the Scriptures recount how you never fail; You always come through. Lord, I pray that You would increase our faith and trust; help us to rest in this love, abide in this love; and then fill us with Your Spirit, so that we will be able, as best we can, submitting to the Spirit, to love others. We pray this in Jesus's name. Amen.

OTHER TITLES BY CASTLE QUAY BOOKS

Other Titles by Castle Quay Books

OTHER TITLES BY CASTLE QUAY BOOKS

www.ingramcontent.com/pod-product-compliance
Lightning Source LLC
Chambersburg PA
CBHW061252110426
42742CB00012BA/1893